Between the Jigs and the Reels

Published in Ireland in 1994 by
Drumlin Publications

Cover Design: EYECON Graphic Design
Front Cover Photo of John Doherty by Connor Sinclair.

ISBN 1 873437 08 0

**Published by Drumlin Publications,
Nure, Manorhamilton, Co. Leitrim, Ireland
(072) 55237**
Printed by Colour Books Ltd.

BETWEEN THE Jigs AND THE Reels

CAOIMHÍN Mac AOIDH

CONTENTS

FOREWORD

by Tommy Peoples

Music and song played an important part in the social life of the area of Donegal, in which I grew up, even into the 1960s. It was the principal form of entertainment, but sadly it declined with the advent of the radio and television. It was not unusual for someone to start up a song, as I remember. This did not apply to the same degree to the musicians. Visiting by relatives, friends and acquaintances was the normal method of socialising, and to my youthful memory, singing seemed a natural part of some of these get togethers.

The principal musical instrument in the area was the violin or fiddle. In the generation previous to mine there were many practitioners but by my time they seemed to have retired from playing altogether and a few of them only just about kept in touch.

Things had changed for these fiddle players. One of my early memories is of cycling to Raphoe to collect insulin for my mother. A grand aunt of mine, Julia Devine, lived alone in Momeen, about half way to Raphoe from our house near St. Johnston. Anytime I made this journey I visited her. One day she reached up to a tin box on the mantlepiece and gave me a document which I still have to this day. She told me that it was a court summons and explained its significance.

Apparently my grandfather, Jimmy Peoples, and his brother-in-law Tommy Devine, brother of Julia, had somehow got the site of a small hall off a farmer in the area. They were brought to court over this. The story goes that the farmer signed over the site when drunk and later regretted his action. Anyhow, the hall was built at the beginning of the century and still stands to the present day, although now it is in disuse. In those days it was used mostly for dancing classes and as the base of a fife and drum, marching band. The principal users of this hall were the young Catholic population hired out to the local farmers through the hiring fairs. For the dancing classes and occasional all night dances held there, the music was provided mostly by fiddle players who used to play in pairs. Some of these players are mentioned in the chapter on *East Donegal and The Lagan* and including Mattha Peoples, my uncle, Bob Peoples, Tommy Coyle and Tommy McMenamin. My own mother's brothers Eddie, John and Barney Martin, also played fiddle and melodeons. I remember hearing most of these players and remember them as good players but, as the dances had stopped by my time they did not play so much anymore.

Dance bands took over in the Fifties with a different type of music. The old dances that I heard mentioned like the Lancers, highlands and sets went into decline. They were even looked on as backward by the younger generations, who generally accepted 'Rock Around the Clock' with enthusiasm. I was one of the few of my generation in my particular area to have the music of the older generation passed on to me through my older cousin, Joe Cassidy. I went to Joe for lessons each Sunday for a couple of years. My father brought me first when I was seven years of age. Previous to this, I used to sit on the bottom step of our stairs, rock and sing. It became a habit with me which I did for several years, so my father decided it would be wrong not to let me learn to play a musical instrument. There were already fiddles in the house from my grandfather's time.

The point about this hall, dances and the fiddle music mentioned, was that the hall became the recreational focal point of the many hired workers in the surrounding areas. The dancing, music and marching band gave them a unity and comraderie that didn't exist previous to the hall being built. It sustained their spirits in the harsh conditions in which they were forced to exist. The only work available in East Donegal, or the Lagan area, was as farm workers, or else in the many flax mills. Farm workers were hired at hiring fairs in Letterkenny or Strabane. The period of hire was of six months duration. The Lagan was very fertile tillage, but the workers lived in poverty. The working day was long, and at night time the hired workers had to be back in their place of hire by 10:30 p.m. I remember hearing my own mother speak of the first morning of her hire, at Alexanders, near to where I was born, and that Davy Alexander was just about to knock on her door as she opened it at 4:45 a.m. Her first task was to get breakfast for the household and afterwards milking etc. So each working day was approximately thirteen or fourteen hours. The term "idle rich" did not apply in The Lagan.

Humour helped to salvage the situation. I heard my father tell of two young men who, having been hired in Strabane, received their first meal at the farmer's house that evening. They got some bread and a little butter, and later the farmer's wife came in with a little bit of honey on a knife. She divided it on both plates. One of the men looked at her and said "I see you keep a bee", to which she replied "Oh, yes! We have quite a few hives out in the back garden". The conversation ended when he retorted "Well Jesus missus, there must be only one of them working".

If the food was reasonable at the place of hire, then generally the workers were happier there as the wages at the end of the six months only allowed them to buy a new pair of boots with something left over.

Another incident which happened in my younger days (long after the hiring fairs had ceased) concerned potato gathering. East Donegal was famous for its seed potato export. Teams of gatherers were hired by farmers. They worked a six-day week. There might be up to ten pairs of gatherers working together as a team, a couple to each box. If there were ten pairs the potato drill was divided in equal lengths, so the pair at the start of the drill gathered up to where the second pair started and so on throughout the ten pairs. Men and women did this work which was back-breaking. Each pair was no sooner finished gathering their section, that the tractor and digger was coming again digging out the next drill without mercy. The farmer's wife would bring out tea and bread for the workers at 10.00 a.m. and 1:00p.m. etc.

This particular farmer's wife was the first woman in the area to introduce margarine on bread rather than the customary butter. Stork margarine was the only brand available at that time, and the packet had a picture of a stork standing on one leg. Anyhow, the gatherers realised that the switch had been made as the margarine did not appeal to their sensitive taste buds. Their reaction the next time they saw the farmer's wife coming with the tea was for each and every one of them to stand on one leg as the stork.

My first experience of traditional music outside my own area was when I was brought to the Comhaltas Ceoltóirí Éireann (The Irish Traditional Music Society that was founded in 1951)sessions which were organised and run by Hugh McGovern and Jimmy Ponsonby in Letterkenny. These happened irregularly and were held in the 'Institute' at the lower end of Main Street. They took the form of a concert and musicians, singers and dancers performed on stage to an audience. The best part of these nights was the playing that went on in a room at the back of the hall. My interest was in fiddle playing, and at these I heard the likes of Charlie Patton, Frank Kelly from Killygordon, and Vincent Campbell of Glenties, all wonderful players. Frank Kelly was a relation of Hugh Gillespie who made recordings in America during the Coleman, Morrison, Killoran era (these last three were famous Sligo fiddlers resident in the States in the early part of the century). Gillespie played in the lilting Sligo style more so than the straighter Donegal style. This is a generalisation as none of the Donegal fiddle players played alike but had their individual touches. Frank Kelly and Hugh Gillespie played as a duet in later years and were wonderful together. Vincent Campbell was a wonderfully unique player, with wonderful ornamentation and the use of both drones and chords by playing two strings together. John Doherty and Danny Meehan, two other Donegal fiddlers whom I got to know in later years also used these techniques. I met other players at these sessions also, like Tony O'Donnell of Brocagh, now resident in England, and Seán Gallagher from Ardara. The effects of these nights on me were enormous.

My National School teacher, a dedicated teacher, who was from Gola Island off the west Donegal coast and taught every subject through Irish, used to have me come to school early as he wanted me to sit an examination which might enable me to get free secondary education by winning a County Council scholarship. Well I remember being up at the school gates on mornings after the Letterkenny music nights. The school stood alone at the top of a hilly area. While standing at the gate, awaiting the teacher, I could hear music coming from the school playsheds as if it really was playing there.

I did get that scholarship and went as a boarder to Saint Eunan's College, Letterkenny, but I did not have much enthusiasm for the obligatory Latin, Greek and other subjects of the formal education system. Music lifted my spirit in Saint Eunan's in the sense that I had discovered Pa and Ma Butler, who owned a little shop near the college in Glencar. Pa, who was an old man then in my childish eyes, played the fiddle some, mostly slow airs, and sold single cigarettes. I got to know him and eventually left my own fiddle at this house. I then slipped out of the college most nights to visit him, when he'd play some tunes and Ma would make a cup of tea. I remember one day the students got a half day off, and that night were allowed to go downtown to see a film – The Nun's Story. We were warned that anyone seen around the town would be expelled. Well, myself and two other lads, Con Logue and Hugh Coll, both from Fanad, and the three of us friends had only six old pennies between us so we walked around the town instead. We saw the Dean of the college pass slowly in his car. He had a good look at us but didn't stop, so we decided to leave town. We walked to Strabane, eighteen miles distant, and got there at 5 a.m., where two RUC men stepped out of a doorway and questioned us. They brought us into the barracks and the following day at 10 a.m. we were handed over to the Dean who met us at the Northern Ireland border. We were brought back to Saint Eunan's and expelled later that day. The President of the college was Dr. Cunnea, a noble Irishman who played the fiddle as well. He later became parish priest in St. Johnston and regularly played at sessions with George Peoples. I grew to like him a lot as I got to know him.

There is a sequel to this story. The two boys who were expelled with me were later taken back by the school. I suppose I was deemed the trouble-maker. I got to know this and with the first money I earned gathering potatoes, I bought chips, chocolate and sweets in Letterkenny and slipped into the college again at approximately midnight, discovered their rooms by wakening others and delivered my present to both. It was as joyful for me to do that as it was for me to slip out of the college previously.

After that I went to a day school for a short while but mostly skipped school. At sixteen years I went to Dublin to find work, any work. I had an older sister there, and I was quite content to work as a labourer as my father before me had done. When in Dublin a couple of weeks, I unknowingly walked into John Kelly's shop (the famous Clare fiddler and concertina player) as I had seen tin whistles in the window and wanted to buy one. I had not brought a fiddle with me on leaving Donegal. John Kelly was a great admirer of Donegal fiddle players, particularly, John Doherty, Vincent Campbell, Seán Gallagher , Ardara, and Neillidh Boyle, Dungloe. I met John's kind-hearted wife first and we got chatting and then John himself appeared from an inside room. The outcome was that I was informed about the sessions in Church Street and the old Piper's Club in 14 Thomas Street. I spent many a happy time at these weekly sessions and can recollect many of the people I met there with love and wonderment that I should meet such people. Peter and Maggie, an aged husband and wife who went each Saturday night to the Piper's Club , Jim Nolan, who acted as master of ceremonies there, John Egan, the Sligo flute player and gentle soul who did likewise at the Church Street sessions on Wednesday nights. Tom Mulligan, Leitrim fiddler, Larry Dillon and Jim Christle, both Dubliners. Jim played and sang. Connie Kelly, a singer, Paddy Ban O Broin, Wicklow flute player, singer and solo dancer, Dan O'Dowd, Dubliner and piper, and numerous other regulars both listeners and musicians. I also met musicians of my own age, like Matt Molloy, a student at Bolton Street Technical College, Liam O Floinn, Seán and James Keane - Seán was a beautiful fiddle player, Paddy O'Brien accordionist from Offaly, Mary Bergin and Tony Smith, the Cavan fiddle player. My own playing at that time differed somewhat both in choice of tunes and method of ornamentation. Donegal was somewhat isolated from the rest of the country due to its extreme north-western position and being almost cut off by the six county border. Emigration from there was traditionally to Scotland so any influences on musicians tended to be Scottish ones.

My own style of playing was to be influenced also in later years by meeting and hearing other Donegal players John and Mickey Doherty, Danny O'Donnell, Dinny McLaughlin and Ciarán Tourish from Buncrana and Kathleen and Martin McGinley from Raphoe. At a Fleadh (music festival) in Listowel, County Kerry I met a Donegal fiddle player, domiciled in England, whom I came to admire greatly. This was Danny Meehan, from Mountcharles, in southwest Donegal. He was a big man with a powerful physique, and a heart and personality to match it. He played wild and wonderfully. The overall package from Danny included folklore, stories, the connections of an overall culture which has now broken down somewhat into segments. Danny was accompanied by Paddy Boyle, originally from Gweebarra, who had spent most of his life in London. I had a special *grá*, or respect for Paddy also as he reminded me a lot of my Uncle Mattha.

I spent a couple of weeks with Paddy Boyle, Danny Meehan and Paddy's son, Paul, a lovely fiddle player born in London, in the mid-Seventies in Donegal. One of my memories of that time was spending an evening and night in the company of John Doherty whom we met walking the road towards the pub at the top of the Blue Stacks, the mountain range in the southwest of Donegal. Also there was Vincent Campbell's father and brother, Columba, another fiddle player. Those memories are sunshine on my rainy days.

When I think of Donegal fiddle playing I think of all these I've mentioned plus Neillidh Boyle, Dungloe, Frank Cassidy, Carrick, Con Cassidy, Teelin. I also think of the O'Byrne brothers, Kilcar. These were incredible musicians and they had their personal individual styles. Most of these last mentioned I have only heard on tape and didn't get to meet, but it is evident that they loved the music and were first class musicians without formal musical training. I agree totally with Neillidh Boyle when he said that Irish music's ornamentation cannot be written or vice versa, played properly from the written notes. It has to be in the blood. The music expresses Joy, Terrible Loss, Hope, Love and Defiance. It has stayed with us when we had our people crushed by oppression, our language killed by force and intimidation.

Irish music was a joy to me, even though it spoke to me of those things, that oppression, terrible sadness, loss, emigration, but also of joy, dance and celebration, but above all the patience, fortitude, nobility and more, love of the people who bore all this hardship, even famine, and came through singing. Nowhere was this more evident than in Donegal as when instruments were unaffordable they even made tin fiddles.

In 1980, on a Sunday morning in Donegal Town at 2.00a.m., I met a man, wearing a long overcoat and cap, walking along. Out of his overcoat stuck the neck of a fiddle which I could clearly see in the street light. I did not know him but I asked him about the fiddle and if he would play a tune. He didn't hesitate but played a beautiful tune on what is probably the last tin fiddle. The man's name was Simi Doherty, nephew of Gentleman John as he called his famous uncle. We adjourned, even at that late hour, to Tom and Rosabelle Kerrigan's, in Saint Joseph's Terrace, both great lovers of traditional music (Rosabelle is a sister of Danny Meehan's and also plays). We spent the entire enjoyable night chatting and playing and the following day left Simi to his home in Stranorlar. He died in 1987. It was a rare privilege to meet him, as I did.

These are some of my feelings on Donegal fiddle players and the music. I have been carried away by even the memories as I have been recalling them. I make no apologies, as the music was a gift to me, freely given, with no charge. I hope I have respected the givers and the gift as the book does and I thank God for every one of those wonderful people.

The music was my ongoing education; it is a lifelong process and I recognise its significance even as I write these recollections. The music was my discipline when I thought I had none. It is the music that has taught me about the human spirit and about life.

This book is a well deserved acknowledgement of those Donegal musicians. It is written in a spirit of appreciation and respect. It can be used to link the musicians to the recorded material stored in archives. It traces the passing on of a music culture in a way that has not been done before.

I congratulate Caoimhín on his endeavours and foresight and wish you, the reader, enjoyment in its reading.

Tommy Peoples,
May 1994

ACKNOWLEDGEMENTS

A number of people have contributed towards the readability and accuracy of this work. To this aim I am deeply grateful to Dermot McLaughlin, Harry Bradshaw, Prionnsíos and Betty Ua Duigneáin, Fidelma Ní Ghallchobhair, Paddy, Kevin and Séamus Glackin, Nicholas Carolan and Jackie Small for having critically read and commented on parts of the manuscript. I am indebted to Seán Donnelly and Mrs. Maureen Glackin for similar assistance and for having supplied, as well as pointed me in the direction of several references. Lawrence Tulloch of Yell, Shetland assisted greatly in providing information on the connections between Donegal and and the rich tradition of Shetland. Cecil Stephens kindly made a number of old books relating to Donegal available to me for examination. Liam O Ronáin and Mary Monaghan of the Donegal County Library assisted in accessing reference works. To Tommy Peoples, I am most grateful for having agreed to write the Foreword.

For too long traditional music enthusiasts have suffered in not being able to further appreciate their music due to a lack of a central repository of material as well as a "closed door" policy in relation to many of the existing archives and collections. This situation has vastly changed with the establishment and growth of the Irish Traditional Music Archive, Merrion Square, Dublin. I am pleased to acknowledge the tremendous assistance and guidance of Nicholas Carolan and Sadhbhh Nic Ionnraic of the Archive for supplying me with a considerable amount of material as well as identifying a number of relevant references which were otherwise unknown to me.

Access to the archives of the Folklore and Folkmusic Department of UCD greatly facilitated my work in researching existing field recordings, particularly those of the Irish Folklore Commission Collection. Ian Lee of the RTE Archives played a major role in clarifying the extent and nature of the material that existed in that collection as well as noting additional material which he had uncovered in his own research in other less well documented collections.

It would be completely unjust for me not to record my huge indebtedness to Danny O'Donnell, who over a number of years meeting and discussing various aspects of the tradition with him, has contributed immensely to the shape, content and style of this work. His detailed, first hand knowledge of the Irish fiddle tradition is, in my opinion, unparalleled and his guidance and information have commonly acted as a beacon when issues and details were less than clear.

My collection efforts have been greatly assisted by a vast array of people who typically assisted in arranging meetings and participating in recordings. Without their help a great deal of information would not have been recorded and several key players would not have been documented to the degree which they deserved. For their help I am deeply indebted to Rosaleen Tourish, Eithne Vallely, Danny Doherty, Dr. Malachy McCloskey, The Boyle (Highlands) Family of Glenties, Pat The Forge Connaghan, the late Frances Doherty, the O'Byrne (Deargs) family of Kilcar as well as Prionnsíos and Citi Ui Mhaonaigh. Tom Donnelly contributed immensely in forming a commitment to the task.

I am deeply indebted to my wife, Catherine and my parents for their unending support. The enjoyment which Eoghan, Ríonach and Niall have shown towards Donegal fiddle music has lent a particular value on producing this work.

For more than two decades I have been privileged to have access to the knowledge, wisdom and opinion of the great body of Donegal fiddlers through conversation, playing and, in particular, field recording sessions. In contributing music, information and folklore it was apparent to me that this diversity of fiddlers always had three things in common; their respect for the generations of players who have gone before them, their great love of the fiddle music of Donegal and lastly, an intense desire to see the tradition carry on and flourish in the hands of a new generation.

This book is warmly dedicated as a small repayment to that vast legion of Donegal fiddlers, whose names are still quoted and others whose names have slowly slipped from our memory. Their playing and crafting of a body and style of traditional fiddle music has resulted in a shining gift which has been passed between generations. Through their memories and preserving acts they, in many ways, have been the unconscious but real authors of this book.

CHAPTER ONE

INTRODUCTION

I well remember having a conversation with the inspired Dublin fiddler Tommie Potts on the nature and attraction of Irish music. He pointed out that in contrast to the general, stereotyped observation that "it all sounds the same", for him, the beauty of the music was that there was always something different and exciting in it.

He felt that there was a cycle in the music. It started with the player hearing and becoming interested in a tune. The next step in the sequence was to learn it. Thereafter the fiddler would work hard on perfecting a setting of the tune. At this point, the piece was very stable for the musician and could possibly become stale and even boring through a routine approach. Here is where the magic lay for Tommie.

When the player was being lulled into disinterest with a tune he or she would, at some unexpected time, hear the same piece played by another player who, by simply altering a note or two, completely transfixed the complexion of the tune and the fiddler's delight with it. This process was an on-going one, Tommie maintained, and he delighted in cautioning that whenever you think you know a tune and may becoming complacent with it, you risk being struck by this pleasurable, unending phenomenon. He described it as "the hidden note". It was there all the time waiting to be discovered and when all around was like a tedious drone it struck the ear and the imagination like a peal of thunder.

In many ways the Donegal fiddle tradition shows remarkable parallels with the hidden note. While the mainstream of traditional Irish music has been developing over the decades the Donegal fiddle tradition has quietly been pulsating out of the limelight. In some cases, such as we will see with its more famous exponents, like John Doherty, there were instances where the searching limelight sent players to scatter for sheltering corners. It is a style which for the vast majority of traditional music enthusiasts has remained un-noticed and grossly mis-understood. Like the 'hidden note', however, it has been recently catapulted into the attention of players, although it has not set out to do so.

From my earliest experiences in playing Donegal fiddle music outside of Donegal, I have found an amazing level of ignorance amongst traditional, and in many cases good traditional players, as regards what is the essence of the style. In contrast, the Sligo style is almost universally known and appreciated within the tradition as is that of Clare, Sliabh Luachra and east Galway. During my years in Dublin in the early 1970s traditional music flourished and the capital, as it was always wont, acted as a melting pot where almost all styles and approaches could be catered for. Even in this setting, with the exception of the Glackin family, Pearl O'Shaughnessy, the newly arrived Tommy Peoples and to a lesser extent the young Kelly brothers, John and James, this vast metropolis had little knowledge of and indeed an even less desire to learn anything about Donegal fiddle music.

During the late 1970s, in what could arguably be claimed as the musical capital of Ireland, Galway, I found there was an infectious and tremendous enthusiasm for fiddle music, accompanied however (Frankie Gavin and Jackie Small excepted), by a dearth of appreciation for Donegal music. My subsequent experiences in Cork, with the marked exceptions of Con Corcoran, Vincent Milne (who had previously struck up a wonderful partnership with Danny Meehan in London) Johnnie McCarthy and Matt Cranitch,proved similar. In these localities I found that players expected the Donegal player to learn the local tunes with no reciprocal arrangements offered. Oddly, this gave rise to the situation where the Donegal player had a significantly greater repertoire and ornamentation range comprising the Donegal element as well as the acquired body of tunes.

My two greatest lessons in some of the appalling levels of ignorance about the Donegal tradition came courtesy of two highly-placed members of Comhaltas Ceoltóirí Éireann, a body which ironically was set up to foster the appreciation and knowledge of the overall tradition.

In the first instance the venue was the Ulster Fleadh in Ballyshannon in the early 1980s. Sitting in the front room of the

Millstone Hotel and surrounded by excellent Donegal fiddlers was an officer of the national executive of Comhaltas. As the small group completed the Teelin version of *Rakish Paddy* the flute-bearing officer enquired concerning the name of the tune. When informed of it's name and Donegal setting, the officer insisted that the only true version of the tune was that recorded by Michael Coleman (the fact that it was of Scottish composition as *Caber Feidh* accounted for nothing). He dogmatically insisted that the Donegal version should never be played as it was not Irish music. In his opinion it was Scottish music, and even worse than that, as Donegal music it was not only Scottish music, but bad Scottish music!

Having delivered his decree he then sought solace in the company of a Teelin man who alone, by virtue of being a native speaker of Irish, was deemed to be more cerebral concerning matters traditional. To the delight of many, the officer was advised in the finest of untempered vernacular Hiberno-English to take himself and his snake-charming instrument back to Kerry. Upon discovering that the officer was not a native of Kerry, the Teelin man extended his public apology at the thought of misconstruing the minstrel of vipers as being a possible member of the decent citizenry of the Kingdom.

The second instance involves another well-placed Comhaltas officer who was entrusted with the task of teaching the fiddle class at the Scoil Éigse, a week long school for talented, developing fiddle players. Strangely enough, it would appear that in this school the pupils are supposed to be given access to the country's best and most informed fiddlers as teachers. In this setting and in the years immediately after the death of John Doherty a pupil once enquired about Donegal music. The teacher emphatically replied that the only real Donegal fiddle player left was Paddy Glackin. This dictum, which I suspect would have brought a great deal of embarrassment to Paddy Glackin, was offered at a time when the likes of Francie Dearg O'Byrne, Con Cassidy, James Byrne, Danny O'Donnell, The Campbells, Prionsias O Maonaigh, Charlie Patton and even Tom Glackin amongst numerous others were still alive and churning out the best of playing!

My point in recounting these occurrences is to indicate that until recently Donegal music was commonly misunderstood, even in what was considered to be enlightened circles. It was often classified as some bewildering form of aberrant Scottish music. Sadly, many also took the easy option of stereotyping it as being a single stylistic form, namely that played by John Doherty. It is almost incredible to note the uniform experience of the middle-aged and young Donegal fiddle players who were told when meeting players outside Donegal that they had not got a Donegal fiddle style because they did not sound like John Doherty!

Things have changed greatly in the past decade however. Like the hidden note, Donegal fiddle music has blossomed into a genuine focus of attention for a diverse number of players, particularly younger ones who wish to become familiar with both repertoire and style. Though it is correctly seen as a natural relative of the Scottish tradition, it is becoming increasingly appreciated within its own unique, valid and exciting identity. Furthermore, the concept that the music must sound like John Doherty's playing to be Donegal music is rapidly running out of currency. There is widening appreciation and understanding for the numerous local styles that exist in the various parts of the county.

The fortunes of Donegal fiddle music have changed quickly. In a discussion with Francie Dearg O'Byrne in the early 1980s he told me he felt that the tradition was one for old men. Though some younger individuals might have an interest, it was dying. Francie lived to see his own music published on a commercially successful recording as well as a considerable number of good, dedicated younger players flock to his door to listen and learn from him. He enjoyed great attention during both the Glencolumcille Summer School and the Donegal Fiddlers Annual Meeting in Glenties. Shortly before his death on June 25, 1987 we were sitting in his home in Kilcar. He was trying to teach me *Jackson's Heigh-ho* and during the proceedings he stopped and remarked that Donegal fiddle music was never so popular as it had then become. In a handful of years he had seen a massive reversal of fortune for the music he had contributed to so greatly.

James Scott Skinner, writing in his book 'A Guide to Bowing', cited a number of influential players who had preceded him. He then went on to remark:

> All these men did good work, but would have soared even higher had they received a good sound training in manual equipment (ie. technique), and still remembered to render their country's music by the light of nature, maintaining its ruggedness and character, and not making it insipid and genteel.[1]

While very few of the Donegal fiddlers have had any form of technique training they have instinctively followed Skinner's direction in seeking to reflect the beauty and ruggedness of their surroundings in their music. They have created a style of music and a body of tunes which can stand comfortably alongside any ethnic music tradition and be considered the envy of most.

1. James Scott Skinner. *A Guide to Bowing.* Glasgow, c. 1900.

CHAPTER TWO

A HISTORY OF DONEGAL FIDDLE MUSIC

Although the fiddle as we know it today has a long and popular history in Donegal, no one can say exactly when it first came into the county. Indeed the very use of the word 'fiddle' can cause some problems. The terms violin and the fiddle are now used to describe the same instrument but this has not always been the case. In the past, a bowed violin-like instrument called a fiddle or fidil existed and is referred to in historical manuscripts. To add to difficulties, a number of other bowed instruments were known to have been in use prior to the arrival of the modern violin. Examples of these are the rebec, a small crude violin; gigga, whose name is more than likely Italian in origin and is the root of the modern word jig; a kit, which was again a small simple forerunner of the violin possibly used to teach children and a cruith or crouwd which was a bowed harp-like instrument.

There are some historical references to these now largely unused instruments. Edward Bunting, the famous collector who published his works between 1796 and 1840 made a conscious effort via his assistant to establish words in the Irish language associated with the harping tradition. The primary source was a Miss O'Reilly from Scarva, County Down who was believed to be the last person instructed in harp playing through Irish. Amongst her terms recorded[1] were cruiteóg which was translated as a small violin; cruith a crowde or violin; and fléasgach (whose root fléasc is currently used to describe a wand or rod) a fiddler.

In contrast, the modern violin was developed by Italian instrument makers around the year 1650. Thus the playing of the instrument postdates this period. For the most likely clues concerning its arrival in Donegal we must look further afield, firstly on a national scale and then to our long established contact with the related tradition in Scotland.

While Ireland has enjoyed a long literary tradition, mass access to the printed word is a relatively recent phenomenon By comparison, the tenure of our oral tradition is certainly extensive. Prior to the beginning of the 1700s the bulk of written records produced in or about Ireland generally come from three sources: ecclesiastical communities for the most part isolated from society whose aims were to produce liturgical and in part genealogical documents; State papers which deal with the general affairs of government; and travelogues from foreign visitors documenting their journeys. Unfortunately, there is precious little in the bulk of these writings regarding Irish music and in the case of the travel writers their comments often come with distinct cultural biases as regards what constitutes music. For example, the English visitor Richard Twiss, writing in his book 'A Tour in Ireland in 1775', tells us[2]:

> "Out of Dublin, and its environs, there is scarcely a single capital picture, statue, or building, to be found in the whole island. Neither is music cultivated out of the above limits, to any degree of perfection; so that nothing is to be expected in making the tour of Ireland, beyond the beauties of nature, a few modern-antiquities, and the ignorance and poverty of the lower class of the inhabitants...".

Based on what is already known about the status and development of all forms of music in the island as a whole at this time it is clear that extreme caution must be observed when depending on the accuracy of such writers.

On a more positive slant, some references do occur which help to reflect on what the early fiddle tradition and its influences may have been. The oldest reference to a fiddle in Ireland is taken to be that found in *The Book of Leinster* describing the 'Fair of Carmen in County Kilkenny'. Eugene O'Curry[3], the noted linguistic scholar of the last century considered this description to relate to an event held in the Seventh Century. On this basis, Grattan Flood[4] in 'A History of Irish Music' suggests a similar age for the fidil's (in this case the intention is apparently the violin) presence in Ireland. It is now considered that the 'Book of Leinster' dates from approximately 1160 and as a result Flood is at least half a millennium premature in his estimation of the existence of such an instrument. Furthermore, due to the age of the reference the fidil as quoted cannot be the modern instrument. What can be concluded from the 'Book of Leinster' is that a bowed instrument generally similar to the violin was known and played in Ireland at least by the mid-1100s and therefore by inference probably was played in Donegal.

There are two bits of direct evidence indicating the form of such primitive fiddles which might have been in use in Donegal before the advent of the violin. In the Cork Public Museum in the Mardyke there is a primitive and unusual violin-like instrument of local manufacture which might easily reflect the design of bowed instruments of this period. Likewise there is evidence of a unique photograph of the late character from the Mountcharles/Inver area, Myles Tinney. Myles can be seen sitting on the step outside a local cottage playing a four-stringed box shaped or trapezoid fiddle of the simplest design and using a bow of approximately eight or nine inches length which was made out of a bent rod and horse hair. Also, Francie Dearg and Mickey Bán O'Byrne of Cashel, Kilcar, who had a rich store of information accumulated over generations, frequently referred to the fact that similar primitive instruments, which fit the description of a rebec, were in use in Donegal prior to the availability of the violin.

In 1674 we find English tourist, Richard Head[5], noting that "in every field a fiddle and lasses footing it till they are all of a foam". Considering the age of the reference it is hard to determine whether he is commenting on the modern instrument or one of its forerunners.

Poetry in Irish affords us the rare reference to instruments. Eoghan O' Donnghaile of Ulster wrote in praise of a harpist named Feidhlimy:

Ní tú Eoghan is olc inníoll
ag a mbí a fidioll maorgáin;
ní hionat bíos an bhocfach
s' ní bhíonn smothfadh an do smaosan.

As this poem is believed to have been composed around 1680 it may or may not be referring to the violin. A version of an anonymous folk poem, Nach Aoibhinn do na hÉiníni[6] however clearly heralds the arrival of the new instrument with the use of the word veidhlin in the lines:

Is báine í na an lile, is deise í na an scéimh,
is binne í na an veidhlín, 's is soilsí náan ghréin;

By the early 1700s the modern violin became firmly established with musicians in Ireland. Nicholas Carolan's research[7] on John and William Neal in his reprinted facsimile version of their 1724 edition of 'A Collection of the Most Celebrated Irish Tunes proper for the German Flute or Hautboy ' shows, via contemporary poetry and newspaper advertisements, that "choice fiddles of all sorts" from England (including some from Barrett of Picadilly) were for sale in the Neals' Christ Church Yard shop and were being played at local gatherings. Indeed, the subtitle of the Neals' collection clearly heralds the modern instrument as the music was seen as "proper for the violin". By 1729 the elder, John Neal, was also advertising as a maker in his own right. As Carolan points out, this is the first known occurrence of a luthier in Ireland.

Fiddlers are occasionally mentioned in the State papers of the Public Records Office. For example, research by Seán Donnelly[8] on a census of the diocese of Elphin taken in 1749 identifies Matthew Cox of the parish of Roscommon and Jeremiah Neale of Fox Taile in the parish of Shankill as fiddlers. The latter would appear to have been somewhat prosperous as he kept two women servants along with his wife and child. On the basis of the date and nature of the information of this reference it can be taken that the instrument alluded to is the modern violin and that as with the Neal's the word fiddle had already become a common alternative name. It would also seem that the playing of the instrument would have become a respectable pastime for the general public and the more affluent members of society alike.

Probably the first reference to the modern fiddle in Donegal comes from the celebrated harpist Arthur O'Neill. Born at Drumstrade, County Tyrone in 1734, he was blinded in a childhood accident and typical of the times was subsequently taught to play the harp as a means of securing a living. At the time, such a practice would have been one of the last vestiges of the patronage system of the old Gaelic society. Shortly before his death O'Neill dictated his memoirs to Thomas Hughes in Belfast. He tells us that during his first tour of Ireland in 1760 when he strayed into the Glenties and Ardara area that [9]

> "I was invited by a gentleman named Nesbitt to go with him to a great wedding (without my harp), where there were plenty of pipers and fiddlers."

O'Neill locates the event in the Barony of Boylagh. Research carried out by the local historian and author the late P. J. Mc Gill[10] shows that the wedding took place in the still extant Woodhill

House, Ardara, the family seat of the Nesbitts.'

O'Neill also records meeting[11] "a good violinist in the person of Captain Boyers of Mount Pleasant, County Longford" in March of 1782. In the same year he attended a large musical gathering in the home of Jones Irwin at Streamstown, County Sligo. A total of forty-six musicians were present, the most numerous being twenty "gentleman fiddlers". Both of these incidents prove the availability and popular use of the modern instrument as well as its acceptability in upper echelons of rural society.

Unlike the situation in Scotland, the cello ceased to be an instrument associated with traditional music early in the evolution process of traditional music in Ireland. This may be due to limited availability of the larger instrument, it's poorer portability or alternatively its significantly greater cost. While it can be questionable whether the music being performed at the Streamstown gathering was traditional music as we think it today, or some mixture of Irish and European Art music with voices for cellos, it is noteworthy that O'Neill records the presence of two "Gentleman Violincello". From a social perspective it is significant that O'Neill makes the reference[12] "It's as common among blind harpers, blind pipers, blind fiddlers and all other blind musicians to say 'I see this. . .' " indicating a lowering by this period of the once lofty status of the harper to one of parity with fiddlers and pipers.

Another confirmation of the existence of the modern fiddle much closer to Donegal is the Stone Fiddle at Castle Cauldwell, County Fermanagh. This was erected to the memory of Denis McCabe who while playing for a party fell off the Cauldwell's barge the 'Saint Patrick' and drowned in Lough Erne. The stone, which measures approximately a metre and a half in height is carved from a local limestone slab into the shape of what is clearly a modern violin. It bears the following inscription:

> TO THE MEMORY OF DENIS MCCABE, FIDLER, WHO FELL OUT OF THE ST PATRICK BARGE BELONGING TO SIR JAMES CALLDWELL BART. AND COUNT OF MILAN & WAS DROWNED OFF THIS POINT AUGUST YE 13, 1770. BEWARE YE FIDLERS OF YE FIDLERS FATE NOT TEMP YE DEEP LEAST YE REPENT TOO LATE. YE EVER HAVE BEEN DEEMED TO WATER FOES THEN SHUN YE LAKE TILL IT WITH WHISKEY FLOES. ON FIRM LAND ONLY EXERCISE YOUR SKILL THERE YOU MAY PLAY AND DRINK YOUR FILL. DDD JJ

It is alleged that the DDD is an abbreviation for Denis Died Drunk.

By the beginning of the 1700's the now familiar pattern of jigs, reels, hornpipes etc. had established itself in traditional music and became the vernacular music of the time. Breandán Breathnach in 'Folk Music and Dances of Ireland'[13] implies that the jig had a slightly earlier popularity than the reel and the hornpipe. The jig, and in particular the slip jig, he argues was mainly of Irish composition while in the early stages in Ireland the reel was largely a Scottish import with the hornpipe brought in from England.

If this is the case there is little doubt that Donegal fiddlers followed the national trend and on their regular working visits to Scotland borrowed heavily from the repertoire of that country. This is not to imply that Donegal music became a minor subclass of Scottish music. Indeed nothing could be further from the truth. As was the case everywhere else in Ireland, Donegal musicians continued to add to the overall repertoire by composing new tunes. Furthermore, they were and continue to be very active in reworking into their own style tunes which originated in Scotland. This is typified by the store of Highlands and Germans played in Donegal which originated as either Scots strathspeys or reels.

Examining the Scottish music story in some depth can give us some clues to the development of fiddle playing in Donegal. Two excellent books have been published in the past few years which between them span the history of Scottish music over the past three centuries. David Johnson in his work 'Scottish Fiddle Music in the Eighteenth Century'[14] estimates that the modern violin arrived in Scotland around 1670 and spread into use very quickly. During the 1700s players moved through an initial period where distinctly Scottish music dominated, to one where local compositions based on European art music came into fashion. This was followed by a period of composition and playing of a mixture of tunes based on Scottish and broader European music. Players adopting this approach were able to satisfy the dancing needs of those who wished to express their national identity through the Scottish sounding tunes while at the same time share in the cosmopolitan pleasures of the new expanding continental art music.

Between 1780 and 1830 however there seemed to be a significant change in the output of Scottish fiddlers. The now recognisable names such as Gow, Dow, Young, McLean, Marshall etc. were coming to prominence and the music and musicians as described in Mary Anne Alburger's book 'The Scottish Fiddlers and Their Music'[15] were emerging. This seemed to mark a period of growing divergence between art and folk music which has continued to the present.

While Donegal society and customs are commonly felt to closely mirror those in Scotland, there are some factors which contributed to important differences. Although it is most likely that the arrival of the fiddle in Donegal was very close to its coming in Scotland, and that the two fiddle traditions from the early 1800s are probably based on very similar lines of development, there must be a serious doubt however that the musical society of the 1700s as described by David Johnson, ever existed in Donegal. This doubt is not based on any form of cultural snobbery which tries to exorcise itself of art music for the driven-snow purity of traditional culture. It is, however, based on the fundamental structural difference between what was effectively a country like Scotland and a limited rural region like Donegal during this period.

Scotland during the 1700s could be divided into two populations, first the geographically dominant rural communities and secondly the populations of cities, like Glasgow and Edinburgh which then were amongst the largest and most cosmopolitan urban centres in the western world. At this time Donegal certainly would have had strong kinship by virtue of its rural setting but was utterly lacking in cities or even towns of considerable population. It is hard to imagine, in the total absence of a sizeable 'high society' which existed in Scottish cities, any demand for unaltered European art music amongst Donegal's rural population with the possible exception of the dispersed, rare big house. The absence of art music in the repertoire of the Donegal fiddler of this time is also suggested by the complete failure of any such music to survive either intact or in memory to the present day.

It would seem most likely therefore that the local equivalents of the ethnic type music described by David Johnson from eighteenth century Scotland were the order of the day in Donegal and possibly only in the rare, exceptional cases as described by Arthur O'Neill as occurring at Streamstown, would art music have been played.

Daily life throughout the 1800s for the people of Donegal was commonly a harsh struggle for existence. It was dominated by physically demanding agricultural labour on precarious, small family tenant farms. Few opportunities existed for social entertainment. In this setting the house dance, barn dance, schoolhouse dance and seasonal crossroads dances formed the primary outlets for enjoyment.

Many of the current older generation of players can recall the art of lilting and also numerous stories of lilters providing music for house dances. Lilters were usually women and several reasons have been quoted for this. Firstly they were usually on hand to give fiddlers breaks during the long hours of dancing or to provide the music in the absence of players in the community. This was frequently the case when many young male musicians, the first-choice players, went to Scotland to work there for for extended periods. Women were also strongly encouraged to lilt as they could be relied upon to always be at home. Secondly, women, generally with lower pitched voices were seen as excellent lilters especially when accompanied by a young girl, who would normally have a high register voice. A girl would often be paired with her mother for lilting in octaves. This is remembered as being a characteristic of the most sought-after and talented lilters and may have had some effect on the development of the strong tradition of fiddle playing in octaves, or as it was sometimes called 'reversing'. Finally and simply, fiddle playing was seen as a male role while, as we shall see in chapter six, the teaching of dancing in the house was the complementary female role. This distinction existed with but the rarest exceptions, one being the Doherty sisters Fanny and Mary. Though noted players it is significant that both ceased to play once they married.

Fiddlers were sometimes brought in to play for reasons other than entertainment such as for dances to raise money for families in dire need. These were sometimes called penny dances where a penny was collected from all attending and passed on to the deserving families. Later on as general conditions improved penny dances tended to lose their basis in fund raising, and the money was spent on paying for the musicians, food, drink and tobacco etc.

Two records from this period provide testimony to these practices. Writing shortly after the Famine in his 'Facts From Gweedore' pamphlet infamous Donegal landlord George Hill gives us an insight into an offshoot of the social roles of fiddlers in the area. It must be remembered that he had a significant vested interest in portraying his tenants enthusiasm for adopting his plan of land reform and thus describes one incident involving the dismantling of the traditional Rundale system and re-location of households as follows[16]:

> "It took about three years to accomplish the divisions, as upwards of twenty thousand acres had to be arranged and distributed. Altogether it was a difficult task, and much thwarted by the people, as they naturally did not like that their old ways should be disturbed or interfered with, nor were they disposed, as yet, to abandon the Rundale system. They did not seem to have a taste for simple plain-dealing, or that matters should be put straight and made easy of apprehension. The greater part of the tenants had to remove their houses (formerly in small clusters) to their new farms. This, though troublesome to them, was not a very expensive affair; as the custom on such occasions is, for the person who has the work to be done, to hire a fiddler, upon which 'engagement' all the neighbours joyously assemble, and carry in an incredibly short time, the stones and timber upon their backs to the new site: men women and children alternately dancing and working while daylight lasts, at the termination of which they adjourn to some dwelling where they finish the night, often prolonging the dance to dawn of day, and with little entertainment but that which a fiddler or two affords."

It is clear from this passage that at this time the fiddler was an integral part of the social life of the typical small community. However the picture as described by Hill of men, women and children happily dismantling their home and carrying timber and stone over long distances on their backs to re-build a cottage followed by an evening of merry dancing till dawn utterly misrepresents the conditions of the period.

On nearby Arranmore Island there was a strong musical heritage. Through her excellent autobiography 'Róise Rua'[17], edited and collated by Pádraig O Cnáimhsí, Róise Rua Nic Gríanna or Róise na nÁmhran (Róise of the songs) as she was sometimes known, gives us a marvellously detailed yet interesting insight into life in the northwest of Donegal and island society in the final quarter of the last century.

We learn of the abundance of song held in store by her mother as well as the existence and popularity of the local warpipes. She gives a brief but glowing account of Féilimí O Baoill, a fiddler from Leidhb Ghairbh who played at her wedding but not before she, the bride, was prevailed upon to lilt *The Swallow's Tail* reel for a step dancer.

Concerning the abundance of fiddlers and the social settings of dances on the island she tells us (my translation):

> "I would say there was up to a dozen fiddlers on the island while I was growing up. We hadn't the likes of the dance halls at that time, but we would often have a dance in a kitchen or a barn. We wouldn't have a dance in the summer since the youth would all be in Scotland during that time of the year. We would have them in the winter and the spring. It wouldn't cost much to go into these dances. Occasionally we'd be let in free, while other times there would be a small charge. It wasn't customary to have a big admission price, maybe three or six old pence. There would only be one musician to play, a fiddler or a melodeon player".

She continues:

> "We would have a fiddler at that time as well. The reason being that a group of men would come together to do work for a poor widow or someone who wasn't able to do work for themselves and they would engage a fiddler for a dance after the days work . . . Usually there would be no charge going into this fiddler but the money collected would be given to the widow or the orphans for whose benefit the dance was held. Sometimes, the dancing would last until six in the morning, but a good deal of the times they put a stop to them at three o'clock".

Elsewhere she recalls memories of bothy life with the potato squads of Scotland. Her account, which generally matches many others from this time, notes the regular occurrence of fiddlers amongst the squads. A translation may read:

> "There were few squads that didn't have a fiddler with them at that time, or someone who could play the melodeon, and they would be playing music for us in the evenings after our work - and again in the evenings at the weekend. We would often have dances in the bothies and people from the other squads could come and visit us, or we would go to them when they had something similar. The old dances were the most common ones we would look for; the Sets, the Lancers, the Maggie Piggy, the (Shoe the) Donkey, the Mazurka, the Barn Dance and their likes. Often as well, we would be interested in learning the Scottish dances: the Gay Gordons, the Highland, the Corn Rigs and others. We would sing songs often also, in the bothies in the evening and at the dances as well. These dances helped to give heart and lift depression from us who were in the midsts of strangers".

Weddings provided another major social role for fiddlers. This whole tradition was generally referred to as 'hauling home' and though it was known throughout Ireland and Scotland it has survived longest in its fullest form in Donegal and outlying parts of Scotland. A bride, her family and guests would be marched from her house to the chapel being led by a fiddler playing *Haste to the Wedding*. After the exchange of vows the fiddler would play *The Girl that Broke my Heart* in respect of all the men who did not win her. Sometimes this would be played after the ceremony was completed and the couple had gone into the sacristy to sign the marriage certificate. The entire wedding party would then be 'hauled home' to the bride's house for a meal and dancing by the fiddler playing *Tá do Mhargadh Déanta* (Your Match has been Made). There were local variations on this tradition with the complex tune *The Wedding Jig* substituting for either the first or last tune in southwest Donegal.

The house dance, barn dance, schoolhouse dance (aimed at raising funds for small local schools without maintenance support) and crossroads dance continued to be the main outlet for fiddlers to meet and play throughout the 1800s and into the first three decades of this century. This practice, as we will see in the chapter dealing with the northwest of the county, was sometimes vigorously opposed by the clergy.

From accounts of fiddlers who played for house dances, it appears that two types of fiddlers evolved in this setting. First was the settled country fiddler who worked full time and provided music for the house dances in his locality. All that was required of him was to have enough tunes to complete the solo or set dances for the evening. In this instance about twenty standard tunes would suffice. Performance for listening purposes would be highly irregular. The second type of fiddler was the travelling fiddle master who combined paid evening playing for dances with daytime employment which ranged from occasional farm labour to more highly skilled journeyman craftwork such as either occasional blacksmithing or more typically whitesmithing (tinsmithing). With these masters, performance of listening music combined with storytelling would be readily expected, particularly in the house where the fiddler got lodgings. In this respect, John Mhosaí McGinley, Anthony Helferty, the McConnells and their relations the Dohertys are the best remembered performers. They spread their music through their travels enriching the local repertoires and as demands of daily work slowly decreased through farm mechanisation in the early part of this century their efforts spawned a third class of fiddler, a local master who excelled to the level of being able to perform solo listening music. The Cassidys, Connie Haughey, Jimmy Lyons and Mick McShane of Teelin as well as Francie Dearg and Mickey Bán O'Byrne of Kilcar would be typical examples of such players.

Arising from the consistency of dancing in houses the very structure of the cottages contributed in determining some aspects of the music. Due to the small size of the room, house dance fiddlers stood while playing to leave as much space as possible for the set. Francie Dearg and Mickey Bán O'Byrne long into their old age after their house dance playing had stopped still regularly stood while playing. House dances commonly lasted for six hours or more and well into the early hours of the morning. Such a demand both physically and for numbers of tunes would be too much for one or two players. To meet this schedule groups of local fiddlers would pair off and play in shifts to fill in the night. To ensure the music could be heard above the noise of the dancers the fiddlers might tune up a half tone and commonly play in octaves to enrich the sound.

Again, the size and shape of typical cottages were less than ideal for practising during an evening at home. With children asleep in very close quarters to the hearth, the powerful volume of the modern fiddle would have been highly disruptive. The incredible skills of the Donegal tinsmiths provided the ideal solution. They made tin, and in one case, a brass fiddle body which would be attached to wooden necks taken from damaged timber instruments. These allowed fiddlers to practise on an instrument which having such a muted volume did not disturb sleeping children or animals in the cottage. There were also spinoff benefits to tin fiddles. Youngsters anxious to play could practise on them and if the instrument was mishandled it would only dent and not shatter as would normally happen with a timber instrument. Repairs if required were very simple.

Prior to the availability of modern mutes another approach to solve the volume problem was practiced by the Teelin players and Neillidh Boyle of Dungloe in the first half of this century. They attached clothes pegs to the bridges of timber fiddles which drew off the sound greatly muting the fiddle. Neillidh Boyle experimented with combinations of pegs to produce different tones for specific airs. His favourite pattern was to place a peg on each side of the bridge running parallel to the belly. A third peg was attached to the end of the peg under the top string and set perpendicular to the belly. This gave a muted sound but a very deep mellow tone highlighting the bottom strings.

The house dance lasted, though in a continuously declining state up until the end of the 1930's. Jazz was coming in and dancing halls were opening. Many players saw financial reward in playing for this new type of dancing and traditional music throughout the country declined. This was experienced in Donegal but to a much lesser extent with house dances lingering on. The leanest time for traditional music was reached during the depression years of the 1950s. The decade of the 1960s saw a strengthening revival in traditional music which was expressed most widely through the ballad boom. During this period the format of playing changed radically. The primary venue changed from what had been the cottage to the new one of the pub. The music was now solely for listening purposes with no dancing. It was typically amplified and no storytelling was associated with the playing of tunes. In Donegal this format was generally adopted but to a much lesser degree than nationally. Figures like John Doherty, who still held the major influence on the music in the county certainly played frequently in pubs but the performances were always to his criteria. Endless strings of reels which were typical of pub playing nationally were ignored. John and others like him chose to stick to the old repertoire of varied rhythms as well as descriptive pieces while chat and storytelling remained every bit as important as it had previously been in the cottages. It is fair to say that this resistance to two-dimensional pub background music in favour of interaction between player and listener ensured the passing on of priceless musical folklore which in other parts of the country was almost totally lost.

The Sixties also saw the consolidation of the Comhaltas Ceoltóirí Éireann movement established in the previous decade. Branches were set up throughout the county and many successful fleadhs were held. There were some areas of friction arising from the Comhaltas movement. Sessions were, and still are, typically organised according to a nationally employed format consisting of a master of ceremonies who would announce the music to be played as well as directing the balance between singing and playing. Often these persons were committee members and not musicians. Older fiddlers often talk about an annoyance of having their playing unnecessarily organised or orchestrated for them. Another area of contention was the division of local music into classes of permitted and non-permitted tunes. In some areas fiddlers were told not to play highlands as these tunes were Scottish and the organisation was there to promote Irish music. Fiddlers, knowing well that a huge amount of the favoured reels played in Ireland were of Scottish origin were frustrated and cynical about being restricted in their choice of repertoire. Feelings of antagonism between certain players and the organisation were sometimes strong.

On balance, however, the impact of Comhaltas in Donegal has been positive, primarily through the teaching efforts of some of its branches. The classes taught by Dinny McLoughlin and Róisín Harrigan in Inishowen, Prionsías O Maonaigh in Gweedore and Ann McRory in Ballyshannon have produced some of the county's most outstanding players and has ensured the transmission of the tradition to a whole new generation of talented players.

During the 1970s the popularity of traditional music exploded. Never was it as strong. In many ways it was the decade of the bands but, with the possible exception of Aileach and Ceoltóirí Altan, groups identified solely with Donegal did not exist. In Donegal the format of the previous decade, involving a mixture of pub and house playing, remained. Some of the famous bands did, however, come under considerable influence from players either from Donegal or with a strong Donegal family connections. For example, the first fiddle player with the legendary Bothy Band was Paddy Glackin who also played along with his brother Séamus in Ceoltóirí Laighean. Paddy's role with the Bothy Band was eventually filled by Tommy Peoples. Máiréad Ní Mhaonaigh also performed briefly with De Danann. Much later, Martin McGinley and Paula Doohan played during different periods with the Sligo-based group Dervish.

The 1980s was a time which saw a drop in overall followers of traditional music but a firming up of the dedication of active players of the music. During this period Cáirdeas na bhFidléirí came into being. This group sought initially to re-establish a performance outlet for the older players in Donegal. This was rapidly achieved by its annual meeting in the Highlands Hotel in Glenties at the beginning of October. The revered older fiddlers were out playing again before audiences which understood and enthusiastically appreciated their music. It became clear during this period that the older generation was being well catered for and that the middle-aged generation of fiddlers was stable. The uptake of the music by the young generation needed to be secured. A week-long summer school involving the active participation of the latter generations was established in Glencolumcille during the first week of August. This has been augmented in recent times by the provision of numerous workshop weekends aimed at younger players throughout the county during the year.

REFERENCES

1 Edward Bunting. *The Ancient Music of Ireland*. Walton's, Dublin, 1969. (facsimile ed.).
2 Richard Twiss. *A Tour in Ireland in 1775*. Dublin, 1776.
3 Eugene O'Curry. *Lectures on the Manuscript Materials of Ancient Irish History*. Hinch and Traynor, Dublin 1878.
4 Grattan Flood. *A History of Irish Music*. Irish University Press, Shannon, 1970. (facsimile ed.).
5 *in* Breandán Brathnach. *Folk Music and Dances of Ireland*. The Educational Company of Ireland. Dublin, 1971, p. 57.
6 Seán O Tuama and Thomas Kinsella. *An Duanaire, Poems of the Dispossessed*. Dolmen, Dublin, pp. 276-277.
7 John Neal and William Neal. *A Collection of the Most Celebrated Irish Tunes*. Folkmusic Society of Ireland, Dublin, 1986 (facsimile ed. with new introduction by Nicholas Carolan).
8 Seán Donnelly. *Musicians in the Diocese of Elphin*. Ceol, Vol 5, part 2, pp 34-36.
9 Arthur O'Neill. *Memoirs of Arthur O'Neill. in Annals of the Irish Harpers*. Charlotte Milligan Fox, John Murray, London, 1911.
10 Pers. comm.
11 Arthur O'Neill. Op. cit.
12 Arthur O'Neill. Op. cit.
13 Breandán Breathnach. Op. cit.
14 David Johnson. *Scottish Music in the 18th Century*. John Donald, Edinburgh, 1984.
15 Mary Ann Alburger. *Scottish Fiddlers and Their Music*. Victor Gollancz, Lonson, 1983.
16 Lord George Hill. *Facts From Gweedore*. Queen's University Belfast, Institute of Irish Studies, Belfast, 1971. (facsimile ed. with new introduction by E. Estyn Evans).
17 Róise Nic Gríanna. *Róise Rua*. Sairseáil O Marcaigh, Baile Átha Cliath. 1988 (Pádraig Ua Cnáimhsí eag.).

CHAPTER 3

INFLUENCES

Because of the basic form of the fiddle as an instrument, it naturally lends itself to certain music features while making others very difficult. This results in traditional fiddle music having certain fundamental characteristics. For example its being played with a bow means that individual notes can be either separated (staccato) or alternatively played in unbroken groups with a long single stroke of the bow (legato). Furthermore, because of the arching of the strings over the bridge, only two strings and thus only two notes, at most can reasonably be sounded at the same time. In Ireland traditional fiddle music is concentrated on a single melodic line, with features like harmony and counterpoint being largely irrelevant. This is not to say, however, that the early fiddle music of Donegal was not influenced by other instruments which were capable of such elements like the harp and pipes. There is abundant evidence to show that in the past Donegal fiddlers were happy to absorb sounds characteristic of other instruments, particularly those of the pipes which may have been significant in giving rise to the fiddler's double stopping patterns.

THE HARP

The harp held a distinguished place within the old Gaelic order. In his extensive research on the Irish harp Robert Armstrong[1] records a reference to Donegal harping in the Accounts of the Lord High Treasurer. He notes that during March 1513, O'Donnell, Prince of Connel (a reference to Tír Chonaill, or generally Donegal), visited the Scottish Court at Linlithgow and while there his harper, the only member of the prince's retinue receiving mention, was paid the handsome gratuity of £7. Armstrong comments that "he was probably a remarkable performer, as only one harper, an Englishman, who may have accompanied the Queen or one of her retinue, received so large a sum".

Concerning events of almost a century later, when the fortunes of the O'Donnells had drastically changed culminating in the flight of the Earls from Rathmullen, Rimmer[2] speculates "that it is possible when the Earls of Tyrone and Tyrconnell and nearly one hundred of the leading Irishmen of Ulster left their native land in 1607 and went into exile on the continent which was increasingly under English domination, they took harpers with them".

Bunting's work[3] indicates a strong presence of harpists in the northern half of Ireland towards the end of the harping era in the closing decades of the 1700s. Although he does not identify any Donegal harpists, if the tradition of playing was as strong as Bunting would indicate we can conjecture that there were harpists in numbers in Donegal who could have contributed in some way to the fiddle repertoire. One confirmation of a Donegal harpist appears in the excellent memoirs of Charles McGlinchey of Inishowen, as collected and edited by Patrick Kavanagh entitled 'The Last of the Name'[4]. In this work McGlinchey recalls the lineage of the poet Seán Mac an Meirge Doherty who lived at Keenagh, Malin and also owned lands in Malin and the Isle of Doagh. He then continues with a story concerning a man who he describes as "a descendant of these Dohertys of Keenagh who was a great harp player, the best in Ireland". Another piece of evidence of an appreciation for harping in Inishowen can be found on one of the two standing stones which accompany the famous Early Christian Carndonagh Cross. The west face of the stone located to the north of the cross clearly shows a harpist.

As we have already seen, Arthur O'Neill was happy to travel to Donegal so it seems reasonable to surmise that there was sufficient understanding and appreciation of his talent to make his trip worthwhile. There is further evidence of Donegal harping in Charlotte Milligan Fox's 'Annals of the Irish Harpers'[5]. In a reprinted correspondence from the Reverend George Sampson of Derry, dated July 3rd, 1805, we learn of Denis Hempson of Magilligan, County Derry, whose second "instructor was John C. Garragher, a blind travelling harper whom he (Hempson) followed to Buncranagh, where his master used to play for Colonel Vaughan". It is unclear whether Garragher was a native of Donegal.

An interesting story concerning the Bishop of Derry and a harpist performing in Ballyshannon can be found in 'Camden's Brittania'[6] published in 1722. In this anecdote a harper was entertaining the Bishop, during his dinner. Not understanding the bard's song in Irish he was given a translation. It included a description of the ceremonial burial site of a warrior complete with gold possessions. So accurate was the geographical reference that some persons present went to the alleged site and excavated. They found two pieces of gold, one of which is illustrated in 'Ware's Antiquities'.

A brief account involving the harp appears in the Ballyshannon folklore recounted in Hugh Allingham's 'Ballyshannon: Its History and Antiquities'[7]. In this instance, Shane O'Neill and four cohorts slay Reginald Maguire, who had just been serenaded with harp music by his betrothed Helen O'Donnell of Donegal. This story is again recounted in two separate accounts recorded from the Carricknahorna National School as part of the Irish Folklore Commission Schools Collection of the 1930s. These accounts may, however, have been based on a familiarity with Allingham's publication.

Breandán Breathnach[8] held the view that popular harp music was amalgamated into the repertoire of other musical instruments, particularly with the adaptation of clan marches into jigs. There is one surprising bit of evidence in Donegal fiddle playing to indicate a minor, yet direct, influence of the harp tradition on the fiddle. While tunes and stories were being collected from John Doherty at Árd McCool in Stranorlar during early 1977 he played a very unusual air. This involved bowing the melody on the bottom strings of the fiddle using only the first and second fingers. In the meantime, he formed a simple chord on the top two strings using open strings and his third finger. He plucked the chords with his little finger, in accompaniment to the simultaneously bowed melody of the air. Doherty later explained that the chord plucking was to imitate a harp, as the piece was originally a harp tune which had come down through the long line of fiddlers in his family and which he learned from his father. Interestingly, this same technique is also employed by Neillidh Boyle in the bird-song imitation portion of his intricate version of *An Londubh*. In a broader sense, airs and marches from what is accepted as the harping tradition are commonly found in Ireland, such as the Carolan repertoire, and the tunes *Tábhair dom do Lámh* and *Tiarna Mhaigh Eo*, the latter being a strong favourite amongst older Donegal fiddlers.

FLUTES, FIFES AND WHISTLES

There is little evidence to suggest that in the past either the concert flute or whistle had any great influence on Donegal fiddling. Charles McGlinchey[9] gives an interesting account of the flute in Inishowen while referring to church choirs. He states:

> Away back in Fr. Shiel's time, about 1820 and before, it was all flutes they had. Seamus Aindréas McCool and his brother Charley played the flutes at that time. They were great singers, too. The Harkins of Clogherna had music in them. Music is a thing that follows tribes of people.

At face value, this passage is very interesting as the older generation of players do not recall flute players and old instruments which would have been used in the past are almost unknown in the county. This apparent concentration of flute players in Inishowen may be easily explained by the fact that even today older people use the word 'flute' interchangeably to describe the timber concert flute and the smaller instrument, the fife. While there is little evidence of concert flute playing, fife bands were very common. McGlinchey's reference to flute players in Inishowen is almost certainly noting the existence of fife players.

While these instruments might not appear to have had any great impact this is not to infer that they were not played. Fifes in particular were played in militia (often pronounced milishee) bands. In Hugh Allingham's[10] book we read of the formation on August 1st, 1779 of 'The Loyal Ballyshannon Volunteers Fife and Drum Band', along with a similar group in Killybegs in order to parade and drill in preparation for a French or Spanish invasion. We also learn that Mr. Oliver, Bandmaster of the 'Donegal Militia Band', composed The Donegal Polka to act as an overture to Carolan's *Hawk of Ballyshannon,* a tune whose title cryptically refers to the Fermanagh Chieftain Philip McGuire. A copy of this work, originally dedicated to Lady Cecilia Conygham and published by Marcus Moses can be found in the Irish Traditional Music Archive in Dublin.

Francie Dearg and Mickey Bán O'Byrne's grandfather was known to have played the fife. Packie Manus Byrne of Corkermore, Ardara, and Paddy Campbell of Glassagh, Glenties, are players associated with the whistle. Other than these individuals there appear to be no significant whistle or flute players in the folk memory of the county.

PIPES

Both uilleann and warpipes have been played in the county for at least three hundred years leaving a lasting mark on fiddle playing. It was common military practice until the current century for warring British armies to engage the services of artists to attend battles and sketch the events. The drawings and paintings produced were geared towards capturing the strategic positions of various sections of both armies, the lie of the land, patterns of attack etc. These paintings, along with the military leaders' diaries - which described the progress and strategies of the confrontation - would then be used in officer training schools to teach classic battle tactics. We know that pipers were strongly associated with Irish armies. A copy of the contemporary drawing by an English artist of the Battle of Ballyshannon on October 17th, 1593 is held in the Convent of Mercy Secondary School, Ballyshannon and figures a player of the warpipes in the ranks of the O'Donnell forces.

No doubt the most famous of Donegal pipers, of both warpipes and uilleann pipes, was Tarlach Mac Suibhne (1818 - 1916), An Píobaire Mór or Searlaí Eamoinn Ruaidh as he was locally known in his native Gweedore. The Píobaire Mór was also a fiddle player and no doubt would have derived part of his fiddle repertoire from his piping. He possessed a copy of 'O'Farrell's Collection of National Music for the Union Pipes' and professed great respect for the music contained in it.

Many relatives of Mac Suibhne, both blood relations and through marriage, played the uilleann pipes as well as the warpipes. These include uilleann pipers in the famous Doherty and related O'Rourke families. Those were Hugh Doherty (born about 1790) and his son Simon (born about 1824) as well as Edward O'Rourke of Ardara (born about 1875 and married to Hugh Doherty's great-great-grand-daughter Fanny). His pipes were still in Ardara until recently and in a playable condition. Paddy Bán Quigley (born about 1870) from Ardara although primarily remembered for his uilleann piping could also play the warpipes. Another Ardara uilleann piper was John Breslin whose pipes are now in the possession of Peter Oliver in Ardara. Hugh Devanney of Newtown Cunningham was also a well-known uilleann piper. Warpipers in the Doherty-Gallagher-McConnell families were Hugh Doherty and Simon Doherty (same as above), Mickey Doherty (brother of the latter Simon), Simi Doherty (born about 1854 and son of the latter Simon), Mickey Doherty (born about 1850 and brother of Simi), Donal Gallagher (born about 1840, son-in-law of Simon Doherty), Mickey (born 1875) and Hugh (born 1876) Gallagher (sons of Donal) and Mickey Mc Connell (born about 1873, a son-in-law of Simon Doherty). The latter player was also a very accomplished fiddler who, like the Píobaire Mór would have had a mixed repertoire deriving from both instruments.

Another warpiper who would have had a direct influence on prominent fiddlers was Charlie Boyle, a younger brother of the famous Cronashallog fiddlers, Neillidh and Con Boyle. Charlie was a highly respected piper and the brothers were fond of playing typical piping tunes together outdoors.

In the late 19th century there lived in Kilcar a family of seven brothers of the surname Campbell, who were famous warpipers and had a great impact on the music of the area. Francie Dearg O'Byrne recalled that they were extremely good players and would perform for dances in the locality throughout spring and summer. They would travel Scotland for work during the remainder of the year but always returned for Christmas where they would be engaged by the local landlord, Lady Ellis, to play for her Christmas Eve Ball. So powerful was the volume of the music that the Campbells would play outside on the lawn while all the windows at the front of the house would be open to let in the music for the dancers inside.

The ability of Micí Mhícheál Bhig Ó Dónaill as a piper is well recounted in Róise Nic Ghrianna's[11] autobiography. On the basis of this information it would appear quite reasonable that he was a noted and influential piper in Arranmore as well as in the bothies of Scotland.

John, Mickey and Simi Doherty have all left impressions in recorded folklore of some influences which the two forms of pipes have had on Donegal fiddling. We know that the still popular *Hiúidí Gallagher's March* (played as a double jig) was a favourite of Hugh (or Hiúidí) Gallagher noted above. While recording a version of the *Tullaghan Lassies* reel (also known in two versions as *Lough Isle Castle* and *Seán sa Cheo,* both of which originate from the Scottish reel *Sleepy Maggie* first published in Scotland in 1734), Simon

(Ballinamore) Doherty tells us that the tune was a piping one which came to him through the many pipers in his family. Further evidence of a piping source for the tune in the Doherty family is found in a field recording made by Breandán Breathnach at the Reelin Bridge in 1965. In the course of this recording John and Mickey played *Tullaghan Lassies* but in this instance Mickey droned by using double stops with trills on the bottoms strings throughout the entire performance. This piece is arguably one of the most exciting recordings of Donegal fiddle music in existence. This format of playing was also used by Francie Dearg and Mickey Bán O'Byrne and a piping origin for the tune was also firmly noted by Neillidh Boyle.

Many typical Scottish piping marches were to be found in the repertoire of the Dohertys and have been passed on to the current generation of players. It is significant that their father, Michael, played warpipes in the Letterkenny Militia Band.

Two jigs, both entitled *Rí na bPíobairí*, played with marvellous droning effect by Francie Dearg and Mickey Bán O'Byrne, are clearly of piping origin, as is another, *Muinneal a' Bhardáil.* Other typical examples of Donegal fiddle music reflecting piping influences are *The March of the Meenatoitin Bull (The Inverness Gathering)* which was played as both a march and a reel, as well as the notable reel *Muilleann na Maide.* Vincent Campbell plays Mickey Doherty's five-part version of the latter tune, in which the droning and piping imitation is very evident in the first part.

A classic piece of pipe imitation was sometimes played at gatherings by the Doherty brothers. This set consisted of the air *The Enniskillen Dragoons*, followed by the jig *Nóra Críonna* and finished with a rousing version of *Miss McLeod's* reel. They were played in scordatura or 'open tuning'. The fiddle strings were tuned as ADAD to give a constant droning sound and the melodies played using very long, unbroken bow strokes. A spirited version of this set (not including the initial air) can be heard on the excellent release of the Irish Folklore Commission's field recordings of Mickey Doherty entitled *The Gravel Walks*. Another trick of some of the older generation of Donegal fiddlers to effect pipe imitation was to place teaspoons or metal bottle tops on the F holes of their fiddles. The loose items would pick up the vibrations from the belly of the fiddle and vibrate giving a drone-like hum. Other

Donegal tunes which characteristically contain long bowed double stops reminiscent of piping include the reel *The Oak Tree* or *Na Saighnean, Jackson's Reel, Maighdean Mhara Mhullaigh Mhór* and *Saitheadh a' Bháid.*

Surprisingly, one of the earliest documented uilleann pipers in Ireland came from south Donegal. Patrick Haly was born at Ballyshannon in 1748. According to an account by Hugh Allingham[12], he was a very jovial individual fond of both piping and singing. He was also a regular visitor to nearby Castlecaldwell, where he played for Sir James Caldwell on his barge, the Saint Patrick. It is almost certain that Haly would have been familiar with the ill-fated fiddler, Denis Mc Cabe, who as noted above came to a watery end off this same vessel. According to Breandán Breathnach[13] the form of pipes available at this time and most likely played by Haly would have comprised two drones and a single tenor regulator. Haly, a prominent Town Burgess in Ballyshannon, died on April 26th, 1813 and is buried in Saint Anne's Churchyard at Mullnashee. There is no record of what became of his pipes.

As we shall see in the next chapter, the inter-twining of fact and folklore is a common occurrence in Donegal. At times, this weaving can be so tight that it becomes impossible to identify and separate the various strands of a story. One family which appears to fit well into this coalescing of myth and reality is the Jacksons.

They are best accounted for by Francie Dearg O'Byrne though the Campbells of the Croaghs also have accounts of the same family, albeit under a different surname. The general story is that it was believed the family was originally from Mayo and came to settle in Bundoran during the first half of the last century at a time when their children were quite young. A boy and girl each took up the fiddle while another of the boys took up the uilleann pipes. The trio travelled Donegal playing at fairs and gatherings. At this time much of the dance music was performed by lilting. The music of the trio so impressed the local lilters that there was a great rush to learn their tunes. In an effort to imitate the full sound of the trio with pipe drones, lilters would hum the Jacksons' tunes through paper and comb. Their repertoire, which bears all the hallmarks of piping origin, is still known today amongst some older players in southwest Donegal as *The Combs* or *Jacksons' Combs*, and many of them include the name Jackson in their title. The majority of the combs which have survived have come through the repertoire of Francie Dearg O'Byrne.

The information provided seems quite plausible and the derivation of the combs image is attractive. There is, however, enough evidence to throw some doubt on this story thus relegating it from the sphere of fact to highly creative folklore.

In his article entitled 'Piper Jackson'[14], Breandán Breathnach gives a broad account of uillean piper Walker Jackson of Lisduan House, Ballingarry, County Limerick. A list of tunes either composed or accredited to this prolific player as well as tunes with the surname Jackson in the title accompanies the article. Amongst these is *Jackson's Hi-Ho* which appears on page 26 of the 'Gunn Collection' from County Fermanagh while Breathnach also notes its existence in County Leitrim. The Gunn Collection transcription is the same as Francie Dearg's version. This in itself does not discredit the Donegal story of the tunes origin as it could still have been circulated by the Bundoran family. Furthermore, taking *Jackson's Hi-Ho* in isolation, the Fermanagh and Leitrim examples combined with the Donegal version could be argued to support a northwestern provenance of the tune. It is another tune title cited by Breathnach which focuses the main doubts on the Bundoran Jacksons. On page 45 of his article Breandán notes six tune titles occurring in the 'Henry Hudson Collection' which were assigned to Walker Jackson but were not associated with any transcriptions. Among these is the *Kitchen Comb*. It is by no means an over-stretch of the imagination to accept that with the passing of time the latter tune became known as *Jackson's Comb* and that ultimately, as Francie Dearg related, the associated Jackson tunes became known under the umbrella title *The Combs*. Whether Walker Jackson of Limerick or alternatively a less documented Jackson family of Bundoran was the source of the Donegal Combs repertoire will almost certainly never be established. What is of great importance however is that these tunes, with their clear piping overtones, were very attractive to Donegal fiddlers who made extremely imaginative additions to their techniques and ornamentation styles to capture piping tones in their music.

The free reed instruments used in traditional music today are relatively recent arrivals. The melodeon is a post-Famine instrument and largely entered the Irish tradition at the end of the last century in its ten key single-row form with stoppers. This instrument went on to be overtaken in popularity by the ubiquitous accordion. Sally Hegarty of Kilcar, a relation of Frank Cassidy, is remembered as being a player of incredible ability on an instrument which had an extra fourth stopper giving a vibrato sound to the music. At least one tune, a slip jig, still bears her name. Mickey (Gollie) Gallagher of Teelin was also a well-respected player who was in popular demand to play with the local fiddlers. His influence can be heard to some degree in the playing of the highly talented Dermot Byrne. In the latter two cases it would be accurate to say that each of the players adapted their styles particularly to suit the sound and settings of Donegal fiddle tunes. As such, their music stands out against the legion of box players who play in a loud, dominating, indistinct style. Kate Sweeney from Meenmore, near Dungloe, was another exponent of the old single row melodeon. She was renowned for her regular playing at convoys throughout the countryside between Dungloe and Ardara. She lived to her 104th year and was known to have traded tunes with the Dohertys. Through her family, Kate passed many of her tunes onto her grandson, Francie McHugh of Lough Doon who like her, is showing every sign of playing into his second century. Another talented player who has based a vast amount of his repertoire on the fiddle music of John Doherty, in particular, is Patsy Wilson who now lives in Donegal Town.

The concertina is currently seen as having had little range outside of County Clare. While Clare is the centre of strength of the instrument today it was certainly to be found in the northern half of the country two generations ago. Several players can be accounted for in the eastern part of County Derry, where again as with the rest of the country it primarily served as a woman's instrument. Grace Orpen claims in her book 'The Dances of Donegal'[15], published in 1931 that "the violin and concertina are the instruments most commonly employed... (for playing for dances)". While Prionsias O Maonaigh's mother, Rosie Sweeney, was a concertina player, there is nothing to indicate that the instrument was played in any numbers or had any impact on the fiddle music of the county.

MISCELLANEOUS INSTRUMENTS

A popular instrument a generation or two ago and by all accounts having had greater popularity before that again was the Jew's Harp or as it was best known in its Irish language form the *Trumpa*. Many of the older fiddlers remember this being most popular during the height of the house dances and lilters. The appeal of the instrument was linked to its continuous drone-like sound. The McMonagle family of Tievealough, by Lough Ea in the heart of the Croaghs, who were famous for their poetry are also strongly associated with excellent playing on the instrument. The title *The Loughside Hornpipe*, a tune made popular by John Doherty, is a literal translation of the townland name Tievealough. John learned this tune from the trumpa playing of the McMonagles' in whose house he was a frequent and very welcome guest. The mouth organ was occasionally played in Donegal but does not appear to have impacted on the fiddle music at all.

ACCOMPANIMENT

Much has been spoken in recent years concerning bodhrán accompaniment to traditional music. In Donegal there appears to be much fewer players compared to most other counties. This seems to suit the existing body of fiddlers since it is generally considered that other than in the hands of three or four very talented individuals throughout the entire country, it is normally a disruptive device. More simply, as one player maintains, the bodhrán best serves two purposes at any session; either as a big communal ashtray or as a large tray for bringing down real musicians a round of drink, preferably paid for by its owner.

My own experience overall of the guitar as an accompanying instrument to Donegal fiddle music is that it is held in only slightly milder disregard than the bodhrán. Fiddlers immediately become suspect on the production of the instrument at any gathering. This is based on a widespread lack of knowledge of the tunes by the accompanist as well a lack of sensitivity for the rhythm of the tunes. There is almost always a question of the volume with which the instrument is played. Fiddlers hold that as an instrument of accompaniment, it should add rhythmically to the music with the volume remaining under the featured fiddles. All too often they lament the insistence by guitarists to play at equal and often greater volume than the fiddles. There are some players however, who are regularly sought as accompanists by fiddlers. These include Gearóid O Maonaigh of Gweedore, Dermot Toland of Gortahork, Paul Kelly of Bundoran and Seán Chon Johnnie Byrne of Teelin while the loss of Ballyshannon's Charlie McGettigan to Leitrim has denied the county of the talents of one of the most gifted guitarists in Ireland today. As for the piano, it never caught on in Donegal to the degree which it did throughout the rest of Ireland. For almost identical reasons of displeasure as cited with guitarists, Donegal fiddlers for the most part would appear to be content with the piano's non-development in the county.

INFLUENCES FROM THE IRISH FIDDLE TRADITION

In terms of the Irish fiddle tradition, Donegal music has been largely isolated until a few years ago. It had little outward effect on the styles and repertoire of the remainder of the country. Likewise, it was largely untouched by external Irish fiddle influences with one minor exception. The fiddle music of Sligo, as popularised by the recordings of Morrison, Killoran and Coleman, swept the country from the time of their original releases in America around the first quarter of the present century. The music of Coleman and Morrison did enter the Donegal repertoire, but in almost every circumstance the tunes were performed in the original Donegal style of the fiddler. This is in stark contrast to the greater portion of Ireland which saw slavish attempts at trying to reproduce the original recording's style. The one Irish fiddler outside of Donegal who seemed to make a direct impact was Paddy Killoran, particularly on Mickey Doherty. Mickey and his brother John would have both been familiar with Paddy Killoran's commercial releases and this is evidenced in several recordings of the brothers. John tended to play the tunes in his own style but often strung Killoran's sets of tunes together as they were originally performed on record. With Mickey, however, there is clearer evidence from recordings that he attempted to bend his rendition of the specific sets to be closer to Killoran's. It is significant to note that during his last visit to Ireland, Paddy Killoran was brought up to

Donegal by Garda Sergeant McGill, a native of Raphoe, who was stationed near Paddy's home locality. During this visit Killoran met Mickey Doherty and they struck up a friendship with the pair having a healthy admiration for each other's abilities.

Another musician to influence the Donegal fiddlers, albeit to a much more direct extent, was the classically trained multi-instrumentalist, Arthur Darley. Well-known in the first half of this century for his arrangements of popular tunes as well as for performances and adjudications at various musical competitions, Darley was a good violinist and had an appreciation for traditional music. He came to live in Dunkineely for some time and is remembered as having been employed as the organist for the Church of Ireland. During this period he was greatly impressed by the Dohertys and made a point of keeping in contact with them. He composed the reel *The Four Mile Stone* which appears in 'Roaches Collection' Volume 1, number 189 as well as a jig entitled *Bruckless Shore* which has become known as *Arthur Darley's* or alternatively by the completely misleading name *The Swedish Jig*. These tunes are still well-remembered today in Donegal and have been passed on largely through the playing of John Doherty and Danny O'Donnell. A jig appearing under the title *The Milestone* in the portion of 'The Northern Fiddler'[16] dealing with Danny O'Donnell is credited to Arthur Darley. This tune in fact is a composition of Darley's which he entitled *The Donegal Jig*. The incorrect title which appears in the book was taken up wrongly from Danny by the collectors when he spoke to them about the reel *The Four Mile Stone*. Apparently Darley composed quite a number of tunes in the traditional style and his manuscripts were kept in a trunk which was inherited and taken to France by his son. There, sadly, the trail ends. Based on the popularity of Darley's three known compositions a great deal would seem to have been lost.

INFLUENCES FROM THE SCOTTISH FIDDLE TRADITION

While the Donegal fiddle tradition absorbed only rare influences from within Ireland it obviously assimilated significant elements, both stylistically and in terms of repertoire, from Scotland whilst managing to maintain its unique identity. This influencing was a natural result of the strong bonds between the two localities through seasonal migrant workers.

As has already been mentioned, the Scottish reel repertoire pervaded all of Ireland during the last century. Another characteristic Scots rhythm, the strathspey, also had an impact in Ireland. It was well known throughout Ulster, and even the Sligo virtuoso, Michael Coleman, was not adverse to recording the strathspey *Stirling Castle* as well as *Lady Mary Ramsey's.* The schottische or as it was sometimes known, the fling or highland, was similarly adopted in numerous localities and can easily be traced back to its introduction via Scotland. Though geographically extensive in Ireland there is no denying that these rhythms found their greatest strongholds in Donegal. The strathspey, german and highland were as much the musical standard with the Donegal fiddler as were jigs, reels and hornpipes. In fact, in some places the highland would certainly have had a stronger currency than jigs and hornpipes.

Perhaps the greatest impact of the bond with Scotland has been the extent of the development of the highland as a rhythm in Donegal. In this case, strathspeys were commonly adapted by levelling out the heavily-dotted Scottish rhythm and to a minor degree reducing the strings of triplets. A good example of this can be found with the popular *Padaí Bhillí na Rópaí's Highland* or *The Low Highland* which has been made out of the Scots strathspey *Miss Stewart of Grantully* and is played elsewhere in Ireland as a reel entitled *The Green Groves of Erin.* The practice of generating highlands from other rhythms also extended to reworking reels into highlands. A typical example of this is one of the most popular highlands *Sporting Paddy* which has been formed by modifying the reel of the same name. Also in terms of melody exchanges, complex Scottish descriptive pieces such as the *Four Poster Bed* and *The Hen's March Over the Midden* thrived in the crossing to Donegal.

It should be pointed out that the trading was neither one-way nor confined to mainland Scotland. During a visit to Shetland by Prionsías and Máireád Uí Mhaonaigh, the late Tom Anderson was able to confidently indicate to them reels which had been left in the islands by Donegal fisherman. Danny O'Donnell recalls when he was a child people from the Rosses would travel to Shetland to take seasonal work as herring salters in Lerwick. While there, the workers lived in labourers huts and like their potato harvesting counterparts, they held dances and exchanged music. With the exception of the war years, George Stark, The Blind Fiddler, from Dundee annually visited the islands during the salting season between 1902 and 1959. Stark held a regular place at the Market Cross playing for listeners[17]. Danny remembers that the Donegal workers took a tremendous interest in his playing and brought back many of his tunes. Stark died in 1960 at the age of 83 years.

In relation to the bow, the marked single stroke styles captured on the recordings of James Scott Skinner and William McKenzie Murdoch had an inspirational effect on many of the great players of Donegal during the first half of this century. While there was no conscious attempt to copy this bowing pattern, many Donegal fiddlers did seek to produce the same attacking feel to their music opting for a generally staccato based bowing. Prior to the availability of these recordings the meeting of Donegal fiddlers working in the seasonal squads with their Scottish counterparts ensured a regular transfer of local stylistic elements.

One element of the Scottish influence which has created a distinguishing mark between Donegal fiddlers and those throughout the rest of Ireland is the abundance and familiarity with playing in positions. The influence of classical technique, particularly during the golden era of James Scott Skinner and William McKenzie Marshall meant a great increase in the use of position technique by Scottish fiddlers. This was clearly picked up by the Donegal fiddlers and maintained in the tunes demanding position work brought back to Donegal. These were further added to by the development of reversing tunes requiring moving up out of the first position to play the octave melody. Position playing is extremely rare outside of Donegal with the fiddler only having a tune or two which rises beyond the first position. In such cases, the note is often C or C sharp on the first string which is achieved by a simple, quick slide with the little finger. In Donegal however, there are a good deal of tunes demanding position work. These have been played and recorded by the great masters of the style and this technique is not viewed as an impediment or overly daunting challenge to the regular player. Position playing is not uncommon and given the fact that the technique was transferred via an oral, as opposed to a formal training medium, the typical level of mastery of the skill is a tribute to the great musicianship of the Donegal fiddlers.

The result of absorption of these various Scottish elements into Donegal fiddle music has been a general preference for an overall staccato style of bowing with a greater, but not total, use of triplets when ornamenting a tune. It must be stressed, however, that this is a generalisation, as many fiddlers employed mixed staccato – legato bowing and fingered rolls in their general execution. Tunes of Scottish piping origin are often treated with liberal double stopping, sometimes combined with finger trills, to effect the drone of pipes. Another feature of the Scots influence has been maintaining tunes and changing others into the key of A major. A typical example of this is the playing of Neil Gow's *Brandlings* in its original key of A in Donegal while throughout the rest of the country it is played in the key of G and titled *The Dogs Amongst the Bushes.* Another example is the transposition of such reels as *Music in the Glen* and *The Woman of the House* into the more suitable fiddle key of A as would be in Scotland.

The Scottish influence in Donegal was strong but it was never more than an influence. Scots music was never passively assimilated without modification into Donegal music. As was the case with all other counties which found themselves exposed to Scottish music, it was always altered to fit comfortably within the local style.

Over the centuries, Donegal music has received influences from several sources. Rare fragments from the harping tradition remain. Outside of existing local pipe bands, the once influential piping tradition in Donegal is generally moribund. The only exception to this would appear to be the take up of Donegal fiddle and piping tunes by inspired uilleann pipers who with few exceptions are largely based outside of Donegal such as Joe McLaughlin, Paul Harrigan, Robbie Hannon, John Murphy and more increasingly Seán Óg Potts. Donegal has internalised little of the fiddle styles of the remainder of Ireland being more naturally exposed through traditional migrant labour routes to our nearest neighbours in Scotland.

REFERENCES

1 Robert Bruce Armstrong. *Irish and Highland Harps.* Irish University Press, Shannon, 1969, p.145.
2 Joan Rimmer. *The Irish Harp - Clairseach na hÉireann.* Mercier Press, Cork,1977. p. 47.
3 Edward Bunting. *The Ancient Music of Ireland.* Walton's, Dublin, 1969. (facs. ed.).
4 Charles McGlinchey. *The Last of the Name,* Blackstaff Press, Belfast, 1986, Patrick Kavanagh (Editor).
5 Charlotte Milligan Fox, . *Annals of the Irish Harpers,* John Murray, London, pp 114-115, 1911.
6 *in* Hugh Allingham. Ballyshannon, *It's History and Antiquities. The Donegal Democrat,* Ballyshannon, 1879.
7 Hugh Allingham, Op. cit.
8 Breandán Breathnach. *Folkmusic and Dances of Ireland,* The Educational Company of Ireland, Dublin, 1971.
9 Charles McGlinchey, Op. Cit.
10 Hugh Allingham, Op. cit.
11 Róise Nic Ghrianna. *Róise Rua.* Sairseál O Marcaigh, Baile Átha Cliath, 1988. Pádraig O Cnáimhse (eag.).
12 Hugh Allingham, Op. cit.
13 Breandán Breathnach, Op. cit.
14 Breandán Breathnach. *Piper Jackson.* Irish Folk Music Studies, vol. 2, 1974-1975, pp 41-52.
15 Grace Orpen. *Dances of Donegal.* D. Wilkie, London, 1931.
16 Allen Feldman, and Eamon O'Doherty. *The Northern Fiddler.* Blackstaff Press, Belfast, 1979.
17 Tom Anderson. *Ringing Strings.* The Shetland Times, Lerwick, 1983.

CHAPTER FOUR

DONEGAL FIDDLE FOLKLORE
AND
TUNE ORIGINS

The social setting for fiddle-playing, as we have already seen, has changed radically in Donegal over the past three decades. The last generation of Donegal fiddlers whose main outlet for home entertainment was storytelling, music-making and dancing, has, for the most part, passed on. It is hard for those of us who are the products of the post-radio, television and now video home-entertainment era to understand the value, let alone, the unwritten performance rules of storytelling and music making of the previous generations.

For example, younger players today sometimes compare tapes of various renderings of a particular tune by John Doherty where he tells a story concerning its origin. At times the tune is credited to different composers or associated with different sets of events. The listeners on occasion hastily conclude that, due to the obvious lack of consistency, John was not a reliable source for either historical or folklore information. This view is what may be expected from a person who has grown up in a technological age of data accuracy. What it fails to recognise is that strict accuracy is not what either storyteller or listeners looked for in their entertainment. What they sought was a good story, well-told and a good performance of the tune afterwards. The only time when a tune had to specifically match a piece of music was when there was a certain sound involved in the tune which would be required to correspond to some facet of the tale, for example, the rhythm of waves in *Tuam na Farraige*, birdsong in *An Londubh* or the cacophony of the hunt in *Seilg a' Mhadaí Rua*. Outside of such circumstances any good story could be matched against any good tune for the pleasure of all involved at any convenience.

In this way, a tune did not have to be strictly associated with any one title. In fact very many tunes are found associated with different names, composers and circumstances of origin. What is important, however, from the folklore point of view are the stories which preceded and gave additional dimension to the performance of the tunes. Here folklore and music remained married in a partnership of mutual support.

To the older generations, fiddle-playing was seen as a gift in itself and the way in which a person came to acquire this craft was commonly enveloped in a mantle of folklore. Two variations of a folklore motif, both of which have been excellently explored in Daithí O hÓgáin's book 'An File'[1], were regularly used to explain how a person came to become gifted in fiddle-playing. In the first instance, a simple person, usually with no formal education or particular talents, is journeying home at night. He decides to sleep in a faerie rath and is mysteriously awoken. Beside him he finds a book, a pen and a fiddle which have been left by the faeries. By expressing interest in the book, the person is given the gift of poetry; the pen signifies the gift of prose while the fiddle bestows the gift of music. The faeries must get something in return however and after choosing, the pen usually leaps up blinding the person in one or both eyes. In the second version, the person is sleeping in the rath and is awoken by faeries who invite him/her into the fort, through a secret door, to attend a dance. The person must be careful not to eat or drink as this will entrap him as one of the faerie folk, and he will be permanently lost from the human world. During the night, he is offered either a book, a pen or a fiddle with the same results as in the first version of the motif. This story was frequently used to explain how a fiddler, poet or writer came to achieve rapid skills in their craft in the absence of any amount of formal education.

The coupling of the gift with some form of blindness was a natural one since sight-impaired children were often taught music or poetry. It was viewed as a profession which was compatible with their available skills even until recent times. In the case of accomplished players and reciters, the supernatural origin of their blindness and talents certainly enhanced the mystique of their reputation.

Two Donegal fiddlers who lived in this century openly claimed that they received their music in such circumstances. A detailed account of how the Píobaire Mór, Tarlach Mac Suibhne, came to learn his music from the faeries in the rath in Gweedore is well documented in Francis O'Neill's 'Irish Minstrels and Musicians'[2]. In that account, the book which the Píobaire Mór reported as having contained the music of the faeries is his copy of 'O'Farrell's Collection of National Irish Music for the Union Pipes'. The second, fiddler Neillidh Boyle, who by coincidence was blind in one eye, likewise was fond of telling the story of how one night, while coming home from a housedance in Dunlewey, met with the King of the Faeries and, after a long discussion about music, had the gift of fiddling bestowed upon him.

In a similar motif, Simi, John and Mickey Doherty often told stories of how a simple fiddler who only had the one tune suddenly came to be a famous player. In this format, the fiddler is reluctantly travelling to play for a housedance or a wedding. He is very unwilling due to his limited repertoire but has agreed as no other fiddler is available. On the way to the house he meets a wee red-haired man who enquires about his ability to play. The man laments his poor skill while the faerie asks to see his fiddle. The faerie draws his fingers over the strings sounding them three times, and hands back the fiddle telling the man he will now be the best player in Ireland. This act of the faerie sounding the strings three times is commonly repeated in similar stories, and is the main ingredient in imparting musical enchantment to the fiddle and fiddler. Following this the fiddler proceeds to the wedding and plays brilliantly for hours without repeating a tune. He continues as a gifted player into old age and as he draws his last breath, the fiddle, which is hanging on the wall bursts into pieces never to be played again. In one telling of the story by Mickey Doherty, he records that such an occurrence took place near Ballykerrigan School, naming Francie Herron from Garvan Hill in Glenfin as the man who was heading for a wedding in Letterhillue[3]. A very close version of the same story appears as recounted by Pádraig Eoghain Phádraig Mac A' Luain in 'Uair a Chloig Cois Teallaigh'[4].

Another variation of this story which I heard recounted by John Doherty involves the faerie warning the fiddler not to let anyone else ever catch the fiddle after the sounding of the strings. If this were to happen then the fiddle would lose its enchantment. The fiddler goes on to the wedding and plays without stop for hours. He is offered tea and a young man, the faerie in disguise, approaches him and asks for the loan of the fiddle to fill in playing while he takes his tea. Having forgotten the agreement, the fiddle immediately loses its enchantment and the poor fiddler is only able to play two tunes for the rest of his days.

Fiddle cases are only recent developments with traditional musicians. In the past, the instrument was carried in a sack when travelling and hung on the wall when kept at home. In folklore the commonest ending for an enchanted fiddle was to burst on the wall with the last breath of its owner. This seemed to ensure that a fiddler who had not been given the gift of music by the faeries would never be able to play the enchanted music. This tradition is also reflected in Scotland where the famous McPherson destroys his fiddle prior to his hanging to make certain no one inherits his instrument. Mickey and John Doherty when recounting the death of their father stated that, though very low, he managed to sit up and strike into *Mac Suibhne's Reel.* So great was the playing that the tip of the bow whistled (according to his sons this occurred regularly and was an indication that he was in good playing form). He gave over the fiddle to be hung up on the wall. Shortly afterwards he took his last breath and the fiddle instantly shattered to bits never to be played again. With this tradition of the non-inheritance of enchanted fiddles in mind it is interesting to note that the great Ballybofey player, Hughie Gillespie who died as recent as 1987, had his fiddle buried with him!

A similar story of fiddle enchantment appears in the book 'Songs of Uladh'[5] concerning the origin of the Scottish fiddler, Largo's, composition *The Fairy Reel* and how the tune came to originate. According to this version, four fiddlers and a piper were playing for dancers at a bonfire gathering on St. John's Eve (one of a handful of dates in Irish folklore when the supernatural and earthly worlds meet) when a stranger came into the company and requested the best of the fiddlers, a Mac Fhionnlach from Falcarragh to play *The Fairy Reel.*

Mac Fhionnlach was unable to play the tune and the stranger took up the fiddle and gave a masterful performance. He handed the fiddle back to the Falcarragh man and told him "Now there's your fidil for you. Turn on the 'Reel'. Play it after me for you're the only man in the Five Kingdoms that can do that same!" Mac Fhionnlach was able to play away at it "without break" while the stranger danced with a young girl. At the finish he slipped a gold coin into her hand and left requesting the company to move the fire seven paces to the north. It is clear from the latter point that the stranger was a faerie and the bonfire was set on one of the faeries' "gentle places".

The same tune again crops up, this time on Tory Island. The folklore of the island is renowned for its richness, and music sometimes features prominently. While working for the Irish Folklore Commission in the 1940's Séamus Ennis collected this version of events from Hughie Dixon concerning the effect that hearing a faerie playing *The Faerie Reel* can have on mortals[6]. I have translated from the original as follows:

> "One of the islandmen was going to collect sheep at Port Glas one day and when he reached Port Glas he heard marvellous music there. The tune that was being played was *The Faerie Reel* and as he was a grand dancer he had to give in and dance to it. He danced away and the music played on until at the end of it all he wasn't able to stop even though he was tired and worn out with the dancing. He tried his best to stop but there was no use in it. Another islander came along the path and saw him dancing but heard no music at all. He asked him what sort of caper was he up to, dancing as he was and the dancer replied that he was unable to stop and he wouldn't be until some mortal laid a hand on him. He would have dropped with exhaustion from dancing only that the other man happened on him. The soles of his shoes and his socks were worn through and his feet were sore to the bone from the roughness of the place he was dancing on".

Another piece of island folklore, in this case concerning a blind fiddler and the supernatural, was collected during the schools collection project by Antoin O Dochartaigh in 1938[7]. The story was told by Nuala Bean Uí Dhómhnaill, a native of Gola Island, who was then in her eighty-ninth year. A translation of her Irish by myself and Fidlema Ní Ghallchóbhair is:

> "There was a girl by the name of Nóra Ní Dhómhnaill who lived here. She was one of the kindest of girls." There was a travelling fiddler going around at that time called 'An Fidléir Caoch' (the blind fiddler). He would usually get accommodation for the night in Nóra's father's house. One night he came in with a pall of death on him and he said "Nóra, you must help me up to Dún Lúiche as I'm not long for this world and my wife is buried up there and I'd like to be buried in the same graveyard as her'. 'Ora, my dear!' said Nóra, 'you're not dying at all, and I need your advice. My father has made a match for me and I have no liking at all for the man he has chosen. My heart is set on another young boy and I wouldn't like to part with him'. 'Take my advice', said the Fidléir Caoch, 'and marry the boy you have chosen and don't marry for riches and I'll play at your wedding'.

> All was well for the time being. Nóra began to put aside some goods from day to day for a wedding meal until she had all made ready. She and her young man eloped and married without anyone being the wiser. There was no word of the fiddler but when they returned from the chapel on the day of the wedding they prepared a little feast and before the guests had all eaten the serving boy looked out the window and said 'You should see the group of people coming up the path and the Fidléir Caoch leading them'! 'O', said Nóra 'Isn't it great that my old friend is coming. We'll have plenty of enjoyment soon, thanks be to God'! The sweetest music that you ever heard began and the gathering strolled around the house taking their time to come in. All became quiet in the end, and when Nóra looked out the window again there was no one there to be seen about the place. Everyone was astonished about this, but it wasn't long before all became clear - the Fidléir Caoch was three weeks dead and buried but he had kept his word to play for Nóra's wedding at the end of it all!"

In international folklore, the fiddle itself is regularly presented as an enchanted instrument. It was sometimes believed that the music actually existed inside the body of the instrument and it was the job or the craft of the fiddler to take it out. This was expressed in the following story from Proinsías O Maonaigh concerning his earliest exposure to the fiddle[8]:

> Well, as a youngster the fiddle was a very rare instrument in this part of the country now, and I remember the first man that ever I saw playing the fiddle and he was Seán Bán Fhéilimí, from Rann na Feirste. He came over of a Sunday evening at that time and he'd play for a good long while and eventually he'd go off with that gang of me brothers and sisters and neighbours. They went off to a dance or something, so he left the fiddle in our house. Me mother took it into the room and left it down on the table and straight away warned me not to lay a finger on that case, for the fiddle was in the case and not to touch the case out of position because the least tampering done to the fiddle would do it harm. There was an old neighbouring man and he told her that the best fiddlers in the world maintain that there's still music in the fiddle that was never taken out of it! And I'd say that's right too!

'Gentle' or enchanted fiddles were not always a welcome instrument. They could be viewed as annoying, sometimes even sinister. John Doherty recounted how his father, Mickey Mór, had a marvellous fiddle onto which a young boy 'took a conceit' and pestered him until he sold it. After a few weeks Mickey sought out a new fiddle in a shop in Strabane[9]. John takes up the story:

> Says my father 'Mister Sweeney, have you 'ere a fiddle for five

shillings or seven and six pence and it would do me rightly for all I want of it now'. 'Well Mickey' says the pawnmaster, 'I have fiddles here from five shillings to five pound and from five pound to twenty pound and so on'. 'Och' says my father 'just give me a fiddle'. 'Well Mickey I'll show you a fiddle here for seven and six pence now'. He showed my father the fiddle and begod it was a good fiddle. 'Oh Mickey' says he, 'it's not a cheap thing like that you should have. You should have a fiddle like what I'm going to show you now' and he went on into a back room and it was in a paper bag that he had the fiddle and it was hung to the roof. 'This is the kind of fiddle' says he, 'that you should have Mickey'. He pulled the fiddle out of the bag as far as the neck you know and when me father looked at the turning of the head and the make of the neck and all, 'Oh God' says me father, 'Mr. Sweeney that'll be too dear an instrument for me'. 'Well now wait Mickey have a look at it anyway until you see'. So he took the fiddle out of the bag and me father played a tune on it and oh God it was ringing like a bell. 'Well now' says Mr. Sweeney, "that's the kind of fiddle you should have'. 'Well Mr. Sweeney' says me father, 'I couldn't reach the price of that fiddle. Oh not at all'. 'Well how do you know Mickey. Hold on till you hear' says Mr. Sweeney. 'Do you like it'? 'Oh surely it's the best instrument ever I drew a bow on'. 'Well Mickey now' says he, 'if you have ten shillings I'll give you the fiddle'. So begod me father thought he was, you know, kind of going off his track a bit. 'Oh God' says he, 'Mr. Sweeney I hope you're not making any mistake now because I know anybody could make a mistake'. 'Oh no Mickey, I'm making no mistake because that's all I'm charging you for the fiddle is ten bob'. So me father pulled out the ten bob and he gave it to Mr. Sweeney. He took the fiddle home with him anyway that evening and oh he was very proud of it. Of course we were all young cubs at the time and we had no knowledge of music or fiddles or nothing you know. And he was very much afraid we would be working at the fiddle or trying to be scraping at it and we might spoil it. 'Now boys', says he 'listen. I want to tell you. There's four of you there now and I want to tell you something. Let me not find that you had put your hand near that fiddle because I have that fiddle tuned to my own taste'. So now we didn't because we were afraid to go near it. So anyway that was alright until bedtime. I remember me father and mother lay in a little offshot room from the kitchen and we'd be in the lower room. But there about the minute to one o'clock, there the music started up in the kitchen and what the divil did me father think only that we were up and working at the fiddle and he called to us. 'Now boys' says he, 'sure I thought I warned ye there in the evening not go near that fiddle'. So we were all sound asleep, oh dead asleep. And he called to us again and at long last he struck a match to the candle and it light up. And as soon as the candle was lit there the music stopped.

So he kept the candle light and he went on down to the room and he examined every one of us and begod he nearly burnt the hair on our eyebrows to see were we asleep. He was satisfied that we were asleep of course and he came up again and went into bed and blew out the candle. As soon as the candle was blown out there the music began again. Says he to me mother 'will you stay there awake for awhile and listen to what's going on'? 'What's that?' says she. 'Oh now listen to what's going on and you'll soon know it'. So she listened and he blew out the candle and there the music started. 'Who's at the fiddle?' says she. 'Oh now' says he 'that's the mystery'. So he light the candle again and the music stopped again. Me mother was one morning after that trying to kindle the fire you see and somehow she was in a hurry to get the breakfast ready and everything. 'Oh' says me father, 'is that fire not going right'? 'It is not' says she, 'for I'm just at it now'. 'Och well we'll soon see to that' says he and he reached for the fiddle and he put the fiddle under the grate and put the whole thing ablaze. Says he, 'now you'll play no more' and he burned the fiddle. So that was the finish of that.

The story of another unwanted enchanted fiddle in my own townland of Tullyhorkey is recounted in the Irish Folklore Commission's Schools Collection. Máire and Cáit Nic a' tSaor who were attending the Tullymore School in 1937 contributed the following account[10] which they had been told by an elderly local informant:

There is a bush growing in our field and it was always known as the faerie bush. Once a little girl was coming past this bush from the well with a can of water. She saw a little violin just the length of her own little hand and a bow beside it for playing it and both were as white as snow. She brought it home with her to show it to her father. She was going to try to play on it but her father stopped her and told her to bring it back and leave it where she found it. When she looked for it next morning it was gone. At other times there were little pipes found at the same place but only very small ones. The heads of the pipes were only as small as my thimble.

The bush which is referred to in the story is almost certainly the lone blackthorn growing out of the wall in the ring fort (circular earthen dwelling structures of early Christian age commonly associated with the faeries throughout Irish folklore) which is located in the field between Lawrence and Brenda Sweeneys' house and the Abbey River. This fort is described as listing number 1155 in 'Archaeological Survey of County Donegal'[11].

Concerning the construction of the fiddle, older players had some beliefs on the making of a good instrument. Proinsías O Maonaigh again relates[12]:

> I remember that at that time they said that the best thing for a soundpost was the bone of a crane's leg. You know the 'corran mór'. It has big long legs on it. That to get one of them, it was the best thing to use as a soundpost.

John Doherty believed that one of the secrets of success of the Stradivarius instruments was in using tonewood cut from the south facing side of the tree. As people in Ireland would know, this drier side of the tree gets maximum sunlight, with dampness and moss growth greatest on the northern faces of trees. When buying a fiddle John cautioned that in the days of his youth he would check for the correct height of the sides of the instrument by settling the fiddle down on its side and placing an old one penny piece in the C bout. If the height was right the penny fit exactly on the side with no gap between the coin and the overlap of the back or belly.

Folklore which touches into classical mythology was not unknown in Donegal and may represent the influence of hedge schools. For example one reel very popular with the Dohertys was *The Three Merry Sisters* of Fate. It is almost certain that this tune was popularised in their eyes through the recording of it by Frank O'Higgins, as they usually played it along with the other reels in his set. They rarely ever used the common title *The Merry Sisters.* The three sisters referred to in the Doherty title are Lachesis, Clotho and Atropos, the daughters of Erebus in Greek mythology. These figures determined the fate or destiny of a man as represented by the carding, spinning and eventually cutting of a string of yarn; the last act representing the severing of the life-line bringing about the death of the person. These figures are represented in the familiar bronze sculpture at the southern entrance to St. Stephen's Green, Dublin.

The renowned classical violinist Paginini was also recalled in a story told by John Doherty. It is a local variation of an international motif. In this instance, a savage bull is kept in the courtyard of a wealthy king's castle. On a table in the centre of the courtyard is a treasure trove containing the king's riches. There was an open challenge that anyone who could get past the bull and remove the treasure would have it. Thousands of heroes were killed in their various attempts to retrieve the store. The frail Paginini was scorned for even attempting to outmanoeuvre the beast. In the end, the great musician slowly marches into the courtyard playing a very soothing and haunting tune, thus mesmerising the bull. Paginini then quietly retreats with his fortune. The appearance of Paginini in Irish folklore is very interesting. The renowned violinist was known to have suffered from an unusual disease which left him very pale and gaunt. His fingers were elongated and bony as a result and in his drawn face was set a pair of bulging, often bloodshot eyes. This appearance combined with his natural technical wizardry on the instrument gave rise to a popular belief that he was possessed and in some cases people strongly believed him to actually be the Devil himself. Folklore about him and his activities rose up after his death and John's story confirms the fact that it spread at least into the remote musical community of the northwest of Ireland.

The Devil has been associated with fiddle-playing in international folklore. I have heard him described as a sinister figure in one of two variations on a story wherein he is an outstandingly gifted fiddler. In the first case a good local fiddler barters his soul for the ability to play as well as the Devil while in the second a contest takes place between the Devil and a very capable local player with the prize being either greater skill and sometimes the Devil's fiddle or with the penalty being the loss of the innocent fiddler's soul. Variations between winning and losing in the latter setting occur.

In the one connection between a Donegal fiddler and the Devil, rather than being a totally evil figure, the Devil actually has a sense of humour. A grand-uncle of mine, Eddie Bradley, now in his nineties of Tullinkesay, Magherafelt, County Derry, himself a fiddler, recalled a story of a fiddler named Mooney from Donegal whom he knew during his youth. Mooney was a good player and travelled throughout the northwest of Ireland and was in great demand for house dances. He was a jolly individual and while revelling in fiddle-playing was not the victim of any social excesses. He had though, a wife, who detested music, in particular fiddle music, and made his life unbearable with an unending barrage of complaints about his livelihood, lifestyle and personal shortcomings.

Finally Mooney could endure no more. He took up his fiddle and set out on the road for himself. After walking for about an hour he stopped to rest against a ditch and was surprised when a small, hooded, sooty individual emerged from the hedge and enquired about what he was carrying. Mooney replied that it was a fiddle. The small character asked for the loan of the instrument and played a fantastic piping-style double jig. Being quick to learn, he picked up the tune after only the second time around. Mooney was delighted exclaiming he had never heard fiddle-playing as good in his life. Trying to make better acquaintance he then asked the small man his name. The hood was thrown back and the horned little man proclaimed "I am Belezabub, the Devil himself!" with an expectation of shock and horror from the fiddler. Instantly Mooney's hand stretched out and as the smile broadened on his face said "shake hands with your relations my friend. I'm married to your sister"! The Devil could only see the humour in Mooney and disappeared laughing but not before Mooney had learned the tune.

After a few weeks of joyful rambling Mooney eventually returned home and there never was a whimper out of his wife again. From that meeting until the day he died, Mooney was famous for playing the jig he had learned from his in-law which has since been known as *The Devil and his Sister.*

According to Eddie Bradley, for some years prior to his wife's miraculous rehabilitation Mooney had been experiencing serious marital difficulties. His neighbours decided that because he was out every night playing for house dances this might be putting an undue strain on his home situation. They thought if he was at home more in the evenings the future might brighten between the spouses.

To achieve this they designed a plan to frighten him about being out on the roads at night, hoping it would result in him staying closer to home. On Halloween they booked him to play at a certain house knowing that he would have to pass by the local chapel and graveyard on his journey home. Mooney accepted and travelled out to the house. While he was playing, three strong young men went to the graveyard and proceeded to dig a deep grave leaving it gaping. One of the men wrapped himself in a sheet and lay in the bottom of the hole. Mooney put in hours of wonderful music and in the middle of the night when all was finished started the long walk home.

As he neared the graveyard the two men in hiding signalled his approach to the third lying in the grave. The "deceased" started to let out the most unholy groans to frighten the fiddler howling "I cannot rest, I cannot rest". The spry Mooney hurdled the wall in one leap and straight away caught hold of the abandoned spade. He shovelled heap upon heap of soil like an engine into the grave saying "It's no wonder you can't rest and you with no mould on you"! The "corpse" struggled madly to escape its confines and a screaming white ghost was reported as having run the roads of the parish in a frenzy the next day. Mooney's rambles were not thwarted in the least by the incident.

The faeries were a group of people from the otherworld about whom the older generation had a healthy respect. Folklore abounds about them in Donegal and many excellent books and collections have been compiled on their activities, most notably those by Áine Ní Dhíoraí[13] as well as Seán O hEochaidh, Máire Mac Neill and Séamus O Cathain[14]. In these works, as in the living lore of the older players, the faeries take an enthusiastic part in the music. This, no doubt, arises from their professed love of it.

One person who is remembered as having directly inherited a store of tunes from the faeries was Bidi a' Mhuc Ros. Bidi was a renowned lilter from Muckros Head near Kilcar, and though she never left her locality she was constantly introducing new and very much sought-after tunes into the local repertoire. This gave rise to speculation amongst her neighbours as to how she, who never left her own parish, could always be getting supplies of new tunes.

Francie Dearg O'Byrne described how it was eventually discovered that one wild wintery night, while still a young woman, a knock came to her door. Before her were two small red-haired men seeking shelter from the storm. She brought them in, giving them lodgings and food for the night. To pass the time the two men took out fiddles and played the grandest music Bidi ever heard. Just before dawn when the storm was abating they told her that they must leave, but to repay her hospitality they would grant her a wish. Bidi told them that she was so fond of their playing that she would love to learn some of their music. The two men told her that whenever she wanted to learn a new tune she should go down and sit on the spink at Muckros Head. The two faeries would appear there to only her and they would give her any tune she liked. This arrangement lasted throughout her lifetime and many of the tunes she learned were picked up by the local lilters and fiddlers, some of which still survive, particularly through the playing of Francie Dearg.

Francie also explained that when Bidi died she was laid out in an open coffin in her cottage. All the local people attended her wake and, as was the custom, there was much music. Towards the end of the night the lid was placed on the coffin. Just at that instant, the door opened and in came the two faeries to pay their respects. They went over to the coffin and tore into a grand droning reel, which they played in octaves long enough for all the locals to learn. When they stopped they walked over to the fireplace and flew up the chimney never to be seen again! That reel is still well known today throughout Donegal and bears the name given by the two faeries *Bean a' Tigh Faoi Chláir (The Woman of the House in the Closed Coffin)*. This tune is also sometimes known as *Bean a' Tigh ar Lar*. Some other tunes which Bidi learned from the two faerie fiddlers and which survive amongst local players are *Slán le Ceol (Farewell to Music*, not to be confused with the Carolan composition of the same name) as well as a slip jig entitled *Bidi a' Mhuc Ros* along with a march and hornpipe of the same title.

The faeries were responsible for many tunes in the Doherty repertoire. Mickey recalled once how, when still very young he was introduced to a reel by his grandfather, Simi Doherty. Simon told him that he had learned it one night while coming home from playing for a house-dance in Glendowan. He had made it to Glenveigh, and was at a dark and lonely spot with not a light of a house to be seen, when at last he spied two wee men, one holding a lamp while the other was calling out sets. There were about a dozen dancers present and the caller announced a reel called *Banríon na Síoga* (The Queen of the Faeries). The dance went on for some time and Simi who hid in the ditch was able to pick up the reel played for it. From that day forward it was one of his favourite tunes to play at dances. This tune was also recorded by Mickey for the Folklore Commission under the title *Paddy's Trip to Scotland*[15].

In another instance Mickey tells of a wedding of a Teelin girl, Máire Bhán, who was married in Carrick[16]. The guests returned to her house for a supper and dancing, when in came a wee red-haired piper. He neither ate nor drank but played from afternoon till daybreak for dancers, and all were taken aback by his playing of a particular reel which has come to be known as *Máire Bhán's*

Wedding reel. When the piper left the cottage he was quickly followed out by the young men present to see where he came from but he had disappeared in a instant. The tune Mickey associated with this story was that which he played in scordatura tuning and also called *An Píobaire a' Chéidigh*, or alternatively, *The Bonnie Bunch of Ferns*.

Faerie abductions whereby babies and less frequently, adults are abducted to swell the ranks of the faerie communities were a common belief with older generations. In this case the person was abducted and not to arouse suspicion was replaced by a changeling with little or no human reactions. Accounts such as those occurring at Derries, near Ballintra and Loughran Rock, near Carrickahorna as recounted in the Irish Folklore Commission's Schools Collection[17] often indicate the abductions took place during a time of great merriment with much music causing a distraction. *The Pinch of Snuff* is a tune well appreciated amongst Donegal fiddlers and its origin is often recounted by southwest Donegal players in an attempted faerie abduction of a bride at a wedding in the Teelin area. In this case, the faeries were trying to trick the bride into saying words which would complete the abduction process. In the meantime hiding in the rafters of the cottage was a young man who had loved but not won the girl. He could see the events taking place and as the girl was almost ready to seal her fate the young man shook down some snuff onto the bride who was dancing below him. She sneezed on breathing in the snuff and the people immediately blessed her with the customary "Dia agus Muire dhuit" (God and Mary bless you). At the mention of the holy names, the faeries instantly took flight. What was happening soon became clear and the tune which the fiddlers had been playing for the dance was then christened *The Pinch of Snuff*.

The motif of the *seachran* is a very familiar one in Irish folklore[18], and typically involves a person wandering onto a faerie path. The "gentleness" or enchantment of the land causes the person to become completely disorientated, straying aimlessly for hours. In some versions, such as that reported to have happened to the great Sligo fiddling brothers Jim and Michael Coleman[19], the person is also overcome by a thick mist. It is this setting and this format which gave rise to the tune *Seán sa Cheo*. The enchantment is commonly broken by the person turning their jacket inside out. They then become instantly familiar with their surroundings, finding that they are at the last spot they recognised before they got lost.

The seachran tradition, though more often associated with faeries, is combined in one instance with the activities of the Banshee, to give us at least one piece of music which comes to us from her singing. The Banshee as Daithí O hÓgain informs us in his monumental work 'Myth, Legend and Romance, An Encyclopaedia of the Irish Folk Tradition'[20] is a female being who commanded a healthy respect. She was best known to eerily foretell and lament the death of a person whose surname was prefixed with the Irish O or Mac.

The air associated with the Banshee was transmitted to the current generation of fiddlers mainly through the playing of John Doherty, who called it *Paddy's Rambles Through the Park*. John's use of the word 'park' was not, of course, intended to mean a recreational park but instead to reflect the Irish term 'pairc' which means a farm field. Furthermore, John's closing observation that the air was weird would appear to be well in keeping with the Banshee lore of eerie wailing. The incident which brought about the origin of the tune is recounted by John[21] as follows:

> It is a known fact that the Banshee was heard in this country (in this sense the word country implies a particular part of Donegal). Oh surely that's no lie. But Paddy was coming past this park anyhow and then at that time the workers, you know, would, if there were stones lying in the park, they would gather them all up and pile them into a pile here and pile there and so on like that. But anyway, Paddy was late on coming home at night and there he heard the Banshee. Oh the people were all sleeping. All the whole country was all asleep. Well they used to call these lumps of stones "carnans" you know. But he heard the Banshee at the first carnan and he just stepped across the ditch very quick to see who was the singer. But when he went as far as the first carnan then the Banshee was at the second carnan. And Paddy followed on and there he was through the park all night 'till a little while before daylight in the morning. And the song that the Banshee sang Paddy had it all learned and it's called *Paddy's Rambles Through the Park*. It's a very old, weird kind of an air.

The Irish term 'cailleach' is normally translated as a hag or a weathered old woman. It is also used to describe a witch. There is a strong body of witch lore in Ireland which associates witches with unfortunate happenings. In these stories the witch is often an old woman suspected by her neighbours as being the cause of many of their problems. The witch is very difficult to catch at her undertakings since she transforms herself into the form of an animal, usually a hare or a cat and roams the countryside at night milking cattle dry and carrying out other mischiefs. She is often found out when she is shot in her animal form and traced by a trail of blood to her cottage where she is found in the morning bleeding in her human form. One typical misdeed she is associated with is entering undetected into a cottage in the form of a hare and sneaking into the milk churn. Here she remains in spirit. Usually for as long as she hides in the churn no amount of churning of the milk would ever produce butter. There was one cure however. John Doherty played a double jig *An Sean Cailleach sa Mhaistrim (The Old Hag in the Churn)* which he learned from his father. According to the father, this tune had a certain sound in it that witches could not tolerate, and if a churn was not producing butter, by playing or lilting the tune to the churning rhythm the witch would be driven out and the churn would produce butter at a rate never seen.

The association of witches with animal forms is also recalled in another tune, though Scottish in origin, which was popular up to a generation ago in Donegal and is still played by Danny O'Donnell. The reel title '*An Cailleach Oiche*' directly translates as '*The Night Hag*' but literally meant '*The Owl*'. It was believed that witches found it very advantageous to take the form of an owl to work their deeds based on the bird's quiet, rapid flight as well as keen night vision. In this way she could move safely and quickly over large areas. Though the tune title recalls the bird the intention of the deeper meaning was clear.

Both Mickey and John Doherty often told a story the events of which correspond to the well-known song *Casadh an tSúgáin*[22] (The Twisting of the Rope). In this setting, a wandering fiddler seeks lodgings for the night from two sisters living on their own. They are very reluctant to accommodate him but he persists. The younger girl devises a trick to get him out of the house. She asks him to make himself useful by twisting a straw rope with a traw-hook. As he twists the hook the girl feeds more straw into the rope. The fiddler keeps backing away as the rope lengthens and eventually is outside on the street. At this point, the elder sister who was hiding behind the door slams it closed and cuts the rope. The fiddler sees the humour in being tricked and composes a reel calling it *The Girl that was too Smart for the Fiddler.* The tune which the Dohertys usually played with this story is the *Boyne Hunt,* which is a Scottish composition commissioned for the Perthshire Hunt Ball and originally titled *The Perthshire Hunt.*

In 'Béaloideas 1989'[23], the Journal of the Folklore Society of Ireland, an extensive review of the folklore motif of the "Musician in the Cave" and its connection with the older "Festival of Lughnasa" tradition is given by Máire Mac Neill. Specific examples of occurrences of the motif from various parts of Ireland and Scotland appear, but the vast majority of these contain only fragments or the barest skeleton of the overall motif. While contributing folklore material in 1977, John Doherty[24] told a long story which, if the elements in Máire Mac Neill's work are any guideline, must constitute the fullest and most exciting account of the motif.

In John's version all the typical elements of the story are present. According to him there was a cave outside Glenties which was never fathomed and those who had tried it never returned. It was believed that living within it was a terrible demon. The local warpiper was a very eccentric character and was eventually challenged to descend to the depth of the cave. He agreed to the challenge and decided to take his pipes and his dog along for courage. The next morning all the people gathered at the mouth of the cave and the piper and his dog journeyed in after the piper announced (in Irish) that "The foal will be a mare and the calf will be a cow before I am seen again". The piper started playing his favourite march and the people hearing it above ground kept vigil until night. A guard was appointed to stay until the morning and all the while the tune became fainter and fainter as the piper descended. This continued for three days until the music could no longer be heard. A guard remained at the mouth of the cave for several weeks but the piper never emerged. It was believed he was killed by the demon. Some weeks later, the piper's dog emerged from a cave in Glencolumcille without his skin (this point is a curious but consistent element in the motif)! The people who had listened to the fading music outside the cave well remembered the piper's tune and went on to name it *Farther and Deeper.* John then played the march and, on this occasion, the tune he played was the march from the air, march and reel set *Fáilte Romhat in do Bhaile a Ghráinne.*

This same format is confirmed in Lochlainn McGill's excellent work 'In Conall's Footsteps'[25] as being associated with Uaimh a' Dorchadais in the Maghery Cave system near Ardara. Máire Mac Neill[26] also mentions the Fiddler's Cave at Castle Archdale, in nearby County Fermanagh. A few of the older people from Glencolumcille associate John Mhosaí McGinley with the "musician in the cave" motif, mentioning the Marble Arch cave. It must be said, though, that these accounts are only fragments of the complete motif.

The tradition of the piper in the cave is also recalled in Inishowen and can be found discussed in Percival Swan's[27] writing on the peninsula. Maps of Inishowen show, on the north shore, a sea-cave marked The Piper's Cave. The story associated with this cave is recounted by Charles McGlinchey in his autobiography 'The Last of the Name'[28]. He tells us: "Round the face of Binnion Hill there's a cave, and nobody knows how far in it goes. Long ago a piper went in there to find out where it led to or what was in it. He arranged with his friends that he would keep playing and they could listen above the ground and find out the direction the cave went. They traced him with the playing of the pipes till he was over under lower Annagh. The tune he was playing was:

Beidh na cailíní óga ina seanmhná
Sul a bhfille mé, sul a bhfille mé,
Beidh na huain óga ina seanchaoraigh,
Nuair a thiocfas mise aráis.

(The young girls will be old women
Before I return, before I return.
The young lambs will be old sheep
Before I come back again.)

They lost track of the piper after that and he never came back. The cave is called *Poll a Phíobaire (The Piper's Cave)* since that time."

There are some genuine grounds for associating musicians, and pipers in particular, with caves. The warpipes are a comparatively loud, droning instrument. Pipers and fiddlers who play outside will often prefer to play in a place which enhances the sound of an instrument. Even today, for example, it is very typical to see street musicians opting to play in archways and shop fronts, thus allowing the musician to shelter off the main footpath, freeing-up passers-by. Furthermore the volume of their instruments, which compete with all the sounds of the street is somewhat amplified by the recess. No doubt, the openings of caves proved excellent sites to practice playing, and may well have been a part of the original formulation of the "musician in the cave" motif.

Like their supernatural partners, the faeries and the Banshee, ghosts also play a part in the origin of some tunes in Donegal. The most prominent of these is Taibhse Chonaill (Conall's Ghost) from the Teelin area. It features in the repertoire of Con Cassidy, who describes[29] its origin as follows:

> "There were these three men from Teelin and they were up the back here making poitín by the stream. They had a still hidden in a small turf hut so it couldn't be seen and the stream came nearby for water. When the first run was through they took off some of the wash and they had a few wee drinks to see how the poitín was coming along and they were satisfied everything was right. There came down a very severe fog from Sliabh Liag and nothing could be seen. The three of them got worried and decided they had better make for home because it would be easy to get lost in such conditions. So away they went but they got separated. One of them, this man Conall, was wandering for a long time and couldn't find his way but all the time he could hear this piper playing this tune. And he was musical himself and he picked up the tune. He was frightened for his life but when he got home he was able to play the full tune. People say that it must have been some kind of faerie piper. But that story's true and the man lived down here and his name was Conall and they called the tune *Taibhse Chonaill* ever since."

Another version of the tune by John Doherty appears in The Northern Fiddler[30] under the title *The Ghost of Bunglass.*

One of the famous Donegal reels is undoubtedly *The Black Fanad Mare,* which is sometimes known as *The Nine Points of Roguery.* This tune originated again from a supernatural vision of an old druid to the famous Fiddler Doyle of Fanad. John Doherty gave the following account of the origin of the tune[31]:

> "It seems at the time there was a vision appearing at a crossroads in Fanad. It was supposed to be a vision of one of the druids. Fiddler Doyle was coming home from a dance party that he was playing at and it seems that he had far to come. He was on horseback and he had his fiddle and case with him. He was coming home alright in every way until he came to this crossroads where this vision was appearing. Well a horse beast is very observant you know and as Doyle was com-

> ing to the crossroads the horse halted and threw back his head. The horse can see what we can't see and the horse saw what was standing at the crossroads. He shired away back you know. Then Doyle still stayed on his back and he got the horse for to go again but when the horse came to this particular spot well Doyle couldn't see anything and the horse was watching this one way at the side. Just like that the horse bolted and Doyle still stayed on his back! On and on the horse kept up that top gallop and the vision was still at his side. Doyle saw the vision then but the horse kept on this top gallop till they reached the house. That was about two miles. Doyle got down off the horse and he stabled the horse. He came and had supper and went to bed. With the rhythm of the animals hooves on the road it gave Doyle the impression of the reel and he got up in the morning and he played this reel over on the fiddle. The name he called it was *The Black Mare of Fanad,* being that the horse was so gallant as to take him away and the vision still right beside the animal and keeping up with her. Well there wasn't a single white hair on her body. That was fiddler Doyle though. They say he was a powerful fiddle player.

Folklore concerning mermaids is internationally widespread. Many of the older fiddlers are well able to remember a reel called *Maighdeán Mhara Mullach Mhóir*. It was said among them that a young captain of a Teelin fishing boat used to fish in Donegal Bay over towards Mullaghmore. There was a beautiful young mermaid who used to come out onto the rocks at Mullaghmore and lilt, thus enchanting the captain. After a time, the mermaid saw and immediately fell in love with the fisherman. She went straight to her father and asked permission to live a life on land with the fisherman, but he angrily denied her. She pleaded so strongly that the father knew that there was no remedy for the situation only to do away with the Teelin man. So he plotted to create a storm which would drown him. In the meantime, the mermaid had stolen her father's magic knife which had the power to calm the seas. She managed to meet the young captain on his next trip and they confessed their mutual love. The mermaid gave the knife to the sailor, and told him if his life was ever in danger on the seas to throw the knife into the water and they would calm. Soon afterwards, the mermaid's father heard that the captain was out fishing. He went to meet the boat and created a terrible storm. The mermaid sought her father on hearing the storm above and found that he had gone to drown the Teelin man, so she rushed off to intercede. By this time the boat was nearly broken and many lives had been lost. The captain feared the worst and decided to throw the knife into the water to save those remaining. As he did the seas immediately calmed but soon afterwards the body of the poor mermaid rose to the surface with the knife in her breast. The Teelin man returned home overcome by anguish and never set out on the sea again. The men of the crew who were spared never forgot the lilting of the mermaid. The tune which she once so happily lilted became known as *Maighdean Mhara Mhullach Mhóir*. This tune title has in recent years been shortened in English to *The Maids of Mullagh.*

Francie Dearg O'Byrne had a marvellous story which connected two great reels that he passed on and made popular with the younger generations of Donegal fiddlers. According to the story the daughter of the local landlord was a very handsome girl. There was an old word in Irish for such a beautiful girl, Mol, and she was known to everyone in the locality as Mol na Tiarna (The Landlord's beautiful daughter). Ever since she was a babe she was tenderly cared for and raised by the landlord's servant woman who was known as Máire na Sop (Máire of the wisp) and was the most sought after lilter in the area. Every night Mol and Máire na Sop would pass the evening by the fire lilting and Mol eventually came to have all of Máire's tunes.

As she grew up, Mol fell deeply in love with a very handsome local boy of whom the landlord disapproved. The two used to meet regularly and the landlord soon warned Mol that he would shoot the boy if she did not stop seeing him. Mol na Tiarna went to Máire na Sop and told her of her plight and begged her for help. As she loved her so much, Máire was not able to refuse her. They devised a plan that Mol would arrange her meetings with the young boy and Máire would keep an eye on the landlord to ensure he did not follow her to hunt the boy. They devised a signal that if all was safe Máire would lilt Mol's favourite reel and that if the landlord was suspicious she would lilt her own favourite reel. This worked well for a long time until eventually during the hay-saving time Mol met her boyfriend out in the bushes and no one expected any trouble until the landlord noticed Mol missing. Without Máire spotting him he grabbed his gun and set out to find her. Máire suddenly noticed him going out and raced away through the back fields whistling the warning tune. Mol heard the reel and the boy escaped safely. Máire found Mol and the two started gathering bundles of haycocks. The landlord met them and asked what where they were at. The two explained that they were out getting some cocks of fresh hay for the calves and the landlord lost his suspicion. Over time, the landlord lost his dislike of the boy and the young pair were happily married. The story of the warning tunes was eventually confessed to the landlord who appreciated the humour of the deceit. The two reels then became great favourites throughout the locality and have been called after the two lilters ever since, *Mol na Tiarna* and *Máire na Sop.*

Another tune which has a romantic connection is the strathspey *The Brown Sailed Boat*. This tune was originally composed and titled *Peter Baillie* in honour of the Loanhead fiddler who lived between 1774 and 1841. The story which is associated with its Donegal name comes from the Kilcar area. A local wealthy man had his daughter betrothed to a rich man whom she did not want to marry. She was deeply in love with a young fisherman from the locality. The father discovered this and forbade the girl from ever seeing the young man. The girl could not stand to be parted from him and constructed a plan by which they could secretly meet.

Well aware of the quick weather changes in Donegal Bay the fisherman sometimes carried an extra small sail in case of emergency. His normal sail was white and the spare sail was brown. The girl sent a secret message to her fisherman to say that whenever it was possible for him, they could meet at a secluded spot at a certain time of the evening. If he could make the meeting he was to signal by hoisting the brown sail on his way back to the harbour. If he could not meet her he would use the white sail. The pair arranged their meetings like this for some time and during their meetings planned out their savings. Soon they had enough money to be able to defy the girl's father. The pair went off and married and the first tune played at the hauling home dance was the strathspey which the fiddlers, not having a title for it, named '*The Brown Sailed Boat*'.

We have already seen poitín and its makers entering into the tradition via Taibhse Chonaill. Poitín was not an uncommon element of social celebrations in past generations and there was and still remains a great deal of intrigue and secrecy concerning its distillation and the people involved in producing it. It is not surprising therefore that the drink has associations with the fiddle music of the county. One such example deals with a highland whose playing acted as a coded signal for poitín at a wedding in the Glenties area. This account of the origin of the *Cul Doras Highland* is from Vincent Campbell[32]:

> That tune got its name more or less from the poitín maker at a time when there used to be weddings in the houses. There was a wedding in a place not far from here up in Graffey and at that time they kept everything very silent. There was a lime kiln at every house. The groom wanted to keep everything very quiet. So the father of the girl told him instead of putting the poitín, we'll say, into big kegs put it instead into small crockery bottles and put it into the lime kiln. And he was letting on that he was going to burn the lime kiln and he had the turf all around the place. When the night came, he said to the two sons, he was a fiddle player himself, that when the whiskey was going short in the kitchen he would play this highland. That left them to know to go out the back to the lime kiln and bring in another crockery bottle of poitín. And the name that tune got to this very day was *An Cúl Doras,* the back door.

Tarlach Mac Suibhne is a character as we have already seen, weaves in and out between fact and folklore. There is one humorous story which concerns his preparations for the famous trip to Chicago which, considering the eccentricities of the man, may well have had some basis in fact. This particular story was recounted by his relation, Simon Doherty[33] of Kilmacrennan, who told it while he was hale and hearty in his ninety second year. He had heard it from his father, Charlie, who knew the Píobaire Mór well. This is how he remembered it:

> Charlie's (the name in English by which all of the Dohertys referred to Mac Suibhne) neighbour was called Biddy and she only lived a short distance away. Well Charlie might be twenty times a day down to her and she might be twenty times a day up with him and they would be up and down like that. But he came up this day and says he, 'Biddy, have you ever a spade about'? 'What would you do with a spade? Sure you never handled a spade in your life!' says she. 'Och for what I'm going to do with the spade today, I'll manage'. Well she went outside and got an old spade and lifted a stone and gave the spade a rub of it to clean it up a bit and brought it in and gave it to Charlie. "Well now" says he, 'would you ever have a parcel of paper and a wee length of string for I'll just need that to complete my work'? 'Sure what work would you be at that's playing music from morning till night and never done a hard turn in all your days'? Well anyway Charlie took the spade and paper and string and went off to his own place and in the front of his cottage he cut a sod of turf. He wrapped it

> in the paper and bound it with the string and went back down to Biddy's. 'Now my good woman' says he 'you may have back your spade for that's all that I needed it for was to cut just the one sod of my own turf'. 'And what would you be wanting with a sod of turf, for that would hardly see you through a winter' says Biddy. 'Well I'm away now 'til America' says Charlie 'and when I sit to play out there I'll put this sod under my feet and I'll be the only man of the lot that's able to play rightly for I'll be the only man playing on Irish soil'!

The Loughanure Reel is one of the few tunes which Neillidh Boyle recorded for collectors. Prior to playing the tune he tells the story of how a fiddler was sitting on the side of the graveyard wall in Loughanure. After a while he heard the keening or lamenting of a a man at his recently deceased wife's grave. The fiddler picked up the keen and eventually transformed the melody into the reel.

Like the music which had a specific function such as wedding marches, tunes were also occasionally associated with some forms of ritual or work. An excellent example of this is the marvellous droning reel from Francie Dearg O'Byrne, *Saitheadh an Bháid.* According to Francie, fishing boats in the Kilcar area were made at a local carpenter's house on the mountainside in the townland of Churchtown. When the boat was finished and ready for launching, all of the able-bodied men of the parish were gathered to shoulder the boat down to the quay. A keg of poitín was bought by the new owner and placed in the centre of the boat. A fiddler would be hired and he would sit on the keg and, the whole distance from the carpenter's house to the quayside, would play *Saitheadh a Bháid*, while the men carried the boat, keg and fiddler. The boat would be placed in the water, given a run to the mouth of the estuary to test her seaworthiness and then brought back to the quay. There would then be a quayside dance with the fiddler providing the music and the poitín liberally served up.

Another reel which has a functional origin is to be found in the repertoire of Vincent Campbell called *Fáscadh a' Léine*. In this instance, two women were washing clothes when in came a local fiddler from the Croaghs. They all began chatting and one of the women started to lilt a reel. The fiddler had forgotten the tune for some time and was keen to play it again. He took down a fiddle off the wall and tore into the reel. The women were then anxious to dance a two hand reel to the tune. They were able to mix work and pleasure by taking the two ends of a shirt and wringing it tight while dancing opposite each other. The fiddler had no name for the tune so it was appropriately christened *Fáscadh a' Léine.*

We might expect that in the past there would have been very few links between Donegal and the far off Land of the Rising Sun yet in the fiddle tradition we find both the dance: the *Tokyo* and a hornpipe made popular by John Doherty entitled *The Japanese Hornpipe.* Little if anything is remembered now about the *Tokyo* but the origin of *The Japanese Hornpipe* can be fully recounted. During the days of John's youth and earlier there were several small, family run circuses which travelled the country. To maximise the potential entertainment one or several of the members would play music to provide accompaniment to actions or simple background music. A small circus which frequented Donegal had a fiddler and one of the routines had a short comic skit acted out during the first part of the tune. As soon as the fiddler changed into the second part of the tune the actors immediately stopped the action and did a comic dance. They resumed the routine on the return to the first part of the tune and this continued as a sort of play with many parts until the skit was concluded. The tune used for this piece was *The Japanese Hornpipe* and was quickly learned by the local players. Again it has been given a renewed lease of life to a whole new generation via John Doherty.

A reel which again has come into the repertoire of younger Donegal fiddlers through the playing of Vincent Campbell as well as John Doherty and James O'Byrne is *Gealach na gCoinnleach (The Harvest Moon).* The Harvest Moon is the full moon closest to the autumnal equinox. At this time of the year, the moon rises about the same time every evening not long after sunset. As a result its orange-yellow glow caused by light filtered through the Earth's atmosphere gives its face a very special colour quality. It was believed that the nature of the waxing and waning Harvest Moon could foretell the amount of rain and the degree of coldness for the coming winter. As such the people had great interest in the aspects of this particular lunar cycle.

The Campbell brothers remember that around the harvest time every year a large band of travellers would gather near Glenties up along the higher portion of the road into the Croaghs. One of these was a very big man who was a very good fiddler and known locally as the 'Gypsy Mór'. He was a great curiosity with the local people as he only shaved once a year on the night of the Harvest Moon. The Gypsy Mór was a great believer in the power of the

Harvest Moon and entitled this, his favourite reel after it in Irish, namely *Gealach na gCoinnleach.*

It must be said that with each passing generation the belief in supernatural dealings is fading rapidly. Likewise the associated respect for customs and traditions is on the decline. Though this is the state of affairs today, it is worthwhile closing this chapter with a strange but true account of an incident which would appear to defy random chance yet happened during the recent construction of the Mickey Doherty Memorial in the Croaghs.

During the time of the Black and Tans in Ireland there was a great amount of activity in the mountains and glens around Glenties. As the Tans were just about the only ones who had motor transport in this part of the country at that time local activists would regularly go out at night and knock down some of the many small bridges spanning the little streams and rivers. This meant that as the Tans were driving around on night patrols they would often find themselves trapped on a remote stretch of road between two broken bridges. Their exploits would be curtailed and they had to sit out a long cold night for the morning before they could repair the bridges. Their main concern at this time was to catch the bridge knockers.

The Campbell brothers recall one night Mickey Doherty was coming from the Ballybofey direction towards Glenties and just as he crossed over a small bridge into the townland of Eadaninfagh he was overtaken by a lorry load of Tans. Seeing a pack on his back they suspected he might be carrying hammers and bars for knocking bridges. They jumped out and were very close to shooting him on sight. Mickey pleaded with them that he was only a travelling tinsmith. He opened his coat and showed them his fiddle and unrolled his pack of smithing tools on the road. Still not believing him they threatened that if he could not make something out of tin there and then they would shoot him. Mickey took out a quarter of a sheet of tin that he had left and scribed out his markings. With his shears he cut out the shapes and tapped out a pandai (a milk jug or creamer) with his hammers on the road surface. The Tans were convinced enough and let him go. He quickly hurried down the road and went into the first house he came upon, namely Peter Campbell's. In relief, he sat and played the whole night. He played a grand tune the boys of the house were not familiar with. He told them the name of the tune was *The Pandai That Saved My Life.*

Years later Cairdeas na bhFidléirí with the tremendous help of the local community built a fine memorial to Mickey encorporating a stone fiddle carved by Josie Campbell at this bridge. I can recall clearly the work was being finished in late September and there were severe squalls blowing. With each squall we would run and shelter under the small bridge. It was remarked a number of times how sheltering under a bridge in such a manner was regularly done by Mickey and his brothers when encountering showers on their journeys. It was strange how we were here under one of the very same bridges that Mickey sheltered under.

The squall subsided and we climbed out to continue work. At that point, Josie Campbell arrived with tea and sandwiches and Jimmy Campbell and I were to sit into the van for the first lunch shift. As we sat in, Jimmy wondered aloud what would Mickey think of the work under way if he had been sheltering there under the bridge with us. Without any speculation he reached forward and turned on the radio which was tuned to Raidió na Gaeltachta. There was complete silence for a second or two and then Mickey played his grand version of *Maggie Pickie* with Conal a' Damhsa dancing from the Cómhairle Béaloideas Éireann recording. At the finish Conal O Dúfaigh simply announced that was the end of programming from Donegal until the evening. Jimmy and I sat eating in silence. Mickey had given a verdict!

REFERENCES

1 Daithí O hÓgain, *An File*, Oifig an tSoláthair, Baile Átha Cliath, 1982, Caibidil 5.

2 Francis O'Neill, Irish Ministrels and Musicians, EP Publishers, Yorkshire, 1973 (facsimile reprint).

3 Mickey Doherty, BBC Sound Archive recording.

4 Seamus O Catháin. *Uair a' Chloig Cois Teallaigh*, Comhairle Bhealoideas Éireann, Baile Átha Cliath, 1985.

5 Padraig Mac Aodh O'Neill and Seosahm Mac Cathmhaoil, *Songs of Uladh*, William Mullen, Belfast, 1904.

6 Séamus Ennis, Irish Folklore Commission collection notes, Dept of Irish Folklore and Folk Music, UCD.

7 Irish Folklore Commission Schools' Collection,Middletown School.

8 *Teip Proinsías Ó Maonaigh*, Cairdeas na bhFidiléirí Collection, An Foras Cultúir Uladh, Gleann Cholm Cille.

9 *Teip John Doherty*, Cairdeas na bhFidiléirí Collection, An Foras Cultúir Uladh, Gleann Cholm Cille.

10 Irish Folklore Commission Schools' Collection, Tullymore School.
11 Brian Lacy, Archaeological Survey of County Donegal, Donegl County Council.
12 *Teip Proinsías Ó Maonaigh,* Cairdeas na bhFidiléirí Collection, An Foras Cultúir Uladh, Gleann Cholm Cille.
13 Áine Ní Dhíoraí. *Na Cruacha Scéalta agus Seanchas*. An Chlochomar. Baile Atha Cliath, 1985.
14. Sean O hÉochaidh, Máire Ni Néill and Séamus ó' Cathain. *Siscéalta o Thír Chonaill,* Comhairle Bhéaloideas Éireann, Baile Átha Cliath, 1977.
15 Mickey Doherty Irish Folklore Commission recording.
16 Mickey Doherty BBC Sound Archive recording.
17 Irish Folklore Commission Schools Collection.
18 Daithí Ó hOgáin, *Myth Legend and Romance, An Encyclopaedia of the Irish Folk Tradition,* Ryan. New York. 1993.
19 Harry Bradshaw. Michael Coleman 1891-1945 Viva Voce. Dublin 1991.
20 Daithí Ó hOgáin, *Myth Legend and Romance, An Encyclopaedia of the Irish Folk Tradition,* Ryan. Op cit.
21 *Teip John Doherty,* Cairdeas na bhFidiléirí Collection, An Foras Cultúir Uladh, Gleann Cholm Cille.
22 Mickey Doherty BBC Sound Archive recording.
23 Máire Mac Néill, The Musician in the Cave. Béaloideas, 1989.
24 *Teip John Doherty,* Cairdeas na bhFidiléirí Collection, An Foras Cultúir Uladh, Gleann Cholm Cille.
25 Lochlann McGill, *In Conall's Footsteps,* Brandon, Dingle, Co. Kerry,1992, pp 316 - 317.
26 Máire Mac Néill, Op cit.
27 Perceval Swan. "Twixt Foyle and Swilly. Hodges Figgis, Dublin 1949.
28 Charles McGlinchey, *The Last of the Name,* Blackstaff Press, Belfast, 1986, Patrick Kavanagh, Editor.
29 *Teip Con Cassidy,* Cairdeas na bhFidiléirí Collection, An Foras Cultúir Uladh, Gleann Cholm Cille.
30. Alan Feldman and Eamon O'Doherty, *The Northern Fiddler,* Blackstaff Press, Belfast, 1979.
31 *Teip John Doherty,* Cairdeas na bhFidiléirí Collection, An Foras Cultúir Uladh, Gleann Cholm Cille.
32 *Teip Vincent Campbell,* Cairdeas na bhFidiléirí Collection, An Foras Cultúir Uladh, Gleann Cholm Cille.
33 *Teip Vincent Doherty,* Cairdeas na bhFidiléirí Collection, An Foras Cultúir Uladh, Gleann Cholm Cille.

CHAPTER FIVE

DONEGAL FIDDLING
AND
MUSIC COLLECTIONS

The collection of traditional music appears to have gone through a series of stages which have been directly related to the development and introduction of new technological advancements. Initially, the gathering of material was limited to the transcription of music by persons commonly taking an "antiquarian" interest in their material. Breathnach[1] comprehensively describes some of the problems involved in working with such material today, noting that many of the early collectors were classically-trained musicians having a preference for noting down tunes in piano settings. As such, pieces were regularly set in keys which the performers could never have availed of. Sometimes the collectors' lack of having acquired their music in the oral tradition resulted in tunes being written in totally unsuitable time signatures. Accepting such inherent flaws, these manuscripts and printed collections are still of immense value.

The invention of sound recording technology towards the end of the last century opened the possibility of committing players performances to some sort of semi-permanent record. The early stage of Irish music sound recordings resulted in a limited number of performances on cylinder devices. These were collected by special interest bodies, such as the Feis Ceoil and public broadcasting authorities, who had the funds to purchase these instruments. Recording activity during this phase grew continually between the 1920s and 1940s with the ultimate involvement of private companies in the production of commercial discs. By the early 1950s mass-produced tape machines became available to the general public. This development saw the collection of sound recordings by many enthusiasts over wide portions of the country. It marked the beginning of a new era of documentation of the broad range of players which could not have been feasibly covered by the larger cultural organisations, broadcasting and academic authorities. In the end, the contribution by a number of visionary devotees of the music through personal recording initiatives during this and subsequent decades has contributed vastly to the documentation of traditional music in the latter half of the present century. Three such activists, whose work has ensured that a significant portion of the Donegal fiddle tradition has been preserved, immediately spring to mind. They are An tAthair Eoghan O Colm, Dr. Alun Evans and Danny O Donnell. Their pioneering recordings, particular of the repertoire of John Doherty as well as Francie Dearg and Mickey O'Bán Byrne, make the often quoted phrase that the vast amount of these artists' tunes went with them to the grave a very hollow statement indeed.

Running parallel with developments in sound recording has been the advancement of visual recording devices. The camera moved gradually from a period of limited availability in the last century to one of being a typical household item by the 1960s. Thankfully, fiddlers became the object of interest on occasion and they have been documented to varying degrees. As with sound, the trend in visual recording technology has continued and the further introduction of widely available developments, such as television and video taping, ensures that a growing number of very valuable performances have been documented.

Outside of the long lineage of folklore and music, the oldest documented form of Irish traditional music is written manuscripts and printed collections. They can take us furthest back through the history of Donegal music. Systematic attempts to note the broad spectrum of Irish traditional music did not begin until the end of the 1700s. Edward Bunting is generally regarded as the first major collector of the music. His efforts were focused on noting the music of the last generation of harpists who had learned their playing through oral transmission. Of Donegal interest is his reference to the existence of the painting of the Battle of Ballyshannon as well as the inclusion of the air *Tiarna Mhaigh Eo*[2] which is a very popular tune with Donegal fiddlers. The latter version, however, is different from that played in Donegal.

In his 'Ancient Music of Ireland'[3] George Petrie includes the song *It Was an Old Beggarman, Weary and Wet* which he had received from William Allingham who had collected it in the Ballyshannon area. In his more substantive work 'The Complete Collection of Ancient Irish Music'[4], posthumously edited by Charles Villiers Stanford, we find eight listings with Donegal connections. *The Death of General Woulfe, 'Twas on the First of May, Brave Boys* and a hymn were obtained from the Reverend J. Mease of Rathmullen, while William Allingham is credited as the source of *Kitty O Hea, It Was an Old Beggarman, Weary and Wet, Van Dieman's Land* and *Mo Cailín Deas Ruaidh.* A song air, *Art McBride,* is also included. Though most are presented as song airs some can be played as dance tunes. It was commonplace until recently for songs to be composed to existing dance tunes. Finally worth noting in this collection is an air supplied in 1864 by P.W. Joyce appearing in Volume III, number 1123 as *Easter Snow.* The title is an anglicisation of the north Roscommon placename Díseart Nuadháin, which can today be found in the form of Estersnow, a District Electoral Division in the Boyle Number One Rural District. Petrie includes what appears to be a literal re-translation from the English form title back into Irish, *Sneachta Cásga* as an alternative name. Airs to this title were, as we shall see, favourites of Tarlach Mac Suibhne and his relations the Dohertys.

A manuscript collection containing transcriptions by Brendan Rogers of forty-two tunes played by some of the performers at the Feis Ceoil competitions held in Belfast in 1898 and 1900 has survived[5]. From a copy now held in the Irish Traditional Music Archive one tune in particular, *Easter Snow,* is significant as it points directly to Tarlach Mac Suibhne who was known to have attended and competed in 1898. The transcription, ignoring the difference in key settings, is the same as that noted above in Petrie. Surprisingly, however, it does not match the air which was played by the Dohertys.

Tarlach Mac Suibhne, or The Píobáire Mór as he is commonly known, clearly played a different air as *Easter Snow* than his relatives the Dohertys. We have good reason to believe he was fond of the piece as a comprehensive account of the early Feis Ceoil gatherings[6] by Breandán Breathnach shows that Mac Suibhne was one of seven pipers at the first Feis in Dublin in 1897. Quoting a contemporaneous extract from the Evening Telegraph he records that the Píobáire Mór won the "unpublished ancient Irish airs competition" playing *MacSweeney's March* (no doubt identical with that subsequently published in Songs of Uladh from his brother Pádraig's playing) as well as *Easter Snow* given under the Irish literal translation title *Sneachta na Cásga.* Finally on this air, it is worth noting that John Doherty used the English form of the name to derive a story of a woman called Ester Snow. Ester, he maintained, was a most beautiful woman of six feet in height. Her skin was as white as snow and thus became known as Ester Snow.

By the turn of the century the travel writer Stephen Gwynn had developed a great interest in and was well acquainted with the northwest corner of Donegal. He came to be very familiar with some of the local inhabitants and it would seem became convinced of the depth of the musical tradition of the area. Through his encouragement two enthusiasts associated with the Irish Folk Song Society, London, namely Pádraig Mac Aodh O'Neill (sometimes published as Herbert Hughes) and to a lesser degree Seosamh Mac Cathmhaoil (Joseph Campbell) were introduced to some of the prominent singers and fiddlers of the district. Mac Aodh O'Neill accepted an invitation from Gwynn to spend his holidays in northwest Donegal inAugust of 1903 and during this period transcribed tunes from musicians introduced by his companion.

The events of this visit left a tremendous impression on him and he returned again the following August to continue collecting. The end result of his efforts was a limited number of tunes published in the society's 'Journal of the Irish Folk Song Society', London[7] and a more comprehensive work jointly published in 1904 with Seosamh Mac Cathmhaoil, 'Songs of Uladh'[8]. The latter marked an extremely valuable early attempt at documenting Donegal music.

During his initial 1903 visit Mac Aodh O'Neill was introduced to farmer and schoolmaster Proinseas Mac Suibhne of Fawans, Kilmacrennan. Mac Suibhne undoubtedly had a major impact on Mac Aodh O'Neill who valued him as a seminal source of music. In fact, the author notes that he took down nearly half of what appears in this book[9] from Mac Suibhne.

The repertoire collected from Proinseas Mac Suibhne is very interesting for a number of reasons, primarily however, as it shows a continuity of the oral transmission of the local repertoire and that which several fiddlers recently passed on to current players. While Mac Aodh O'Neill in his Preface remarks the decline and disappearance of much valuable music from this area, the tunes noted show some striking connections with material circulated to today's Donegal fiddlers by the Dohertys. The observations of decline noted by Mac Aodh O'Neill could not have anticipated the significant handing-on impact which was even then being carried out by this family.

For example, the Scottish reel composition, *The Perthshire Hunt* is almost universally known in Ireland as *The Boyne Hunt.* A version learned by Proinseas Mac Suibhne from an old fiddler Aodh Gordon of Ceis Lionáin appears in 'Songs of Uladh' under the title *The Sailor's Trip to Liverpool.* I am familiar with only one other instance where that title is used, namely, a private recording by Mickey Doherty. Another tune, *The Muineachán Switch* was learned by Mac Suibhne from an old Glenswilly fiddler named *Uilliam Ua Curthainn* and was noted as being popular with the older people of Kilmacrennan. The version noted is in the key of A and is the same tune as that played in the key of D by the Dohertys which they titled *The Monaghan Twig* or *The Monaghan Switch.* It must be said that this tune had a circulation almost limited to Donegal until recently introduced to a wider audience through the playing of the current generation of young Donegal players.

Through Mac Aodh O'Neill's accompanying notes to Mac Suibhne's tunes we are fortunately introduced to a number of other fiddlers from the district who would otherwise have been lost to memory. He learned *The March of the Clan Suibhne* from a Fanad fiddler named Seághan Mac Giolla Carr. At the time of passing on the tune Mac Giolla Carr was over eighty. The tune is intended as a clan march and it is clear from the transcription it was performed in piping imitation style. On the basis of this piece it would appear justifiable to infer that the current Donegal practice of pipe imitation in the fiddle playing of performance pieces dates back to at least the mid - 1800's as Mac Giolla Carr was over eighty years old when he taught it to Mac Suibhne.

Mac Suibhne also contributed tunes he had learned from Nabla Ní hAnlúain who was then an elderly fiddler. Two reels are passed on from her playing, namely, *Burn's Reel* (a version of *Within a Mile of Clonbur)* and Miss Oddison which is a very unusual tune with triplets accented by bouncing the bow off the strings. This latter technique was well-known in Donegal and John Doherty demonstrated how he had learned it from his father for use in playing pipe imitation triplets in strathspeys and highlands. Another elderly fiddler, Dómhnall An Tailliúr Mór Mac Lochlainn of Druim Lurga, Kilmacrennan contributed *The Green Fields of Éire* (a version of *The Morning Star*) which he had learned from Séumas O' Dómhnall, a fiddler from Cluain Cille, Termon.

Two other tunes contributed by Proinseas Mac Suibhne are the jigs *The Humours of Baile na Fead* learned from Robert Sproule of Dromore, Kilmacrennan and *The Maidens of Tír Eoghain* (*Mac Ardle's Favourite* in 'O'Neill's Music of Ireland') learned from Antoine Mac Suibhne of Bearnas Gap. The latter is a three-part version in the key of A which is identical to one of two settings commonly played today throughout the country as *Out on the Ocean*. Dómhnall O' hArcáin of Ramelton contributed a piping air *Céad Bliadháin Ó Shin* which he had learned from Pádraig Mac Suibhne, the fiddle playing brother of Tarlach Mac Suibhne. This tune was apparently used as an introductory piece to a longer descriptive piece *Brian Boroimhe's March*. An untitled air was also contributed by Séamus Óg Mac Fhionnlaoich, a young sailor and fiddler from Port na Bláth who took Mac Aodh O'Neill out to Tory Island during the course of the collector's holiday.

Other tunes appearing in this collection from Proinseas Mac Suibhne's playing and not noted as having been learned from other sources include a jig *The Maidens of Derry* and the reel *Over the Bridge to Peggy*.

Lastly, we are introduced to a fiddler from the area about whom there is surprisingly no other information considering the manner in which he is portrayed. The collection contains numerous drawings by Seaghán Mac Cathmhaoil, brother of the joint author. The centrepiece of the cover is one of his line drawings. It shows a capped man with clay pipe and walking stick against a wall and nearby a bunch of sally rods for making creels. Slightly protruding from under his coat is clearly a fiddle. The sketch is titled Dómhnaill O Gallchóbhair The Dark Fidiler of Falcarragh. As there is no reference anywhere in the text of the collection to this figure it cannot be ascertained whether O Gallchóbhair lived at the time of the collecting or the drawing was based on a player who had passed on and was strongly remembered in the locality. Considering the manner in which he is portrayed and his nickname it is surprising he escapes discussion.

The 1904 articles appearing in the 'Journal of the Irish Folk Song Society', London[10] contains a reprint of the portion on *The Fair Reel,* as in 'Songs of Uladh' as well as three dance tunes and an air collected in August and September 1904. The first is a jig *Seol na nGeabhaigh* from Dán An Taillúir Mór Mac Lochlainn, a reel *Mary Will You Do It Again*? from Proinseas Mac Suibhne which we are told was used for the Clap Dance and a reel entitled *The Letterkenny Frolic* from Andrew MacIntyre of Ballymore who also composed the lyrics of *The Maids of Bearnas Gap* in 'Songs of Uladh'. Lastly is the air *Lionn Dubh Buidhe (Cuach Mo Londubh Buí)* from Cassie Sweeney, a sister of Proinseas Mac Suibhne.

The jig from Mac Lochlainn had been known to him since at least the 1860's also with an alternative title *My Grandfather's Nightcap.* It is commonly known today as one of several different jigs entitled *The Geese in the Bog.* It is very interesting in that, again, this tune has connections with the Dohertys as it is harmonic version of one which was played by John and particularly favoured by Mickey. Mac Lochlainn's version is in the key of G and clearly a fiddle version as it makes ample use of the bottom strings, well below the range of the pipes, whistle or flute. It is also curious for another reason. As we have already seen, pipers were encouraged at the early Feiseanna in Dublin and Belfast to perform pieces not thought to have been previously published or of "archaeological value". One of the most significant players to appear in the first few Feiseanna Ceoil was the blind Galway piper Dinny Delaney. A performance of one of his double jigs entitled the *Kid on the Mountain* (not today's well known slip jig) is amongst the transcriptions made by Brendan Rogers and is extremely similar to Mac Lochlainn's. This version, as noted by Breathnach[11], is problematic as the original transcription of the tune extends well below the range of Delaney's pipes. In this case, it is clear that Rogers transcribed Delaney's playing based on the pitch of his chanter, which was typically set in a flat key, and did not relate to the fingering of the chanter. A corrected transcription of how the jig must have been originally performed by Delaney has been made by Terry Moylan in 'Ceol an Phíobáire'[12]. This setting is extremely close to that played by the Dohertys' with the exception of the fiddlers availing of some melodic variations available on the fourth string.

Concerning *Mary, Will You Do It Again?*, Mac Aodh O'Neill notes the tune was used for the Clap Dance. From his accompanying notes it is clear he was not familiar with the dance, which still survives in a few localities in Donegal, west Fermanagh, Cavan and Monaghan. The tune would appear to have been performed quickly by Mac Suibhne in that it is classified as a reel. The dance is usually done as a hornpipe to the tune *The Soldier's Joy* with the partners standing opposite and clapping each others palms to the final two crotchets of the second, fourth and sixth bars.

Mac Aodh O'Neill's enthusiasm for collecting traditional music would appear to have been transmitted to the aforementioned Andrew Mac Intyre. In 'The Journal of The Irish Folk Song Society', London[13] in 1905 he contributed two tunes from local players with which he would have been well acquainted. The first is *Coll's Reel* which he learned from the playing of John Coll of Derryherriff in the parish of Doe. The second is *Glacan's Reel* which was a tune well-known locally and associated with the playing of Padraic Glacan of Doe who flourished in the 1870's. The second part of this reel is clearly a close variation of the turn of *Miss Thornton's Reel.* Immediately following these reels is a double jig contributed by Herbert Hughes (Pádraig Mac Aodh O'Neill) from the playing of Proinseas Mac Suibhne in August 1903. It appears under the title *The Geese in the Bog* or *The Jolly Old Wife.* He notes that it was one of the most popular of all dance tunes in Donegal. It is the familiar *Three Little Drummers of O'Neill's* collections.

In the 1905 -1906 volume of the Journal a number of items of Donegal interest appear. The words and music to a song entitled *The Sailor's Farewell* which was learned from a girl in Moville as well as the air and fragments of the lyric of *Bonagee* from a Culdaff girl are contributed by Honoria Galway[14]. A tune which resembles a double jig, with the exception of having too many bars, entitled *Hey, My Kitten My Kitten* was collected by Major Dulap[15] from an old woman in Donegal and included in a contribution by Charlotte Milligan Fox[16] entitled a 'Sheaf of Irish Dance Tunes'. Also appearing is a double jig which she collected in 1904 from T. Sweeny in Mountcharles entitled *Arthur McBride.* The tune is that commonly referred to today as *The Rakes of Kildare* and shows no relation at all to the *Arthur McBride* published (and referred to above) by both Petrie and Joyce. In the same edition, Edith Wheeler[17] provided an article on the song *The Irish Girl.* In discussing its variations she notes a set of words from Michael Devlin of Rosapenna with an additional verse heard from a young woman in Mountcharles in 1903. She also noted the existence of another air to the song from Mary Sweeny of Rosapenna. Lastly, she adds an air entitled *The Bouchal Roe* which she offers as an alternative air to *The Irish Girl* which she heard in Mountcharles, presumably during her 1903 visit.

In a 1910 volume of the 'Journal of the Irish Folk Song Society', London[18], Charlotte Milligan Fox included an article entitled 'Folk Song in County Tyrone'. In the course of the article she notes the work of Henry Morris (Enrí O Muirgheasa) who had been collecting from elder farmers Eamon and Anne Tracey. This brother and sister were native Irish speakers and lived at An Caisleán Glas, outside of Omagh. Milligan Fox lists a number of songs Morris had collected from the Tracey's and amongst these is *Briseadh Eachdhruim,* which O Muirgheasa eventually published in 'Dhá Chéad de Cheoltaibh Uladh'[19]. The inclusion of this is interesting in that it is a very rare piece and the only known recording of the air of it to my mind is that made by Ciarán Mac Mathúna from the playing of Francie Dearg O'Byrne of Kilcar.

P.W. Joyce's work 'Old Irish Folk Music and Songs'[20] contains no references to Donegal dance music but does note four songs with Donegal connections. These are the Jacobite song *Ye Natives of this Nation* obtained from Barnaby O'Hanlon *O, Where are you going my Pretty Fair Maid,* and *Am I the Doctor You Wished For to See?* while he speculates on Donegal origins for the sea-faring song *Strike Up, Ye Lusty Gallants, Charming Mary Neill,* and *Arthur McBride* which is almost identical to that noted by Petrie.

Incorporated into Joyce's book are two other collections which existed in manuscript form, namely the 'Forde Collection' and the 'Pigot Collection'. In the 'Forde Collection' he notes the air title *Castle Finn* and associates this with the east Donegal village. Also printed is an interesting air entitled *My Love She is Living in Donegal Town* which had been supplied by the Reverend Alexander Ross of Dungiven, County Derry. It would appear from the absence of editorial notes that Joyce did not recognise its inclusion in the 'Pigot Collection', number 712, as an untitled air where it was sourced from a native of Donegal. This tune is very unusual as I have only heard it played by two fiddlers, namely John Doherty and Vincent McLoughlin of Ballymaguigan, County Derry. The evidence would seem to indicate that this tune was in circulation in the northwest of Ireland during the last century and has lost currency during the present one.

The most notable collection of Irish music published is comprised of the combined works of Francis O'Neill written while resident in Chicago during the early decades of this century. These works centred on the music provided by the host of emigrant musicians based in that city as well as music collected by a handful of his collaborators mainly living in other American cities. Considering the vast emigration from Donegal and the large number of fiddlers known to have existed in the county it is very strange, that with the exception of Tarlach Mac Suibhne, who is featured solely as a piper, we are not directly introduced to any Donegal fiddlers by O'Neill. Writing elsewhere[21], I have discovered the music of one such Donegal player in Francis O'Neill's works, that of Joe Timoney (O'Neill uses a typical American version of the surname - Tamoney), or as he was known at home, Joe Pheadar Shéain O Tiománaí. Joe was born and raised in in Mín a tSamhaidh, Fintown and emigrated to the United States in the earliest years of this century. He was a great-great-great-great-great grandson of the famous poet Tadhg An Fhile O'Tiománaí An Aighe who came to settle in Fintown from nearby Aighe outside of Ardara and who married a daughter of one of the O'Donnell chieftains. After a brief spell on the east coast Joe made his way west to San Francisco arriving in that city on April 19th, 1906 - the day after the great earthquake!

He became prominent in the Irish music circles of San Francisco coming to the attention of Francis Walsh, a former member of the Irish Music Club of Chicago. From his days in Chicago Walsh was well aware of Francis O'Neill's efforts in collecting and collaborated with his friend sending him biographical sketches on the players as well as transcriptions of their tunes.

No information is offered by either Walsh or O'Neill on O'Tiománaí but five of his tunes do appear in 'Waifs and Strays of Gaelic Melody' first published in 1922. The title of *The Glendowan Reel* belies its Donegal connection through its reference to the mountainous area in the centre of the county. It is identical to the popular *Sligo Maid's Lament*. The former name, however, was that used amongst older players and is still a common title in Donegal. The second reel is *The Fairy Hurlers*. Three hornpipes are also credited to O'Tiománaí. *Dan Lowry's* refers to the very well known

Dublin theatrical establishment of the period while the second is *Raftery's Hornpipe*. The final tune is the key of A major and entitled *Tamony's Hornpipe*. It is interesting that upon close inspection it is identical to *The Smith's Hornpipe* which appears in 'O'Neill's Irish Music for Piano and Violin'[23] as well as a setting in the key of G major entitled *The Friendly Visit* printed in 'The Dance Music of Ireland'[24]. This tune, in its A major version is still very popular in Donegal and hardly ever played in this key outside the county.

The information on Joe Pheadar Shéain which confirmed his Donegal origins came to light again through the efforts of Danny O'Donnell. While still living on the east coast of America in the 1950s he became aware of a thriving music environment in San Francisco and the existence of Joe in particular. To satisfy his desire to meet musicians he travelled to the west coast and sought him out. Danny stayed in San Francisco for some time and played at length with O'Tiománaí learning many of his tunes.

Though O'Neill does not record any acquaintance of Donegal fiddlers this does not preclude his correspondents being familiar with Donegal fiddlers as we have seen with Walsh. Another correspondent of O'Neill whose contributions appear in 'Waifs and Strays of Gaelic Melody'[25] was Pat Dunne, a farmer originally from Kilbraugh, Thurles. It is more than likely that he played music as he did supply O'Neill with a small collection of manuscripts in the years prior to the 1920s. While it remains completely in the realm of speculation, a number of tunes published by O'Neill from Dunnes' manuscripts indicate that he may have got some of them from a Donegal player. For example, number 264 is entitled *The Donegal Reel* and is identical to that popularly played under that title or more commonly in Donegal as *Úna Bháin Ní Chuinneagáin*. The reel immediately preceding it is entitled *Irish Pat* and is identical to that played today in both a reel and highland versions as *Sporting Paddy*. While this tune is found in the repertoires of the musicians of other counties only in Donegal is it usually found as a reel and a highland.

Published in Glasgow, 'Allen's Irish Fiddler', contains tunes collected and arranged by Hugh Mc Dermott[26]. Available until recently, it is a very unusual collection of dance music. As in other collections, *Úna Bhán Ní Chuinneagáin* appears as *The Donegall Reel.* Two tunes by name give a tenuous hint to Donegal, namely, *Sweeney's Hornpipe* and the *Glendoan Reel (The Sligo Maids Lament).*

The Donegal links however are significantly firmer with the transcriptions of two other reels, namely *The Wild Irishman* and *The Pidgeon on the Gate*. In the first case, the reel is that version which existed only in Donegal until recently. *The Pidgeon on the Gate* appearing in 'Allen's Irish Fiddler' is unique in that it corresponds with none of the popular settings of the tune. It is in the key of G Minor, that which was almost unique to the playing of Neillidh Boyle. In fact, the setting is so close to that played by Neillidh, it would be tempting to conclude that it was transcribed either from him or from his recordings. Unfortunately I have not been able to trace anything about the collector and arranger of the tunes in this book, Hugh McDermott, but based on some of the diagnostic material in the collection it would appear he may have had some familiarity with Donegal players in Scotland.

While Donegal fiddlers may have escaped the attention of Francis O'Neill, those based in Philadelphia during the early decades of this century certainly received the notice and respect of Cavan-born fiddler and composer Ed Reavy. Reavy, whose abundant compositions have comfortably slotted into the mainstream repertoire of traditional music today, was born in Barnagrove, County Cavan in 1898. He emigrated to Philadelphia in 1912 and quickly established himself there as a player of significance becoming familiar with all of the great players of that era. He is best remembered, however, for his numerous compositions.

These appear primarily in two volumes, 'Where the Shannon Rises'[27] and 'Ed Reavy, The collected Compositions'[28] edited by his son Joseph. In the latter collection, Joseph Reavy includes an appendix wherein the background to either the selection of the tune title or the original influence of the melody appears.

It can be seen from these notes that the Donegal fiddlers Ed Reavy met during his years in America left a significant impression on him. Neil and his son John Doherty (or Dougherty as they were known in America) of Glenties were held in very high regard by Reavy and the fame of the Dohertys' had also reached Ed via his close friend Louis Quinn of Armagh who was well acquainted with the brothers John, Mickey and Simon (Ballinamore). This respect resulted in the titling of a reel *The Donegal Doughertys*. In the background notes on this tune Ed is quoted as acknowledging Neil Doherty as "a little known master of his trade ... a superb player of highlands and a great Donegal fiddler... a true traditional player who knew how to brighten tunes in the right places". Neil is further commemorated in the highland *Neil of the Glenties*[29].

The famous Pádaí Bhillí na Rópaí of Kiltyfanad also spent some time in Philadelphia and had a reel entitled in his honour *Pat Boyle of Glencolumkill.* Again we are told in the notes to this tune that Pádaí "was special", and even more complimentary, that "some of Ed's best compositions were inspired by the playing of Pat Boyle"[30].

Three other players from Donegal are briefly alluded to, namely, Charlie Doherty (also in *The Donegal Doughertys*'), John Roarty *(John Roarty's Reel)* who owned a pub and played in Irish dance halls in west Philadelphia during the 'twenties and Charlie Mc Devitt (*Charlie Mc Devitt's Reel)* who though not necessarily a gifted player is noted as having been "an important influence on the tradition at that time"[31].

Ed Reavy's composition legacy is prolific by any standard throughout the history of the Irish fiddling tradition. The 127 pieces appearing in the larger collection are admittedly only those which could be remembered. Many more were known to have been forgotten. A very small number of old tunes (ie *The Irish Washerwoman*) which had been significantly altered to the degree that they were considered worthy of re-introduction via the Reavy touch were included. Considering the large amount of material and the vast timescale over which both the composer and the editor were working with it is not surprising that a non-original piece should accidentally slip in as a composition. *The Merry Wives Highland* appears in the key of C Major. This tune is identical to the reel *An Baintreach Mná* which was learned by the late Francie Dearg O'Byrne as a youth from his father. It is still well known in the Kilcar –Teelin–Glencolumbcille area where it is played as a reel in the key of D Major as Francie had it. In nearby Glencolumcille, it can also be found in the repertoire of James Byrne who learned it from his father John and uncle, Pádaí Hiúidaí.

Pádraig Mac Seáin's work 'Ceolta Theilinn'[32] is of particular interest to Donegal fiddlers. It contains the musical notation of the airs and lyrics to thirty six songs in Irish from the Teelin–Carrick – Glencolumcille area. The version of *Maidin Fhómhair* is interesting in that it differs from that which was a particular favourite of John Doherty.

Volumes one and two of the tutors 'Whistle and Sing!' by Eamonn Jordan[33] contain some material which was obtained from Donegal players. The first volume includes transcriptions of *The Gweebara Reel* under the title (John) *Doherty's Reel* as well as *The Four Poster Bed. The Broken Bridge* hornpipe, a great favourite in west Donegal also appears but its source is not noted. Volume Two[34] contains a transcription of *Tuam na Farraige* from the playing of John Doherty under the title *The Atlantic Waves* as well as one of his versions of *The Heathery Braes* under the title *The Heathery Breeze.* Two germans and a version of the *Pinch of Snuff,* almost certainly of Donegal origin, also appear as do two mazurkas transcribed from the 78 RPM recording of Hughie Gillespie. An untitled highland (p. 86) noted as being from Donegal may well have been sourced from *An Fhidil Ghaelach*[35]. The last tune of the collection is a mazurka titled after Alec Murphy of Aboligan, Maghery, Dungloe. A comment following the tune shows Alec was the source for many of the hornpipes in this volume.

As noted in Chapter Two there have been some direct connections between Donegal and Shetland. Tom Anderson's second collection of Shetland tunes *Ringing Strings*[36] contains a transcription of a tune and its associated dance entitled the *Seven Step Polka.* This tune is a 12 bar, single part close version of a tune which is still played in west Donegal entitled the *Eight Step Polka.* The Donegal version is also a single part tune with eight bars. Tom notes that variations of the tune are to be found in Sweden, England, Denmark and parts of America.

Two similar tutor type publications also contain Donegal material. 'The Ros na Rí Collection of Irish Traditional Music', Vol. 137 (no subsequent volumes were issued) contains a transcription of Hughie Gillespie's recording of *The Donegal Traveller.* The Armagh Pipers publication'Play 50 Reels'[38] contains a number of tunes from Tommy Peoples and John Doherty. Their three volume 'Learn to Play the Tin Whistle' tutors[39] also contain tunes which were sourced in part from John Doherty and Tommy Peoples. Grace Orpen's book 'The Dances of Donegal'[40] is discussed in detail in Chapter Five as it is primarily concerned with the dance forms of the county. However, it does contain a number of tunes which were commonly used for the dances described. Also of interest will be the occasional transcriptions from Donegal fiddlers, generally Tommy Peoples and John Doherty, which have appeared over the years in 'Treoir'[41], the journal of Comhaltas Ceoltóirí Éireann. Volumes one to four of 'Music from Ireland'[42] contain dance tunes sourced from Donegal fiddlers, namely Tommy Peoples, Jimmy McHugh, Hughie Gillespie and John Doherty. With the exception of the items from Jimmy McHugh all of the material appears to be transcriptions from commercial recordings.

A very brief account of John Doherty and his association with Frosses is recounted in Anthony O'Callaghan's 'Here's To My Friends - Songs and Stories of Jim Burke'[43]. A song entitled *Johnny Doherty in Kellys (The Glen Eany Bar)* which was composed by the subject of the collection, Jim Burke of Croagh, near Dunkineely who settled in Frosses, is also included. It recounts the events of an evening's session with John playing and Mickey Brown, Dickie Wilson and Tommy Boyle dancing to his music. Interestingly in the account of John the author recounts a story from Jim Burke about a local Frosses man who made a tin fiddle. His identity is not recorded.

A short collection of tunes was issued in conjunction with a commercially released tape of the playing of Tommy Peoples. The contents of the booklet, entitled 'Fifty Irish Fiddle Tunes- arranged and played by Tommy Peoples'[44], reflects the broad range of influences on Tommy's repertoire. While the transcriptions do not shed any light on Tommy's personal style, a standard mazurka which he learned from John Doherty, *Jackson's Reel, The Laird of Drumblair* and *The Merry Sisters Reel* are of Donegal interest.

A relevant publication in relation to Donegal fiddle music is 'The Northern Fiddler'[45]. This work attempted to document the repertoire, social history of the music and its associated folklore as well as the brief biographies of some of the musicians of Counties Donegal and Tyrone. The Donegal element of the book is clearly dominant and the musicians detailed are John Doherty, Simon (Stranorlar) Doherty, Francie Dearg and Mickey Bán O'Byrne, Con Cassidy and Danny O'Donnell. The decidedly negative review it received on it's release from Breandán Breathnach[46] would appear to be well-justified. While much valuable information is afforded in recorded conversations with the musicians, the music transcriptions presented in the collection vary remarkably. In enough cases so as to warrant concern, tunes in very common circulation with standard titles are transcribed and listed as untitled. This is in direct conflict with one of the primary stated aims for the inclusion of material, namely that "they (the tunes) were unknown outside their immediate environment. In other words, they were either not in print in any major tune collections or they were not played by the younger generation of Irish musicians..." [47]

An example which contradicts all of the latter aims is the inclusion of the classic, commonly printed, and widely-familiar Michael Coleman setting of *The Lads of Laois* appearing as an *Untitled Reel* on page 170. Similarly, an *Untitled Slip Jig* from the playing of John Doherty appears on page 61. The first bar is in 9/8 time changing to 12/8 in the second. The third bar is again in 9/8 returning in the fourth bar to 12/8. The tune is not a slip jig at all but the first two parts of the common four part double jig *Langstrom's Pony* (sometimes *Langstern's Pony*). When the piece, as written, is treated in 6/8 time the fluctuating time signatures become totally irrelevant and the tune conforms to the normal format of a double jig. Elsewhere, on page 82 an*Untitled Strathspey* appears which is the same as that printed only two pages previously as the *Ladies of Gormond Highland*. Furthermore, tunes appear under one title as played by one fiddler and under a different name from another without any mention of the connection, such as with *The Black Fanad Mare* of John Doherty and *The Kiltyfanad Reel of Francie Dearg* and *Mickey Bán O'Byrne*. While the photographs and sketches are much in sympathy with the original material, the significant lack of overall editing is again evident with at least one appearing upside down and a sketch of John Doherty not being reversed in the printing process so he comes out looking decidedly awkward as a left-handed fiddler.

Lastly is the collection of the music from the Cairdeas na bhFidléirí Donegal Fiddlers Summer School in Glencolumbcille. These appear in two volumes[48] and comprise that music taught between the years 1986 and 1990 at summer school. Excepting those tunes which have a wide circulation, the tunes are almost entirely of Donegal provenance and the majority are transcribed from the playing of the older fiddlers who have acted as the sources of the music. An accompanying tutor tape containing the playing of the teachers has also been produced.

Lastly, the most significant development in the area of collections has been the recent founding of the Irish Traditional Music Archive in Merrion Square, Dublin as well as the Donegal Fiddle

Archive in Foras Chultúir Uladh, Glencolumcille. The archive in Dublin serves as the national repository for material relating to traditional music in its broadest sense. It is a most professional body whose collecting and archiving techniques are of the highest standards and in its short lifetime has proven to be one of the most significant resources to traditional musicians. Happily its interest in Donegal material has been considerable and is growing all the time. The Donegal Fiddlers Archive is a joint venture between Cairdeas na bhFidiléirí and An Foras Chultúir Uladh. It aims to collect the broadest amount of material relating to Donegal fiddle music, making it available for consultation by the public in the An Foras Chultúir Uladh building. The material collected to date includes a wide range of photographs, video material and audio tapes. The latter material forms the bulk of the collection and is growing all the time.

REFERENCES

1 Breandan Breathnach. *The Feis Ceoil and Piping. Ceol,* V8, nos 1 and 2, p. 19.

2 Edward Bunting. *The Ancient Music of Ireland.* Walton's, Dublin, 1969 (reprint edition).

3 George Petrie. *Ancient Music of Ireland.* M. H. Gill, 1855. Facsimile reprint Gregg International Publishers Ltd. Farnborough, 1967.

4 George Petrie. *The Complete Petrie Collection of Ancient Irish Music.* Charles Villiers Stanford (Ed.), Boosey and Co. London and New York, Vols I+II (1902), Vol III (1905).

5 Breandán Breathnach. *The Feis Ceoil and Piping.* Ceol, V8, nos 1 and 2.

6 Breandán Breathnach. Op. cit.

7 Herbert Hughes. *Journal of the Irish Folk Song Society,* London, Vol. 1904.

8 Pádraig Mac Aodh O Neill and Seosamh Mac Cathmhaoil, *Songs of Uladh.* William Mullan, Belfast, 1904.

9 Op. cit. Preface.

10 Op. cit. pp 19-21.

11 Op.cit.

12 Terry Moylan (editor). *Ceol an Phíobáire.* Na Píobairí Uilleann, Dublin, 1981. Tune no. 62.

13 Andrew McIntyre. *Journal of the Irish Folk Song Society,* London. Vol. 2, nos. 1-2, p. 13, 1905.

14 Honoria Galway. *Journal of the Irish Folk Song Society,* London. Vol. 3, nos. 3-4 1905-1906, p. 14.

15 Charlotte Milligan Fox. *Journal of the Irish Folk Song Society,* London, Vol. 3, nos. 3-4, 1905-1906, p. 15.

16 Charlotte Milligan Fox. *Journal of the Irish Folk Song Society,* London, Vol. 3, nos 3-4, 1905-1906, pp15-17.

17 Edith Wheeler. *Notes on an Irish Song (The Irish Girl).* Journal of the Irish Folk Song Society, London, Vol. 3, nos. 3-4, 1905-1906, p. 26.

18 Charlotte Milligan Fox. *Folk Song in County Tyrone.* Journal of the Irish Folk Song Society, London, Vol. 8, 1910, p. 25.

19 Enrí O Muirgheasa. *Dhá Chéad de Cheoltaibh Uladh.* Oifig Dhíolta Foilseachan Ríaltais, Baile Átha Cliath, 1933, lch 22 - 24.

20 P.W. Joyce. Old Irish Folk Music and Songs. Cooper Square, New York, 1965 - a facsimile reprint of the 1909 edition.

21 Caoimhín Mac Aoidh. *Joe Pheadair Shéain.* Ceol, vol.8, nos 1+2, 1986. pp 37-39.

22 Francis O'Neill. *Waifs and Strays of Gaelic Melody.* Chicago, 1922.

23 Francis O'Neill. O'Neill's *Irish Music for Piano and Violin.* Chicago, 1915.

24 Op. Cit, no. 894, p. 154.

25 Op. cit., p 140.

26 Hugh McDermott. *Allan's Irish Fiddler.* Mozart Allen, Glasgow (no date).

27 Joseph Reavey (editor). *Where the Shannon Rises.* Philadelphia, 1971.

28 Joseph Reavey (editor). Ed Reavey, *The Collected Compositions.* Philadelphia, 1984.
29 Op. Cit., p. 115.
30 Op. Cit., p. 147.
31 Op. Cit., p. 148.
32 Pádraig Mac Seáin. *Ceolta Theilinn.* Institute of Irish Studies, Queen's University, Belfast, 1973.
33 Eamonn Jordan. *Whistle and Sing! Book One,* Whistle and Sing, Ashardan, Portadown, Armagh, 1975.
34 Eamonn Jordan. *Whistle and Sing! Book Two.* Ashardan, Portadown, Armagh, 1988.
35 Caoimhín Mac Aoidh. *Highlands o Thír Chonaill.* An Fhidil Ghaelach. An Crann Darach. 1982.
36 Tom Anderson. *Ringing Strings. The Shetland Times Ltd.,* Lerwick, 1983.
37 Daithí O Ríseach agus Donnchadh Mac Suibhne. *The Ros na Rí Collection of Irish Traditional Music,* Vol. 1. Ros na Rí Productions, Suffolk, Dunmurry, Co. Antrim (no date)
38 Brian and Eithne Vallely. *Play 50 Reels.* The Armagh Pipers' Club, Armagh, 1982.
39 Brian and Eithne Vallely. *Learn to Play the Tin Whistle,* Parts 1-3. The Armagh Piper's Club. Armagh, 1973.
40 Grace Orpen. *The Dances of Donegal.* D. Wilkie. London. 1931.
41 *Treoir.* Cómhaltas Ceoltóirí Éireann, Monkstown, County Dublin.
42 Dave Bulmer and Neil Sharpley. *Music From Ireland* Vols 1-4.Celtic Music, Lincolnshire, 1976.
43 Anthony O'Callaghan. *Here's to My Friends - Songs and Stories of Jim Burke.* Donegal Democrat, Ballyshannon, 1986.
44 *Fifty Irish Fiddle Tunes -arranged and played by Tommy Peoples,* Waltons, Dublin, 1986.
45 Allen Feldman and Eamonn O'Doherty. *The Northern Fiddler.* Blackstaff Press, Belfast, 1979.
46 Breandán Breathnach. *The Northern Fiddler - A Review.* Ceol, vol.5, no.2, p.64, 1982.
47 Op. Cit., p. 250-251.
48 Caoimhín Mac Aoidh (editor). *An Ceol - The Music of the Donegal Fiddlers Summer School,* Vols 1-2. Cairdeas na bhFidléirí, Beal Átha Seannaigh, 1990.

Jimmy Peoples. Grandfather of Tommy Peoples of St. Johnston.

Pat Mulhearne of Fallash, Drumfries playing at home shortly after his ninety fourth birthday.

Neillidh Boyle at his home in Cronashallog, Dungloe

Myles Tinney of Mountcharles with his box fiddle.

Mickey Mór Doherty and three of his son Mickey's children (Frances in centre)

Simon (Kilmacrennan) Doherty

Frank Cassidy of Teelin

CHAPTER SIX

DANCING

The music played by the Donegal fiddlers did not originate as either listening or solo 'performance' music. It began its life and can still be described as dance music. Dancing was one of the major social outlets for the people of Donegal through the generations and as we have already seen in the first chapter, the main venues were primarily the cottages followed by schools, barns and cross roads. This pattern continued in Donegal up until the 1930s and from this period the house dance declined with the introduction, often by the clergy, of large parish-based dance halls. By the 1960s the separation of dancing and music was largely completed. House dances, though still extant, were rare and the pub became the new venue for fiddle playing.

A variety of dance forms were produced during the decades when traditional dancing was popular in Donegal. Evidence among today's elder fiddlers indicates that unlike the rest of the country itinerant dancing masters were not as important a factor in the spread of dance forms. In parts of Donegal it is remembered that within the family, the fiddle was typically played and taught by the father to the sons while it was the traditional role of the mother to teach all the children to dance. With few exceptions, the introduction of dancing masters appears to have occurred in the southern end of the county. Tarlach Mac Suibhne was known to have taught dancing during his travels about the northwest of the county and more recently Francie McHugh of Lough Doon also gave lessons. Eddie Moore, now in his nineties, remembers that during the closing decades of the last century two brothers by the name of McCabe used to travel and give dancing lessons. When in the Ballyshannon area they would organise classes in the early evenings for children and young adults in Terry McCauley's barn in Corlea and then hold a barn dance to which they charged admission for adults at night. This particular barn was always chosen as it was flag floored and a favourite with the dancers. During the 1940s or 1950s dancehall-based dances were growing in Bundoran and in the Marine Ballroom, fiddler Dick Mulready used to play and teach dancing. It would appear that Mulready was from north Connacht and travelled to teach in Bundoran on a seasonal basis.

One significant fiddler from the second half of the last century, Neil Coll, from the Dunfanaghy area combined his living as a fiddler along with that of dancing master and was subsequently succeeded by his son, John. An anonymous account of Neil is as follows[1]:

> In the 1870's Irish dancing was held in a barn near Faugher House. There, Robbie Algeo, of Rockhill, was one of the pupils and became as well known stepdancer. He died in 1949 in his ninety-second year. The dancing master in the school was Neil Coll, of Derryherriff. The fee was one shilling a week - six pence a week for girls and all paid a half penny a week for candles. On Saturday nights the class would take the form of a céilí mór. . . There was a case of the boy, unwilling to pay one shilling, who tried to learn the steps peeping through the keyhole. Neil Coll also taught dancing in Derryherriff and Horn Head. Some of the steps he taught still survive. His hornpipes and jigs had twelve steps. One of them called 'The Crab's Walk' another the 'Pidgeon's Wing', still others, 'The Buachaillí Forward','The Bracing of the Hornpipe' and 'The Twisting Hornpipe'. Robbie was still able to execute the steps into his eighties.

In other areas of the country during the past, the impact of the presence of military regiments was significant. Many of the sets popularly danced today such as the Lancers and the Caledonian owe their introduction into Ireland via the British Army[2]. The degree to which the military influenced dancing in Donegal is uncertain as the current older generation of players well remember the traditional dances but generally do not recall their origins. As noted above, the transmission of local dances seems to be much to the credit of the women of Donegal.

Dances in Donegal fall into two categories regarding their popularity in the county. Firstly those which were well established and widespread throughout the county such as the Highland and secondly those which had a more restricted distribution and were popular for the shorter duration of a decade or two. When looking at specific dances it is worthwhile, if possible, establishing to which type of popularity group it belongs.

Unlike most other counties, Donegal is fortunate in having

received the attentions of a contemporary collector specifically interested in the dances of the first three decades of this century. A book entitled 'The Dances of Donegal' was published by Grace Orpen in 1931[3]. The introduction does not afford any clues as to where she sourced the dances described and as already discussed in Chapter One, there is a doubt raised about her familiarity with traditional music performance in the county by virtue of her observation that along with the violin, the concertina was the most common instrument. Orpen's record of the dances however still gives us some valuable information.

She describes fifteen dances, some of which are familiar, while others are more obscure. Appearing first is the 'Fairy Reel' which was danced to the tune of the same name by two men and four women. 'The Six Hand Duke' was done by three men and three women with the jig *Saint Patrick's Day* as the tune cited for playing. 'The Irish Reel', done by two men and two women was done, oddly enough, to the hornpipe *The Flowers of Edinburgh.* Orpen records the widely known 'Trip to the Cottage' for two couples and gives *Merrily Kissed the Quaker* as the tune for it. The vernacularly titled 'Strathsperry Reel' for two couples is described to *Miss McLeod* indicating that the tune might have been played to a dotted rhythm. 'The Irish National' or 'The Petticoat Swish' was done by two couples and the recommended tune given was the double jig *Smash the Windows.* The next two dances described are group dances namely 'The Waves of Tory' with the Scots tune *The One Hundred Pipers* being recommended followed by 'The Six Hand Reel' which oddly enough was done to the jig *Paddy Whack.* The next dance seems a curious one and appears to have been rare as none of today's older players are familiar with the name. It was entitled 'The Pin Dance' and the music provided was the jig *The Young May Moon.* According to the description the dancers made a ring around an individual man who stood in the centre. This man represented the 'pin'. The next dance is the well known 'Shoe the Donkey'. A 'Military Two Step' followed with the double jig *The Top of the Cork Road* noted as suitable. A 'Highland' to be done to *The Girl I Left Behind Me* followed by a 'Barndance' to *Paddy Mc Ginty* appear next.

The familiar 'Corn Rigs' is then described. However, the accompanying tune is the reel *The Green Groves of Erin.* In this case it is surprising that the 'Corn Rigs' itself is not used and though the reel is suitable it would have to have been played more slowly in a highland setting. To finish, Orpen describes an obscure dance entitled 'The Berlin Polky' to which the jig *Off She Goes* is provided as the suitable music. Older Donegal fiddlers to a man and many of the middle generation of players use the word "polkey" for the 'polka'. What is more interesting about this documentation of the 'Berlin Polky' by Orpen is the tune she cites to be played for it. *Off She Goes* is a double jig which also easily fits into slide rhythm. Its basic 6/8 time signature is totally uncharacteristic of the 2/4 rhythm used throughout the country for polkas. The tune which Danny O'Donnell, who had vast experience playing at house dances, clearly remembers as being played for the 'Berlin Polky' was that which appears in 'Kerr's First Collection of Merry Melodie's'[4] under the title *The Krakoviak.* This tune is in 2/4 time and the pattern of triplets are completely characteristic of a polka. It may well be the case that the dance described by Orpen was something other than a polka to which her sources simply, yet mistakenly referred to as the 'Berlin Polky'.

Some of these dances such as the 'Highland', 'Barndance', 'Shoe the Donkey' and 'Corn Rigs' belong to the widespread and long lasting popularity group of dances and are not surprising by their inclusion. Alternatively, others now less familiar, can be clarified to some degree by players such as Danny O'Donnell. 'The Berlin Polky' he remembers as being danced in the Dungloe area but only during the 1920s and 1930s, after which it waned. This dance would seem therefore to belong to the group of dances which had short term popularity and were geographically restricted. According to Orpen's description, 'The Trip to the Cottage' is not that developed by the dancing boards and commissions arising out of the Gaelic League movement which sought to standardise and re-define Irish dancing in the early decades of this century. Danny remembers this older dance was done, but only in the area around Downings. Conversely, the 'Waves of Tory' as illustrated in this collection corresponds to the dancing commission design.

Today Donegal is probably unique amongst the counties by virtue of the degree of popularity of the highland amongst traditional dancers. This rhythm would appear to have a very interesting history. Though universally called a highland in the musical fraternity it appears to have originated from the Schottische, a dance of German origin[5]. This spread throughout Europe and became quite popular in Scotland. It is thought amongst older players that Scottish fiddlers composed and also reshaped existing tunes to play for the dance. As a gesture of national pride they referred not only to these tunes but also to the dance as a 'Highland Schottische' or occasionally a 'Highland Fling'. It is typical of collections of Scottish music of the last century to find these terms used to classify bodies of tunes in common time. In Donegal, they quickly spread and were played for a similar dance. However the 'schottische' element of the name was dropped and the title for both tune classification and dance became known as a 'highland'. The term 'fling', while correctly used in other parts of the country to describe the same set of tunes and probably the dance, is not used in Donegal.

The 'Highland' as commonly performed throughout Donegal today is a couple dance (ie. a girl and a boy) where the first part of the tune is danced side by side with footwork being important and the second half is face to face. It is clear that minor variations in the dance existed between localities. A second form, the 'Irish Highland' is still well remembered and occasionally danced. It is done to the exact same type of tune with identical speed and rhythm but it is performed by a boy and two girls. Cití Bean Uí Mhaonaigh of Gweedore can also recall two types of couple dance highlands from her locality. She remembers their names as the 'Highland Beag', which corresponded to the normal highland of today and the 'Highland Garbh', which she recalls, had an additional step in it.

The barn dance in Donegal has the unusual title of the 'german'. It is in common time and rhythmically there is little to distinguish between the playing of a german and a highland. The dance, again a couple dance, involving side by side and face to face halves, is however markedly different to a highland. The origin of the title is thought to refer to the appearance of 'German Schottisches' in collections from the last century. In this instance tunes played for the highland were thought to be 'Highland Schottisches' and thus named highlands while the tunes played for barn dances were considered 'German Schottisches' and thus named germans. Danny O'Donnell remembers that the 'German Schottische' and the 'Barn Dance' were originally similar but separate dances which later merged to become the german.

The 'Shoe the Donkey', a version of 'Alonzo's Varsovienne' was another very popular couple dance and today's dancers of it in the county perform it in a manner largely identical to that done in other parts of the country. The similar rhythm the 'Mazurka' appeared to have a greater popularity in Donegal than in other areas of the country. Though apparently Polish in origin[6] it appears to have had a rapid and popular uptake throughout the county and in relation to other areas, Donegal has a much greater depth of 'Mazurkas' in the fiddle repertoire. Also of continental origin and popular with both fiddlers and dancers was the waltz.

Another couple dance was the 'Clap Dance'. This was well known in other northern counties but was certainly popular in Donegal where it was typically done to the hornpipe *The Soldier's Joy.* In it, two persons would face each other and during accented notes in the second bar of the tune the persons would clap each others open palms in time to the music. While basically a skillful dance some like Francie Dearg O'Byrne remember the clapping could get rough, particularly amongst the women!

As with the fiddle music, many dances were directly brought home to Donegal from Scotland. Large scale emigration from Donegal was one result of the rapid industrialisation in southern Scotland during the second half of the last century and the first few decades of the present. To cater for the social needs of the influx of rural Irish and indeed highland Scots in cities like Glasgow and Edinburgh dance halls or 'ballrooms' sprang up. In these venues bands would play various selections of tunes to which newly arrived urban dwellers could perform the dances of their home areas. Competition between halls grew and to generate a greater interest and customer loyalty to a particular hall, resident dancing masters, whose job it was to call out the movements of the figures for set dances, were commissioned by owners to formulate new dances which would heighten appeal with the regular customers. Some of these did make their way back to Donegal via returning emigrants, one being 'The Marine'. This again is a couple dance involving alternating side by side and face to face dancing[7]. The title was thought by some to indicate a military origin. In fact, it was the creation of the Irishman, James Fitzgerald, who was the very popular resident dancing master in the Marine Ballroom, Edinburgh. The title is taken from the venue it was designed to popularise. Today the dance is totally forgotten. However, two versions of the tune, one from Glenties and the other from

Glencolumcille, are still popular with fiddlers. They are both titled *The Marine* and are in fact local versions of the Scots tune *The Braes of Argyll.*

In light of the clergys' attitude towards the moral acceptability of house dancing versus the more supervised conditions of ballroom dancing it is ironic to note that the types of dances which arose out house dances were a mixture of couple and group dances while those which came out of the larger venues tended to be couple dances which provided a greater opportunity for boy to meet girl on close terms and vice versa.

The 'Kitty O'Connor' was another couple dance done to a specific marching tune. Though rare now, it appears to have survived best throughout the northern and western coastal areas of the county. During this dance the couple alternate between face to face waltzing and side by side marching[8].

While capable of being played for a highland, the well known Scottish composition *The Corn Rigs* was played for a dance of its own in Donegal. Its popularity may be inferred by the existence of at least three versions of the tune which is widespread throughout the county including a very masterful one by Mickey Doherty. Surprisingly this is one dance which Róise Rua Nic Grianna[9] of Arranmore did not know from her own locality but associated it firmly with Scotland.

Group dances, usually made up of four couples facing each other and forming a square, are commonly referred to in traditional dancing today as sets. These were well known throughout Ireland and were danced in Donegal. They typically contain up to five and sometimes six or more parts usually with mixed rhythms between the parts. The main sets in Donegal would appear to have been the 'Lancer' and 'Quadrille' sets. Set dancing is currently enjoying a massive revival in popularity throughout the country and Donegal is no exception. It is unfortunate however, that despite the proliferation of set dancing classes and workshops which are ideally in a position to explore local sets, the vast majority of those which are now being dispersed are of Munster and Connacht origin. With the exception of the Glenfin and Arranmore areas very little would appear to have been done to investigate the nature of local Donegal sets despite the availability of elderly persons who are able to perform them. During a field taping session a lively set dance was recorded in the Croaghs. Mickey Doherty is playing exceptional fiddle music and the atmosphere is clearly one of great enjoyment and enthusiasm. This Comhairle Bhéaloideas Éireann release of Mickey's fiddling documents the quick speed and rhythm needed to play for set dancing to reels in Donegal[10].

Evidence indicates that group dances have a long history in Donegal. One of the strongest houses for house dancing in the county was that of Peter Campbell of the Croaghs. This house was a favourite stopping point for all of the Doherty family and in this social atmosphere Peter's sons Jimmy, Vincent, Columba and Josie came to be intensely versed in the intricacies of Donegal fiddling. While contributing in June of 1980 to the collection of folklore and information on Donegal fiddle music he recalled the setting of dances in his house[11]. Speaking in Irish, Peter named two particular group dances which were very popular. He referred to the first as 'An tOllman' (pronounced: uhn tullamon) and the second as 'An Cotílan' (pronounced: uhn ko-tee-laan). In the first case, the use of the "t" before the vowel clearly indicates the word was fully integrated into the Irish language on grammatical lines alone. The significance here being that it would appear the word, and thus the dance, had been in local use for some time. After describing the dance it is clear that the former is the 'Allamande', a dance of possible German origin which travelled to and flourished in France by the eighteenth century where it received its name in French meaning "German". The 'Oxford Companion to Music' notes a form of the dance compatible with 6/8 time is still done today in rural Germany and Switzerland[12]. It is also interesting to note that the Irish harper Cormac MacDermott who died in 1618 is credited with composing an untitled, the bass line of which survives in a manuscript in the Library of Christ Church, Oxford[13]. It is tempting to equate this piece of music with the Allamande.

The second dance described by Peter Campbell is undoubtedly the 'Cotillon' and while the name derives from French the dance is again of probable German origin. A contemporary painting of a Cotillon by the artist Collet in 1771 depicts a group dance with four males and four females moving in a counter-clockwise circle[14]. Interestingly Peter's son, Vincent, plays a double jig which he simply titles in the Irish pronunciation, *An Cotiían.* This tune was the appropriate one for the dance confirming a 6/8 measure in Donegal. Likewise, John Doherty and James Byrne play jigs for what they both identify in Irish as *An Cotiían*. Lastly, the Scottish double jig *The Wee Pickle Tow*, which was widely known in at least two versions, each in different keys, in Donegal is noted in 'Songs of Uladh 'as a cotillan[15].

Through the memories of Peter Campbell and his use of the dance titles in a fully naturalised Irish language form it is possible to imagine the development of continental group dances in Donegal. Like the integration of their titles into the local culture it is certain that the dance structures themselves were also adapted and altered to suit local customs and the confined venues in which they were performed.

The 'Barnesmore reel', which was done to the tune *The Wind That Shakes The Barley*, was another popular group dance in the Croaghs along with the 'Four', 'Six' and 'Eight Hand Reels'. 'The Polka' as a rhythm is very strongly connected with the Sliabh Luachra area of Ireland today. Indeed, it is often the case when musicians play polkas today they refer to them as "Kerry Polkas" regardless of the locality of origin of the tune. This situation grossly distorts the impression of the range of the polka in Ireland in the past. It was a well known and danced tune in Donegal where it was performed with a slower, more even beat rhythm. The polka was very popular both in the Campbell house as well as in Cruit Island where Danny O'Donnell recalls exceptional dancers of the rhythm. As noted above, it is almost consistently referred to by older players and dancers as "the polky". A simple dance, the 'Eight Step Polka' was done throughout west Donegal to an unusual tune which had only one part. A version of the tune can be found in Tom Anderson's Ringing Strings[16] collection under the title The 'Seven Step Polka' where it was noted as being for a couple dance. Though largely the same tune, the Shetland version has twelve bars. Tom noted that variations of the tune could be found in Sweden, England, Denmark and parts of America.

Dances remembered by the Campbells but long since having lost popularity are the 'Éire Óg', the 'Paddy Cat', and a double jig entitled the 'Larry O' Gaff' which was danced to the tune of the same title. Finally, they also recall the 'Tokyo', which clearly falls into the group of dances with limited range and popular life-span. The name of the latter may also indicate a late arrival in the county.

In terms of couple dances, the 'Military Two Step' was also

danced. On Tory island to this day can be found an unusual dance; the 'Maidrín Rua' while a dance by the name of 'de Alberts' is remembered from the early decades of this century by Eddie Moore of Ballyshannon. It was done by a boy and two girls and is not to be confused with the 'Irish Highland'. Another interesting title of a dance, 'Rogha an File' is recalled by Proinnsías O'Maonaigh[17]. This title, though in the slightly different from 'Rogha na bhFile' can also be found associated with a tune as written by the Sliabh Luachra fiddler Pádraig O'Keefe in the manuscript collection of his pupil, Paddy Connell[18]. While little is known today of this dance its range between Donegal and Sliabh Luachra suggests at one time it enjoyed a good deal of popularity.

So far the dancing discussed has been largely focused on the house dances. There was one form of house dance which varied from the normal and this took place on the eve of an emigrant's departure. In most areas of the country this type of dance and social event was called an American Wake. In Donegal it was invariably called a Convoy. The first of these two names derived from the fact that before the advent of mass transport, the chances of an emigrant returning were almost non-existent and thus their social testimonial was as good as the final farewell of a wake. The intention of the Donegal name was that the festivities were to speed, lighten and make safe the impending journey.

Francie McHugh of Lough Doon who regularly played at them remembers that convoys differed from standard house dances in that tricks and games had a greater role than normal. While there would be an underlying sadness due to the emigrant's leaving this would be suppressed and there would be a conscious effort at keeping spirits as high as possible in order to leave the person with the fondest and happiest memories of their locality and friends. The humour of the convoy was in stark contrast to the final parting for trains or boats the following day.

A good account of the emigrant's final departure following a convoy is given by Francie when he described a custom of his maternal grandmother, Kate Sweeney, a renowned single row melodeon player from Meenore, Dungloe who lived into her 104th year. Francie relates the events as follows[19]:

> She used to play at the convoys going away till America. And she used to leave here in the morning before the break of day and go a couple of miles along the road with the ones going till

America. She would play music till she would go to the oak bush over at Maas here, over at Clooney. And then she would put her melodeon on her back and take out the rosary beads and she would say the rosary then 'til she went to the Maas Bridge. That bridge was called the 'filleadh (returning) bridge, the last filleadh'. And then she left the goodbye with them and came home.

Dancing was a main ingredient of the convoy but in the Narin and Portnoo district competitions to compose humorous rhymes telling of recent events which took place at convoys would be held. These rhymes were to be sung to the standard tunes played for the dancing. While few of these have survived with the waning of convoys over the last four decades some still exist in the memory of Francie McHugh. He was also well known to compose several rhymes himself.

Together with the couple and group dances there existed the step or solo dances. Solo dancing today, conjures up images of coiffured girls, in ornate costumes, with gymnasically leaping lower bodies incompatibly attached to torsos beset by rigor mortis. This was not the case in the past. The fashion display of the traditional solo dancer counted for nothing. The performance concentrated on adroit footwork in direct interaction with the music and tolerated arm movement to some degree.

Solo step dancers had a number of different choices of where and how they danced. The most basic was the flagstone floor. Some houses which where used for dancing had built into the floor a hollow area under a large flag in front of the fire. Thrown into it were a few farm animals' skulls. This stone was called the clinker stone and its purpose was to act as a resonator to the impact of the steps[20]. The inclusion of the skulls was meant to increase the degree of resonance. A good step dancer on a flagstone floor could enhance his performance by knocking sparks off a sandstone flag with the steel cleats of his hobnail boots giving rise to the expression "knocking sparks out of it" for a good performance. Another method of solo step dancing was on a door or a half door which had been taken down off its hinges and placed on four blocks or bricks at the corners. In this way the door gave a hollow sound with the striking of the dancer's feet.

The intricate reel *Muileann na Maide* was the chosen tune for a famous step dancer who frequented the Croaghs by the name of Fear na Rópaí (Man of the ropes) who is still well-remembered in the area. This dancer always carried a short length of rope with him. When requested to dance he would lay it out in a circle on the floor and have the fiddlers play his reel. He would then dance within the circle and the challenge for him was to not step outside the rope. If he was successful the rope was drawn into a tighter circle and this continued until the circle was no bigger than the area naturally covered by his feet.

A solo dance in Donegal which was done occasionally to highlands and taking its introduction from Scotland was an imitation sword dance. This was done with an open set of tongs taking the place of crossed swords which were laid on the floor. The challenge to the dancer was to perform his or her most intricate steps moving over and between the four quadrants formed by the tongs; going as close as possible without touching them. To make any kind of contact with the tongs during the performance was considered poor dancing.

Possibly the most challenging and demanding of solo step dances in Donegal was that which was known under the various titles of 'The Maggie Pickie', 'The Maggie Pickens', 'The Maggie Piggy' etc. This dance, to which the first figure had a song sung to it[21], could similarly be done as an imitation sword dance. It had in some local versions up to twenty four different parts and was considered not only a great test of dancing skill but of stamina as well. A legendary dancer of this piece was the late Conall a' Dámhsa Mac a' Luain of Croveenananta in the Croaghs who learned his dancing from his neighbour Dan Breslin. Fortunately some of his footwork has been preserved in at least three field recordings [22].

This dance was widely believed by the older generation of players to be of Scottish origin arising from the tune *Whistle o'er the Lave o't*. It is briefly discussed by W. H. Grattan Flood[23] who, without any firm foundation, seems to credit it as a native Donegal tune. He writes:

> A few years later (early 1780s) another tourist alludes to a popular Donegal pipe-melody, *Maggie Pickins,* which went back to the seventeenth century. It was cribbed by the Scotch between the years 1715 and 1740, and adapted to a song called *Whistle o'er the Lave o't* - so indelicate that it had to be rewritten by Robert Burns in 1790. Neither Bunting nor Petrie noticed the interesting fact that this fine pipe-melody was utilised by the Volunteers (presumably 1798 Volunteers) as a marching-tune.

With the exception of his observation on the tune being used as a Volunteers pipe march, which may well have been the case, Grattan Flood's version of the history of the tune appears based on unsteady ground. His implied Donegal provenance for *Maggie Pickins* can be seen to be founded on the diary of an un-named tourist. His evidence for a seventeenth century date of composition is not supplied nor is his information regarding a Scottish cribbing of the tune between 1715 and 1740. About the only thing of fact in this passage is that the Scottish poet Robert Burns did compose a set of words to what was a very popular, simple air; an act which was commonplace until very recently. In leaving this tune it should be noted that sets of Scots Gaelic words exist for this same tune.

In summary, traditional dancing as done in Donegal was rich and diverse with a variety of dances to the various rhythms. Though dancing in the county has been at a low point for the past thirty years the current wave of enthusiasm for set dancing which is manifest throughout the country is having an impact in Donegal.

REFERENCES

1 Anon. *The Duck Street Boys From Cashelmore.* Tirchonaill Tribune, August, 1993.
2 Breandán Breathnach, *Folkmusic and Dances of Ireland,* Educational Company of Ireland, Dublin, 1971, pp 48-49.
3 Grace Orpen, *The Dances of Donegal,* D. M. Wilkie, London, 1931.
4 Kerr's First Collection of *Merry Melodies,* Glasgow, p 46.
5 Percy A. Scholes, *The Oxford Companion to Music,* Oxford University Press, London, 1944, pp 22-23.
6 Percy A. Scholes, op.cit.
7 Bill McAllister, *Dances for the House Dance - Descriptions of the Mazurka, Polka, Highland and Other Round Dances,* (Unpublished Manuscript).
8 Bill McAllister, op.cit.
9 Róise Rua Nic Ghrianna, *Róise Rua.* Pádraig Ua Cnáimhsi (eag.), Sairseál O Marcaigh, Baile Átha Cliath, 1988.
10 *The Gravel Walks - The Fiddle Music of Mickey Doherty,* Cómhairle Bhéaloideas Éireann, CBE002, Dublin, 1990.
11 *Teip Q3,* Cairdeas na bhFidléirí Archive, An Foras Chuiltúr Uladh, Glencolumbcille.
12 Percy A. Scholes, op.cit.
13 Seán Donnelly, *An Irish Harper and Composer Cormac MacDermott (? - 1618),* in Ceol, Vol. VIII, Nos 1+2, 1986, pp 40 - 50.

14 Percy A. Scholes, op.cit., plate 35, figure 8.
15 Pádraig Mac Aodh O'Neill and Seaosamh Mac Cathmhaoil, *Songs of Uladh*. William Miller, Belfast, 1904.
16 Tom Anderson, *Ringing Strings*. Shetland Times Ltd., Lerwick, 1983.
17 *Teip D*, Cairdeas na bhFidléirí Archive, Foras Chultúir Uladh, Glencolumbcille.
18 These manuscripts, written in the hand of O'Keefe exists in a private collection belonging to his student, Paddy Connell, Cordal, Castleisland, Co. Kerry.
19 *Teip E4*, Cairdeas na bhFidléirí Archives, Foras Chultúir Uladh, Glencolumbcille.
20 *Where Songs do Thunder - Travels in Traditional Song*. Paddy Tunney, Appletree Press, Belfast, 1991, pp 153 - 154.
21 *The Lark in the Morning* - Songs and Dances from the Irish Countryside. Tradition Records, TLP 1004.
22 *The Gravel Walks* - The Fiddle Music of Mickey Doherty, Cómhairle Bhéaloideas Éireann, CBE002, Dublin, 1990, also RTÉ Archives recording of Maggie Pickens to the fiddle playing of Felix Kearney (fiddler, Omagh, Co. Tyrone).
23 *A History of Irish Music*. W. H. Gratten Flood, Irish University Press, Shannon, 1970 reprint of 1913 third edition, pp 261-262.

CHAPTER SEVEN

NORTHWEST DONEGAL

On first arriving in the northwest corner of Donegal, the harpist Arthur O'Neill[1] described it as being amongst the remotest and wildest countrysides in Ireland. It is understandable how the first-time visitor to this area might perceive it as extremely desolate. Carpeted by lowland boulder strewn bog, it is surrounded by the raging Atlantic on the northern and western sides, rising to the Glendowan Mountain range in the east and the deep cutting Gweebarra River to the south. For those who come to know the region better, however, it is the epitome of the raw, rugged majesty of western Ireland. The power and beauty of the natural elements can be experienced to the fullest here; from overwhelming gales screeching off a wintry North Atlantic to blistering days in a summer bog. As a Gaeltacht area it is one of the most prominent in the country. Amongst these speakers can be heard some of the most splendid and delicate Irish; whose words are to the ear as the first sip of porter is to the tongue after a Lenten abstinence.

The tradition of fiddle playing here is a long one and listening to the fiddlers of northwest Donegal is to experience a musical mirroring of the environment. For many, the playing has resulted in a wild, impassioned and vibrant style. Several of the greatest names in traditional music are native to this area.

NEILLIDH BOYLE

The golden age of fiddle playing in this area was to begin in far-off Pennsylvania with the arrival of one of the princes of Donegal fiddlers, Neillidh Boyle, or Neillidh Phádaí Neillidh as he was known locally. His parents, Pádraig, from Cruit Island, and his mother Annie Sweeney, from Keadue, near Dungloe, had emigrated to America in search of employment settling in the Irish community of eastern Pennsylvania. They were married by Father James McGowan in Saint Bernard's Parish Church, Easton, Pennsylvania, on October 17th, 1888. While official birth records for Neillidh were destroyed by fire, a sworn oath made to John Sweeney, Commissioner for Oaths in Burtonport and signed by his father on October 4th, 1934 identifies Neillidh as his first child, born on November 26th, 1889 in Easton. Furthermore, an affidavit made on June 25th, 1934 by his cousins, John and Neil Boyle, then residents of the large Dungloe emigrant community centred around the Sun Oil Company in Bayonne, New Jersey, re-confirms he was born on November 26th, 1889, specifying the location as Chane Dam with Dr. Zeiner in attendance. The correct name of the site is Chain Dam, or Dam Number 8, on the Lehigh Navigation System. This is now within the boundaries of the City of Easton's Hugh Moore Park, about three miles west of the city centre. During the end of the last century the area was heavily industrialised and, based on the location of the birth, it is likely that Neillidh's father worked either as a locktender on the Lehigh Navigation System or alternatively laboured in either the Keystone or Lucy Iron Furnaces adjacent to Chain Dam.

In his memoir, 'Rotha Mór an tSaoil'[2], Mici Mac Gabhainn gives us a good picture of the Easton into which Neillidh was born. Mac Gabhainn was born in November of 1865 in Doire Chonaire, Gortahork, not far from Neillidh's parents home. After spending several seasons in farm-hand squads, first in the Lagan and then as a teenager in Scotland, he ultimately decided he had a better chance of fair reward for his hard labours in America. Eventually he found fortune in the gold fields of the Klondyke before returning to Donegal to see out his days.

After arriving in New York Mac Gabhainn quickly made his way to his relatives on the south side of Bethlehem, Pennsylvania. From Mici's first-hand observations we learn that there was a high concentration of Irish labourers, both from Donegal and Connacht in the iron, copper, flour and clothing mills of the area and the Irish language was quite commonly spoken. The railways brought a surge of Irish immigrants to the locality and along with them the need for construction workers to build the new factories and, more importantly, housing. Mici initially secured work unloading barrows of sand for making concrete off barges on the Lehigh Canal before moving into the more demanding iron works.

At this time, the period during which Neillidh Boyle was born, Mac Gabhainn notes that Bethlehem was burgeoning. Yet, when shopping or religious duties needed to be attended, the immigrants would furtively jump the strings of passing coal trains and travel the fifteen miles to Easton where they would congregate and exchange news and experiences.

Neillidh spent the first eight years of his life in Easton before the family returned home to Donegal. Even while in America his parents' devotion to their native culture was so strong that they undertook to speak Irish to their children and expose them to as much music as they could learn.

On arriving back in the townland of Cronashallog, just outside Dungloe, Neillidh's neighbours and schoolmaster were surprised at his fluency in the language. His musical prowess, however, was the true source of astonishment. We are told in a credible account in a local newspaper article[3] written at the time of his mother's death that "even as a child just over from America the greatest of traditional players of the day listened to him in awe". Even at this young age he was reputed to be capable of learning upwards of ten pieces from his mother in an evening.

Neillidh came from very musical people. His maternal grandfather was Pádraig Mac Suibhne from the townland of Keadue, Dungloe, a noted singer and storyteller who was well known to the Irish scholar, Myles Dillon. Pádraig reputedly had the largest store of songs in Irish in the Rosses during his time. (Though it is a recurring motif in Irish musical folklore, several stories recount a singing contest which took place between himself and a traveller from the west of Ireland. The two battled out song for song for two days. Finally, when Mac Suibhne could go no further, the traveller countered with one more song and was declared the winner. He then admitted he too had come to his limit and had won by a single song.) In a recorded interview[4] Neillidh credited his grandfather as the source of some of his airs and in particular lullabies.

It must be said that Neillidh's mother, Nancy, could lay claim to an even greater reputation in the Rosses for music. There is no doubt from the memories of family and local people today, as well as the information recorded by Neillidh himself, that his mother was the most dominant influence on his music. Like her father, Nancy had a rich store of songs as well as dance tunes which she lilted. Professor O Máille from the Irish College in Rannafast regularly brought his summer school students to her cottage during her waning years and urged his pupils to learn from her as they could find no better and more skilled instructress in all Ireland in language, singing or lilting. With the help of the folklorist Fíonán McCollum, O Máille succeeded in having some of her songs recorded; however have not been traced.

Neillidh had two brothers, Charlie and Con, and a sister, Grace, who died very young in America. Con, who was also a renowned fiddler, eventually returned to America settling in Bayonne, New Jersey. He established a céilí band there which was popular for many years.

The youngest brother, Charlie, was an accomplished warpiper and fiddler. Danny O'Donnell remembers his own mother praising Neillidh and Charlie's duet playing when they featured as leading performers at the outdoor concert for Feis Tír Chonaill. The concert was held at the Fair Green in Dungloe and was a major cultural showpiece as it was attended by the recently appointed Bishop O'Donnell. Charlie had an interest in the political developments of the early decades of this century. Though it appears he never actively took part in any local initiatives, his beliefs were enough to bring him to the attention of the authorities. Fearing imminent arrest, he decided to follow Con to America. Knowing that it was unlikely he would ever return or see his parents again, on the day he left he went into the field behind the family home and carved CHAS. BOYLE, 19/9/1919 into a large granite boulder. This stone now stands at the rear of his niece (Neillidh's daughter), Anna Philbin's, house in Cronashallog. Charlie then went into Dungloe and bought a box of matches. That night was mild but very dark. He bade his parents farewell and under cover of darkness strode out the road towards Fintown. As he went, he continued to light up one match after another throwing each one up in the air. His parents stood at the door until no more lights could be seen. That was the last they would ever see of Charlie. He died of tuberculosis within six months of his arrival in Bayonne .

Unlike his brothers, Neillidh seems not to have expressed any strong political beliefs yet he did appear to accidentally get caught up in a daring rescue ambush[5]. On the second of January, 1918, Jimmy Duffy of Meenbannad, who had deserted from the British

Army, was captured by the RIC and imprisoned in Burtonport Barracks. This situation was quickly reported to Joe Sweeney, then chief organiser of the Irish Volunteers in the Dungloe area. He formulated an ambush plan which sought to rescue Duffy and his highly valued rifle while he was being transported by train to Derry Gaol. At Meenbannad (Kincasslagh Road) Station a number of volunteers boarded the train and set upon Duffy's escorts. In a subsequent account, Duffy[6] recalled that he appeared to be struck by 'Neil Boyle, Fiddler', who was not one of the volunteers, but who had mistaken Duffy as a member of the prisoner's escort party.

Neillidh's mother's influence can be seen in the material collected by Séamus Ennis during a visit to Neillidh in 1943. Séamus was then working for the Irish Folklore Commission and recorded the locally composed *Amhrán a' Boxty,* the rare *Éire Mo Thír* (a version of *An Suisín Ban), Cailíní 'n Chéidi,* and the poitín song *Rad na mBurcach.* Ennis also wrote down in his official collector's diary words, or in some cases, fragments of songs which Neillidh could remember from his mother's singing. These include *Seán Mhag Uidhre a' Ghleanna* and *Séamus 'ac Murchaidh.* The former is clearly a version of *Seán O Duibhir a' Ghleanna* while the fragments (a verse and a half) of the latter confirms it is a version of the song known as *Séamus 'ac Mhuirfigh* in east Ulster which can be found in 'Amhráin Chúige Uladh'[7]. The fragment that Neillidh contributed to Séamus Ennis equates with verse fifteen and half of verse twelve in this publication. J. N. Hamilton's work 'The Irish of Tory Island'[8] also contains a version of the song which appears under the title *Séamus 'ic Murchaidh,* the second verse of which corresponds very closely to the complete verse recorded by Neillidh.

The effect of Nancy's influence on Neillidh's music was to convince him that true traditional music had a definite, unique tonal quality which the ear could immediately recognise. Neillidh was certain that this sound was a lonely or haunting one which he felt pervaded his mother's lilting. In an early attempt to reproduce this effect on the fiddle, he discovered that by changing both airs and dance tunes from major into minor keys, particularly G Minor, he could achieve the melodic colouring he sought. His classic piece, *The Pigeon on the Gate* is the best example of this approach. Similarly, the highland *A Stór, a Stór, a Ghrá,* normally played in A Major is transposed into a minor key.

While Neillidh was exceptionally conscious of seeking this specific haunting sound in his music, he was not adverse to playing spirited, driving music in the standard keys as performed by the general body of fiddlers. In a recorded interview[9] conducted by Seán O'Boyle during the visit by BBC collector, Peter Kennedy, in which he illustrates his ideas on Irish music, Neillidh demonstrates how "to properly put beef onto the bones of a tune with the help of *Miss McLeod's* reel".

During a visit to Glasgow, at the age of fifteen, Neillidh had the opportunity to hear the famous Scottish violinist, William McKenzie Murdoch, play in concert. The experience was to prove vital to his musical development. He was deeply impressed by his playing, particularly the Irish air *Aileen Alannah* (which McKenzie Murdoch subsequently recorded on a commercially released 78 RPM disc). The Scottish violinist immediately rose to near par in musical admiration with Neillidh's mother. In a subsequent local newspaper quote[10], Neillidh recalled the impact of hearing McKenzie Murdoch: "I was entranced by his playing, so much that I watched his every movement of his fingers, and I have since made him my headline ...."

His early exposure to classically-trained players like McKenzie Murdoch meant that Neillidh became convinced of the need to master playing in positions. By all accounts, he rigorously practiced position-playing as well as a range of scale exercises in keys, particularly those not normally used in traditional playing. Though still occupied as a farmer in early manhood Neillidh's devotion to music was full-time. This drive to establish a livelihood as a concert performer was quite uncommon since such a profession was largely unknown within the Irish rural community.

An unusual performing opportunity soon came his way. During the 1920's the early popular cinema was developing. In the spring of 1925 Danny Coyle, a Glaswegian son of a Donegal emigrant, was transferred from his employment in Scotland to east Donegal. At the time of leaving Scotland the company's social club was replacing its carbide illuminated silent film projector. This appeared to Danny to be an ideal entrepreneurial opportunity. He, along with a friend, Joe Greigg, bought it knowing that such items must be rare in Donegal and on arrival in Ireland sourced a film supplier in Dublin. A travelling route was mapped out starting in Letterkenny, running through towns along the north coast to

Gweedore, turning south to Glenties and back to Letterkenny through Ballybofey. The partners would rent local halls and show three or four short films per night. While love stories were popular with the women and all were entertained by Chaplin, the westerns were clear favourites among the men who would sometimes side differently between rival cowboy gangs and occasionally end up brawling themselves! Such was the novelty of film at this time that when one scene, depicting a head-on shot of an on-coming train about to run over the damsel in distress strapped onto the railway tracks, was projected onto the back wall of a hall in a small village, near fatalities occurred in the rapid mass exodus of viewers. All were convinced that the train would burst through the back wall at any second killing everyone inside!

As was the custom in large urban cinemas, it was quickly apparent to Danny and his partner that a musical accompanist was required. Travelling through the towns he made enquiries for a suitable piano player but to no avail. When he reached Dungloe he was told that there were no piano players but that there was only one man for the job - Neillidh Boyle. Danny sought out the house and was met by Neillidh's mother who informed him that the artist was not within. She did such a selling job on his ability to meet the demands of the work, however, that on returning home Neillidh found himself employed in the film industry.

Danny Coyle recalls first meeting him and explaining to him what was required. Mood music, accompaniment to the rhythms in the action, and imitation of animal sounds would be the mainstay. Neillidh, at this stage already adept at performing bird imitations from his intricate version of *An Londubh* as well as barking and horse trotting in *Seilig a' Mhadaí Rua*, astounded Coyle with his skill. According to Danny, Neillidh was as much a popular feature of the evening with the audiences as the new technical wonder of cinema, particularly for his lion imitations.

Remaining fully focused on following a career as a performing traditional musician, Neillidh quickly realised the limited potential for earning a comfortable living. Rather than relegate his playing to a part-time status he was satisfied that diversification was the key to success. His incredible technical command of the instrument, which by this time had been noted and publicly lauded in Dublin by the touring violinist Jan Kubelick[11], permitted him immediate access to performing other types of music. By the late

1920s and early 1930s Ireland was going through what was called 'The Jazz Era'. The type of music played was not what we now associate with jazz but consisted of popular, newly-composed dancehall or vaudeville melodies which had mass exposure via the rapidly expanding record and radio media. With the 'Dance Hall Act' Dancing moved quickly from house and barn dances onto a much larger scale in local halls to cater for the bigger crowds and new dance patterns. With larger attendances, a night's take in admissions could make playing for such functions lucrative for the musician who could reproduce the latest popular releases.

During this period Neillidh took his opportunity and joined a jazz band, 'The Dungloe Quartet', which concentrated on playing various halls around the northwest of the county. Amplification was non-existent in almost all of the venues and there were initial difficulties for Neillidh in producing a sound which could first of all rise over his accompanists, and then go on to fill a crowded hall. He overcame this by standing well to the front of the stage, tuning the instrument one or two notes above concert pitch for greater volume and more brilliant tone, drawing the bow very hard to achieve the maximum volume, and then fingering the melodies in upper positions to produce a high-pitch sound that would carry throughout the hall. Under normal circumstances such high tuning would have resulted in the strings regularly breaking. Fiddle maker and repairer Rab Cherry, however, recently overhauled Neillidh's personal fiddle and noted that the bridge had been arched into an almost flat shape. The drastically reduced angle of the strings over the bridge allowed the almost straight strings to be tuned to his characteristic high pitch minimising the risk of frequent breakage.

Neillidh's private attitude at this period of his performing career is not clear. Fans of 'The Dungloe Quartet' extol his virtuosity and paint a picture of an artist quite happy with his craft. Others who greatly respected him for his playing of traditional music suggest that he felt some indignity having to play jazz to see him through. Indeed, much later in the Seán O'Boyle/Peter Kennedy interview, Neillidh[12] himself decried jazz as a low form of "jungle music" (a popular catchphrase of anti-jazz lobbyists, particularly clerics, in rural Ireland during this era who saw the musical form as being potentially morally corruptive).

During this time Neillidh still commanded the utmost respect as a traditional fiddler in his native district but his fame had not managed to spread further afield. All this was to change radically for him arising from his trip to Dublin during the Eucharistic Congress in Summer, 1932. It was in this setting that he met Frank O'Higgins, the famous County Meath fiddler who, at that time, would have been the mainstay broadcasting fiddler with the national radio station, 2RN. Frank was highly impressed with Neillidh's playing and considered him very worthy of wider recognition. Neillidh's much desired high profile performing career was about to be launched.

O'Higgins arranged a hasty meeting between Neillidh and some of the chief administrators in 2RN. Neillidh played an informal audition of three minutes duration for Dr. Vincent O'Brien and Séamus Clandillon. The following contemporary newspaper account from an 'Irish Press' correspondent clearly shows the unexpected and astronomic rise of Neillidh before the nation's listening public[13]:

"A small farmer from the far Rosses of Donegal will give a violin broadcast of Irish music from 2RN on Thursday night and incidentally will show what treasures of the musical Irish race lie hidden in out-of-the-way corners of Ireland.

He is Mr. Neil Boyle, of Dungloe, and for years his skill as a traditional fiddler has been little known except in parts of Donegal. His only tutors, one of his friends told me, were the winds, the waves, the birds and the murmuring brooks.

Then, dramatically, he made his appearance in Dublin. He was one of the many who went from the North-West to the Eucharistic Congress, and, on Tuesday morning following its close, he met Mr. Frank O'Higgins, the well known exponent of traditional fiddling, and they visited the recording studio, over which they were conducted by the director, Mr. Séamus Clandillon at whose request Mr. Boyle played some Donegal airs.

Mr. Clandillon was so pleased by the performance that when he learned that Mr. Boyle intended returning to Donegal on the following day he insisted on his broadcast that night.The carefully-prepared programme for that night was hurriedly re-arranged to include Mr. Boyle's broadcast. The Rosses fiddler had risen to national fame in a day. Back to his native hills that night went the strains of his music, to be captured by the small number of his friends who possess wireless sets.

On Thursday he will play three reels of his own composition - *The Wild Hills of Donegal, Doe Castle Reel* and *The Atlantic Breakers* !"

As is evident from this account, Neillidh broadcast on both the Tuesday and Thursday evenings following the Congress and greatly impressed the broadcasters and the listening public. He became one of an elite group of players brought back at regular intervals amongst a flurry of publicity to perform for live broadcasts. To broadcast at that time was to effectively confer superstar status on a musician. There is no doubt that Neillidh's performances on radio did much to enhance the prestige of Donegal fiddle music and to this day people throughout the county who heard his broadcasts heartily recall feelings of pride which they experienced knowing a Donegalman was capable of standing before the listeners of the nation and playing to the highest standard.

Local press reviews of his broadcasts give a clear idea of the respect he was commanding. Words like "genius" and "virtuoso" are commonly invoked to describe him. Interestingly, in keeping with the broadcast methods of the time, it was decided beforehand which tunes the fiddler would play and heavy advance media publicity[14] from 2RN would herald the performances of such pieces. Neillidh, with only rare exceptions, chose to play his own compositions, and press cuttings reveal that in addition to the three cited above he also composed the air *Cam na hAbhann* which was based on the babbling sounds in a small bend in the stream near Neillidh's front door. Sadly with the exception of *Cam na hAbhann* and *The Moving Cloud* none of Neillidh's compositions survive today. Other pieces which we know from press reviews of radio performances as well as friends' and listeners' memories that he was noted for playing on radio were *Seilig a' Mhadaí Rua, An Londubh, Tiarna Mhaigh Eo* and *Sliabh Sneacht.*

An appearance receipt showing the contents of a fifteen minute broadacast which went out at 7:35 PM on November 16th (the year is not recorded) includes three sets. The first features the B flat reel trio of *The Moving Clouds, Miss Crawford's* and *Fair Haired Mary* (the latter two from O'Neill's collections) which were performed in four minutes. A four and a half minute air - hornpipe - reel set was then played comprising *Erin My Country* (undoubtedly *Éire Mo Thií* from his mother), *The Quarrelsome Piper and Rakish Paddy.* Lastly, was another four minute air - hornpipe - reels set with *O'Donnell's Farewell, The Flowers of Spring, The Boys of the Lough* and *The Dublin Reel.* The first tune is cited as being from an unpublished, traditional source indicating that it was more than likely a local tune. The remainder of the set indicates the influence of the Sligo fiddlers' recordings.

On Thursday, September 30th, 1937, Neillidh married local girl Annie Sweeney, a daughter of Hugh Sweeney of Cronashallog in the chapel at Lettermacaward. A local newspaper edition of the following day notes that by that time he had also travelled to Belfast to broadcast for the BBC. Neillidh and Annie went on to have six children, Paddy, Anna, Mary, Hughie, Charlie and Bella. Paddy studied the fiddle closely under his father and is discussed below while Hughie, now living in Glasgow, took up the accordian.

During his broadcasting period Neillidh's popularity was clearly growing as a local press cutting from this time shows. It reveals that he travelled to Dublin to play live on 2RN on a Friday night. Immediately following the broadcast he was taken to play for the 'An Craobh Ruadh' Branch of Conradh na Gaeilge in the Teachers' Club. The next evening he was presented by the song publisher, Colm O Lochlainn, to play at 'An Claisceadal' and on the Sunday night he played in the 'Round Room' of the Mansion House at a céilí for Craobh an Cheitinnigh Branch of Conradh na Gaeilge.

At this time, the Innishkeel Co-op, through its Glenties base, was the area's most important outlet for commercial recordings. Suppliers such as this often acted as the music companies talent-spotters, recommending players who they felt commanded sufficient local interest to warrant a commercially viable release. Mr. Hueston, the co-op manager, who was well aware of Neillidh's continually growing radio-based reputation, contacted Leslie Thorn of The Gramophone Company, 20-21 Eustace Street, Dublin by letter with the view towards encouraging them to audition him. In an undated reply to Mr. Hueston, Neillidh was requested to present himself at their studios at 3PM on May 3rd, 1937. The session would consist of an audition and, providing he proved suitable, he was to record four selections for test pressings, each to be four minutes in duration.

This session clearly went well for him and on that afternoon he recorded six unaccompanied selections later released on the Regal Zonophone label. One contained a spirited set of *The Swallow's Tail* and *The Strawberry Blossom* (ie.*The Blackberry Blossom*) reels. The former is much like Mickey Doherty's version, employing a three-crotchet finish to the first part which was popular amongst the house-dance players in Donegal. The reverse side included *The Dublin Hornpipe* and *The Liverpool Hornpipe.* Another disc featured the *Harvest Home* hornpipe followed by the *Green Mountain* reel, and the jigs *Haste to the Wedding* and *Over the Hills* on the opposite side. The third had *Biddy from Sligo* and the standard setting of the *Connachtman's Rambles* jigs (though the first conforms to single jig time) on one side, and the *Pidgeon on the Gate* and *Jenny Picking Cockles* on the other.

The recording of the last two tunes was to leave an indelible mark on the body of traditional music. His performance of the *Pidgeon on the Gate,* learned from his mother's lilting and again in his favourite key of G Minor, has become his hallmark. His technical wizardry is fully revealed in his ability to execute the complex fingering at such great speed while not slipping a note. Furthermore, on the first number of hearings, the tune, with its heavily syncopated first two bars, appears to have incomplete timing. When the tune is played or written it is found to be full.

Correspondence between the Gramophone Record Company and Neillidh following the release of his 78s shows the company had a keen interest in making additional recordings of him. However, by March of 1938, difficulties between the two parties concerning the distribution of his recordings and the associated royalties had made working relations impossible.

Local people remember that in preparation for his broadcasts and recording sessions Neillidh would comb the houses of the locality looking for the best available fiddle. Three fiddlers houses he would have called into were those of Neily Gallagher, Joe Gallagher (no relation to the latter), from Loughanure, whom Neillidh held in high regard and Eddie O'Donnell who also step-danced regularly to Neillidh's playing.

The recorded material of Neillidh Boyle which exists today is comprised of the six commercial sets as well as a limited number of tunes gathered in the early 1940s during two separate visits by the collectors Séamus Ennis, then working for the Irish Folklore Commission, and Peter Kennedy in conjunction with Seán O Boyle working for the BBC. The Ennis material is kept in the Irish Folklore Commission collection in the Department of Folklore and Folk Music in University College Dublin, Earlsfort Terrace. It is quite valuable as the sound quality of the recordings is quite good and in some cases can be matched with song words taken down by Séamus in his official collector's diary.

Family memories and transcripts of Ennis' own broadcasts clearly show the two musicians had a very friendly relationship. Ennis stayed with the Boyles and during the day saved hay with Neillidh. The nights were marked by almost endless music, topped up with a huge fry, and then a few short hours sleep before resuming farm work in the morning. Shortly after his recording visit, Séamus Ennis jointly presented a traditional music programme with Seán O Súilleabháin which featured the best of the material obtained by Ennis during his fieldwork. The third programme in the series was broadcast on February 26th, 1946, and featured the singing of Cití Ní Ghallchóbhair from Dore and Neillidh Boyle. The script of the radio programme survives[15] and shows they broadcast *Seán sa Cheo, Éire Mo Thír, Cailíní a' Chéididh, Rad na mBurcach, The Loughanure Reel, Tiarna Mhaigh Eo* and finished with *The Moving Cloud*. On the last piece Séamus commented "Neil plays it with great style and with great wealth of ornaments. As a demonstration of what the old fiddlers could do in ornamenting a reel, this can hardly be surpassed".

The material collected by Peter Kennedy is unusual for the period when it was recorded. Normally musicians at this time would simply play their tunes and contribute no more than titles, if they were known. In this case, Neillidh gave a detailed discourse on the failing state of Irish traditional music, followed by an analysis and demonstration of the hallmarks of traditional playing ending with a series of tunes, many of which had been previously recorded on his commercial discs. These recordings are clearly below the lofty standard of playing on his 78s and unfortunately do little justice to his genius. His discourse, however, is extremely important as it does confirm his overall outlook on music and that his flirtation with jazz was totally finished by this time as his denouncement of it is unequivocal.

The legacy of his recordings prove Neillidh to be very much a fiddler in the Donegal style with incredible speed, drive and attack. His gift with melodic variation is clear. Neillidh's association with the Doherty brothers, John and Mickey, is somewhat evident in his recordings of the reel *The Wild Irishman* (which he titled *The Irishman*) for the Folklore Commission as well as his version of *The Swallow's Tail* reel. The Dohertys had a great respect for Neillidh's playing and frequently played his recorded setting of *The Harvest Home* and *The Green Mountain*. His liberal use of the roll in ornamentation completely debunks the stereotype image of Donegal fiddlers as singularly employing triplets to the exclusion of the roll. Another typical feature of Neillidh's recordings is his consistent use of extremely high pitched tunings, a hangover from his days of playing in halls for dances and films where the high pitch assisted in filling the unamplified building. His use of double-stopped slides and syncopated rhythms may belie some lingering influence of his jazz days but there because no denying the mastery of his playing.

One very unusual aspect of these recordings, and particularly the Irish Folklore Commission material, is the amazing parallel with the limited recordings of Frank Cassidy of Teelin. Both men were extremely bright and gifted individuals. Musically they were very pensive and gave long hours of thought and analysis to their music. Each was also rightly regarded during their lifetimes as masters of traditional technique. Listening to their recordings it is surprising to see when requested to perform for noted collectors each chose to focus their contributions on airs. In both cases they are played with great sensitivity and the precision of their position playing establishes their ease with the technique. The incredible tonal quality of the Cassidy material, which is still remembered today as his hallmark is also much reflected in the Neillidh Boyle pieces. Listening back and forth to the two players, particularly to their performances of *Tiarna Mhaigh Eo,* certainly leads one to conclude a kinship of gifted spirit would have existed between these two giants.

Neillidh continued to play and broadcast throughout the 1950s to shrinking and less widespread audiences, though it must be said that this decade was a lean one nationally for traditional music. Correspondence from April, 1952 shows he broadcast on Radio Éireann a fifteen minute slot starting at 6:50 PM on May 5th for which he was paid £5. His submitted programme of tunes included the air *Seán Dún na nGall* which he was requested to substitute with a dance tune.

Eventually he sought more lucrative pastures and moved to 256 Cumberland Street in the Gorbels, south Glasgow, where he played as a popular and well-remembered solo traditional performer, as well as in small orchestras. Regular visitors to this house included Joe Bonnar originally from Loughanure who played a bit on the fiddle and another fiddler who made a point to call weekly, Manus Boyle, originally from Inishowen. It would appear that towards the end of his life Neillidh had become convinced that his potential was never fulfilled and remained somewhat embittered by events. There was some respite during his last year as the extremely gifted Danny O'Donnell came to live nearby and made contact with Neillidh. These meetings served to raise the Cronashallog Master's spirits greatly. Neillidh Boyle died in Glasgow on August 8th, 1961 aged 71 years and is buried in Dungloe.

PADDY BOYLE

For some time the reputation of Neillidh's son, Paddy, has been uncertain. Those who remember him readily acknowledge his status as a very gifted player. Only a few, however, would be willing to place him on a par with his father. This may be a result of Neillidh's much stronger personality and greater involvement in professional playing. A tape made in Dungloe in 1962 at a house party for returned emigrants to America was only recently discovered. It contains some seven solo, unaccompanied pieces by Paddy. The playing shows a remarkable similarity to Neillidh's. The style could be described as identical to his father even to the use of very high pitched tuning. The music is fast, vibrant, attacking and executed with a fluidity of the bow that is exceptional. There is no doubting that Neillidh had an excellent pupil in Paddy and, on the strength of these performances, quite arguably his equal. Taking into account the rise in the status of traditional music during the 'Sixties, Paddy Boyle was ideally positioned to re-kindle the blazing Boyle style, and would undoubtedly have become one of the seminal national players during the boom decade of the 'Seventies. With his untimely death in 1972 at the early age of 33 years, the Donegal fiddle tradition arguably suffered its greatest set back in modern times. Fortunately a line of Boyle fiddle-playing lives on. Neillidh's grandchildren Geraldine Boyle (Paddy's daughter) and Jason Philbin (Anna's son), now both in their twenties have benefited under the tutelage of Proinsías O Maonaigh and are both active, vibrant players in their own right.

DANNY O'DONNELL

Danny O'Donnell would certainly have been a very welcome visitor to the Boyle household, whether in the Rosses or in Glasgow. He was born in Meenbannad, in the upper Rosses in the first decade of this century. From his early childhood he can recall that the name of Neillidh Boyle was held in high esteem in musical circles. When Danny took an interest in learning the fiddle in the early 1920s, it was within his own family that he sought his first instructions. By that time his older brothers John and Anthony were both well able to play and read music. His maternal uncle, Jimmy Doherty of Cruit Island, was then at home and also greatly assisted Danny in starting. Cruit at that time was a stronghold of music and dancing. Many of the dance tunes and polkas from this locality have come down to us from Jimmy Doherty through his nephew, Danny. Jimmy had emigrated to Scotland when he was fifteen years of age, and while there took lessons, eventually, developing a pronounced Scottish style. Furthermore, 'The Strathspey, Reel and Hornpipe Tutor' by William C. Honeyman was well respected in the O'Donnell household and Danny applied himself to the tunes and bowing instructions therein.

Other significant early influences on him were Paddy Bonner of Crickamore, James Sheáin Mhór O Dómhnaill (a paternal relation), and John Glackin. Bonner learned his music from his mother Síle, an extremely well-respected lilter from below Burtonport, and O Dómhnaill, father of the writer Peadar O'Donnell, played in a simple unornamented style. James Sheáin Mhór's older brother Johnnie was the more sought-after player in the area, and is remembered as playing with a long 'slurred' bow in a simple, straight style. He was also known to have played with Tarlach Mac Suibhne, whose piping influences he adopted. Though Danny never met Johnnie Sheáin Mhór, many of his tunes, which are highly distinct Donegal versions of polkas and single jigs, have survived in Danny's repertoire. John Glackin, was a blacksmith from Glenswilly who had come to spend time around Dungloe. At least one of his barndances and a hornpipe have been passed on through Danny O'Donnell's playing and recordings.

Danny remembers the fiddle style of his locality during his youth as being a very simple, mostly unornamented one with an accent on the rhythm of the tune. There was also a major difference in the repertoire from that which he would eventually come to experience in the southwest of the county. For example, the Rosses repertoire was dominated by simple polkas, mazurkas, barn-dances or germans and highlands. In stark contrast to the south-west, there was a minimum of jigs, hornpipes and reels. Players often only learned enough of the latter rhythms to be able to complete a Quadrille or Lancer set. Typical reels played by the Rosses fiddlers of the house-dance period were the *Swallow's Tail, the Green Groves of Erin* and the (originally Scottish) reel *Loch Levan Castle* (which appears in O'Neill's collections as the *Tomgreaney Hornpipe*), while other common tunes for dancing were *Teviot Bridge,* the *White Cockade* and *The Muckin' o' Geordie's Byre.*

Danny's youth would have coincided with the waning days of the house, barn and local schoolhouse dances. The players he recalls as being heavily sought-after for such dances were Pádaí Beag Gallagher and his sons from Keadue. These were Eoghan (the eldest), Eddie (who died tragically in America), Patrick (who went on to become the best player of the family), and a younger brother. Other Rosses players of the period were John Patterson, Barney Doogan and the noted fiddler Owen Ward who lived just across the lough from Meenbannad in the townland of Kerrytown. Danny recalls[16]:

> He used to play seated outside his house on a good spring or summer evening and his music would carry across the lake to Meenbannad where he was much appreciated. He was one of the Ward family whose residence became famous as the spot where the vision or apparition was supposed to have been seen in 1939 just before the war. He spent most of his life in Scotland and absorbed a great deal of Scottish dance tunes. Neillidh Boyle remembered him and I think he thought pretty highly of his playing.

At this time, while the rest of the country was being exposed to a strong Sligo influence via the commercial recordings of James Morrison, Michael Coleman and, eventually, Paddy Killoran, it is interesting to note that the recordings which were popular around the Rosses were those of James Scott Skinner and William McKenzie Murdoch.

When Danny O'Donnell was about eighteen years old he spent some time as a student in Killybegs. There he came into contact with Connie Gallagher, a full-time music teacher, who taught

Danny some tunes and re-arranged his approach to others. Connie was a "note player" (learned from printed collections) and was a nephew of the famous Connie McCahill of the Fintra Braes outside Killybegs. Also attending these classes was Danny's fellow student Johnnie Doherty (no relation of the Simis) of Gweedore who was then developing into a fine player.

Danny was a highly enthusiastic fiddler from the start and by the early 1930s had made a name for himself as a 'named' (well-respected) player in the northwest of the county. Around this time Neillidh Boyle was at the height of his recording and broadcasting period, and local fiddling enthusiasts started to encourage Danny to seek similar recognition.

In 1937 he travelled to Dublin, and recorded four unaccompanied single-sided acetate audition discs in the Henry Street Studios of the then fledgling national radio service, 2RN. One of these contained the hornpipes *Slievenamon* and the *Dublin Hornpipe.* Danny learned the latter tune initially from John Glackin and then its refined version, as performed on the recording, from Connie Gallagher. The style of these recordings confirms the great ability Danny had developed by his early twenties, particularly with his accuracy when moving up out of the first position. It is extremely consistent with that which he still plays today.

By early 1939 Danny had decided to move to London and quickly secured a recording offer from Regal Zonophone. In May 1939 he recorded three double-sided 78 RPM commercial discs, with Leo Molloy on piano. One of the sides was identical to the hornpipes he recorded in Dublin two years previously, but when released the *Dublin Hornpipe* appeared on the label under its alternative title *The Cuckoo*. While the playing on these discs is clearly louder than those made in Dublin this is no doubt due to the advanced technical facilities in Abbey Road, then the international leader in sound recording studios. On the other hand, the playing is notably more lively and attacking than the Dublin performances. This may well be a result of either natural improvement in Danny's playing or else increased confidence arising from the presence of a backing player with whom Danny was very pleased. Six years later Danny was back in Dublin and again recorded for Regal Zonophone in Jury's Hotel in Dame Street. This time he recorded four double-sided 78 RPM discs, with Albert Healy on piano.

The repertoire of Danny's early recordings would appear to have been selected for the greatest spectrum of appeal within the Irish music market. There seems to be an even mixture between nationally well-known tunes, arising from collections such as O'Neill's, and those which he would have learned in his locality. The Scottish composition *Rachel Rae,* which was a very familiar tune in the Dungloe area, appears under its Irish title *The Moving Bog. The Irish Barndance(s)* which are still common amongst Donegal fiddlers he learned from Connie Gallagher of Killybegs and John Glackin respectively. *The Glendowan reel* is a Donegal setting of the otherwise familiar *Sligo Maid's Lament,* while Neil Gow's composition *Brandlings* is played in its Donegal setting under the familiar Irish name *Colonel Rodney. The Cobbler jig* was locally well-known and was followed by *Close to the Floor* which again Danny learned from Connie Gallagher of Killybegs. Perhaps the most representative of Danny's local repertoire was the inclusion of a set of highlands under the umbrella title *The Thistle and Shamrock.* This set is comprised of three highlands. The second of these is widely known in south Donegal as *The Bundoran Highland* and popularised by Paddy Kelly. It is the Scottish tune *Louden's Bonnie Woods,* while the last tune of the trio is the Neil Gow composition *Neil Gow's Wife.* In this case Danny plays it in the Donegal key.

In 1948 Danny had a desire to extend his horizons and set off for America. He lived in New York for eight years where he became well integrated into the musical community of the northeastern seaboard, meeting and playing with all the great names of Irish fiddling at that time such as Paddy Killoran, Larry Redigan, Paddy Reynolds, Louis Quinn, Hughie Gillespie and many more. Interestingly, while in New York Danny took classical guitar lessons with the aim of achieving a better understanding of the principles of accompaniment. In 1956 he moved to San Francisco, where his playing centred around the Knights of the Red Branch Irish club. Here he came into contact with two Donegal fiddlers Joe Tamony, of Fintown and Dudley Byrne, a first cousin of Francie and Mickey O'Byrne of Kilcar. During his time on the west coast he made some private acetate recordings on a machine owned by the Knights of the Red Branch. A surviving copy includes the set of reels *Music in the Glen, Farewell to Ireland* and *The Dawn.* The first tune is clearly in its preferred Donegal fiddle setting in the key of A, while the last tune shows Danny's continued mastery of playing in positions.

Danny returned to Ireland in 1958, where he renewed old acquaintances in the Dublin musical circle. He was then again off to Glasgow where he lived until 1970. During this time he visited the Boyle household, occasionally playing with his revered old Rosses friend until Neillidh's death. Another player with whom Danny associated during this period was Tyrone-born Jimmy McHugh, who has very strong Donegal connections. His time in Glasgow permitted Danny O'Donnell ample opportunity to enhance his already extensive knowledge of Scottish fiddle music and he spent two happy seasons playing with the Caledonian Strathspey and Reel Society. While in Glasgow he also meticulously combed a local museum which contained the manuscripts of the compositions of Skinner, and identified many tunes which he had learned in his youth in the Rosses.

Danny returned permanently to Ireland in 1970, basing himself in Donegal. In 1973 he was again asked to record commercially, this time for the Philips recording company. The resultant LP shows a balance between Donegal tunes and other more widely circulated material. Of particular note in terms of the Donegal tradition are his versions of the airs *The Blackbird* and *The Dear Irish Boy.*

Since coming home to Donegal, Danny has remained a dedicated, enthusiastic traditional fiddle player. He spent extended periods in Kilcar where he played regularly with Francie and Mickey O'Byrne. He also spent time in Ballyshannon and for over the past decade, his base has been Ballybofey, where he met almost daily with John Doherty until the latter's death in 1979. Danny has been afforded an insight and access to the Donegal fiddle tradition which remains unparalleled. Since John Doherty's death Danny's playing has centred on informal sessions at home. His playing with his close friend, Charlie Patton, is some of the most pleasing and tasteful duet music ever heard in Donegal. Others who have close musical ties to Danny are Martin and Kathleen McGinley, the Harper sisters and flute player Seán Lee. Prior to his death, Hughie Gillespie enjoyed playing with Danny and reminiscing about their years in America.

Throughout his life Danny O'Donnell has played with a precise and accurate style, which is underlined by remarkable tone. The latter is almost universally described as very sweet by Donegal fiddlers. If his style differs in anyway from that of his native locality, it would be in his slightly greater use of fingered triplets played on a single bow, or "slurred triplets", as compared to staccato or "single bowed" triplets where each of the three notes are played with separate strokes of the bow.

Danny O'Donnell has always lived in continuous pursuit of learning, playing and experiencing traditional fiddle music. He has played with the broadest spectrum of fiddlers possible, and at the highest artistic level. While many players have an in-depth understanding of a particular musical circle or region no one else can claim the direct experience of having first-hand knowledge of the west coast of America, playing with the foremost players on the northeastern coast of the United States, having a detailed knowledge of the Scottish scene, enjoying familiarity with Dublin-based players over the years as well as a close personal acquaintance with the greatest of Donegal players of the last and current generation. In his pursuit of learning more about Irish fiddle playing, Danny has researched countless printed collections, resulting in an ability to recognise and source many obscure tunes from memory. Those who have had the good fortune to befriend Danny O'Donnell are unanimous in concluding there is no more knowledgeable person about Irish fiddle music than himself.

THE GLACKINS

Another Rosses fiddler who played a critical role in the improved fortunes of Donegal fiddle music in the second half of this century was the eldest son of Pat Glackin, of Falmore, Maghery, Dungloe and Catherine O'Reilly of Cavan. Pat and Catherine met while both were working in Scotland and their second child, Tom, was born in Sterling on February 25th, 1925. The family returned to Falmore when Tom was only four years of age and it was there that he grew to manhood. His mother, Catherine, was a fiddle player and it was on her fiddle that Tom first began to play. His paternal grandmother, Sally McBride from Dunlewey was also a fiddler and had an important influence on him.

Amongst others to influence him in his early playing days was neighbour Hughie Devanney who was approximately eight years Tom's senior. He was a good house-dance player and took lessons from Neillidh Boyle for a short period. Hughie, who emigrated relatively late in life at the age of forty-five to New Jersey, was for the most part taught by Hughie Bonar. In his prime, Bonar was one of the fiddlers in greatest demand around this locality. At the age of thirty-five he felt strongly enough about political developments of that period to join the XV Brigade of the International Brigades fighting on the Republican side in the Spanish Civil War[17]. He attained the rank of Section-Commander and sadly lost his life in one of the bitterest engagements, the Battle of Jarama, in February, 1937.

In 1947 Tom Glackin moved to Dublin and became a career Garda rising to the rank of Sergeant at the age of 34 years. Tom and Maureen Healy, a native of Dublin with Ballycastle, County Mayo parentage married on December 29th, 1952 and had three children Paddy, Séamus and Kevin. He played in a straight, largely unornamented style but with a strong sense of rhythm and attack which corresponds closely to the style Danny O'Donnell describes as typical of the Rosses players. Tom Glackin was amply gifted with a remarkable ability to teach. A gentleman by nature, with a considerable amount of patience, he was able to transmit his music in stages, firstly imparting the simple melody, then filling in the tune with basic ornamentation. He then encouraged the player and built his confidence to ultimately flesh-out the tune. Tom's guidance and help as a teacher of traditional fiddle music undoubtedly contributed to the development of many of the great players of the generation which followed him.

Since the early 1950s Tom Glackin was an influential figure in Irish music. At this time Donegal music was very poorly known and understood outside of the county. Dublin, the centre of musical trends and events, was still firmly receiving its major influences from western and southern musicians resident there. A chance meeting with Clare fiddler, John Kelly, while on the beat resulted in Tom being introduced to the musical fraternity of the St. Mary's Club in Church Street, then a hive of traditional music activity in the capital. Tom Glackin freely circulated in this setting and forged many lifelong friendships with the musicians of his era, yet at times, he may have felt a little musically isolated. It is clear that during this period, when Donegal fiddle music was not yet widely appreciated, Tom proudly promoted the genius of his Rosses neighbour Neillidh Boyle with whom he was socially quite familiar. He also played a central role in bringing the largely unsung talents of the Dohertys to the attention of those who were then instrumental in shaping the future of traditional music.

In this latter capacity, he would eventually become the key figure in creating a ripple which inevitably would spread and grow, becoming the present wave of interest and development in the popularity of Donegal fiddle playing. Though the Dohertys and other Donegal fiddlers had received the collecting attentions of Séamus Ennis, Caoimhín O Danachair, Ciarán Mac Mathúna and Peter Kennedy during the late 1940s and early 1950s, these recordings have remained largely unexplored in the archives of the various collecting bodies. Nothing existed in a format which was accessible to enthusiastic players keen to learn more about Donegal music.

In the mid-1960s Tom Glackin arranged to bring his friend, the collector Breandán Breathnach, to meet and record the music of the Dohertys. Breandán had just undertaken a massive nationwide traditional dance music collection project. The aim was to document and publish the music as it existed in the hands of its practitioners. The historic recording took place at the Reelin Bridge in October of 1965, and included solo and duet playing by John and Mickey Doherty. These tapes reveal some of their best playing, particularly a powerful duet performance of *Lough Isle Castle* with Mickey providing low pitched droning against John's melody in the first part of the tune. Besides Tom and Breandán, Clare fiddler, John Kelly, and Tom's son Paddy were present at this recording. Breathnach and Kelly were, by their own subsequent accounts, astounded at the ability and the repertoire of John and Mickey. Not only the virtuosity but the sincere interest shown by John in the young Paddy Glackin was to leave a lasting mark on the aspiring fiddler.

Breandán Breathnach and John Kelly unhesitatingly recognised the virtuosity and importance of the Dohertys. The message was carried by these two seminal figures that Donegal had fiddlers of the highest degree. The seed had been planted and would continue to grow. Breandán Breathnach eventually published selections from this recording session, as well as some taken from John Byrne and his son James, of Glencolumcille in his renowned three-part collection 'Ceol Rince na hÉireann'[18]. Tom Glackin continued further in the development of Donegal fiddle music by playing a strategic role in bringing about the issuing of the first widely available commercial recording of John Doherty, which appeared on the Comhaltas Ceoltóirí Éireann label.

In his later years, Tom began to spend increasingly more time back in Donegal. He strengthened his ties with his long-time friend, Proinsias O Maonaigh and they started to develop a marvellous duet repertoire. A few holiday trips with Proinsias to the Fortwilliam area of the Scottish Highlands also saw a growing friendship with Angus Grant. With the death of Tom Glackin on May 22nd, 1988, traditional music experienced the loss of a fine player, one of its most gifted teachers and the man whose efforts set in train the sustained growth of respect for Donegal fiddle playing in the last half of this century.

Paddy Glackin was born in Dublin in September, 1954. It would be accurate to state that in his youth he was surrounded by music. His maternal grandfather, Mick Healy came from Behy near the now famous Céidí Fields while his grandmother, Brigid (Curran) Healy, originally from Ballinrobe, County Mayo played the melodeon. Paddy remembers hearing her a number of times. On his sixth birthday he started to receive lessons from his father. These continued for some years and eventually developed into a less formal, yet continuous process of consultation and advice as regards the general approach and details of playing tunes. Through years of exposure and his tremendous ability to teach Tom Glackin clearly acted as the greatest moulding force on Paddy's playing.

An event of great importance to Paddy would have been the 1965 trip to Donegal and meeting with John Doherty previously mentioned. This occurance seems to have left a lasting impression on him and marked the start of a sincere commitment to fiddle playing. The influence of John's and to a lesser extent, Mickey's, style of playing is evident in Paddy's playing as is their repertoire. Paddy went on to take classical lessons at the College of Music in Dublin and within a year or two of the Reelin Bridge meeting a friend of Tom's, Jim Carroll of Cork, was home from America on a visit. Jim called to the Glackin house on several occasions and spent some time with Paddy clarifying some points of technique. Other frequent visitors to the Glackin home at this time included the Meath and Sligo fiddlers Frank O'Higgins and John Joe Gardiner respectively. These players were established, senior figures in traditional music having not only recorded commercially but repeatedly broadcast on national radio. They were again to have inspired Paddy in his youth.

Despite being in contact with some of the most influential players of the day, Paddy remembers that participation in traditional music was not such a fashionable pursuit amongst his peers. The idea of going off to music lessons with a fiddle under your arm left a young fellow open to ridicule. It took some fortitude to keep on in the pursuit of the music. Eventually Paddy started attending some of the sessions at the St. Mary's Club. He was greatly taken by the flute playing of Sligoman John Egan who was a central figure at that venue. Paddy warmly recalls that his first public performance was a duet with John who bolstered him with a great deal of encouragement.

Traditional music was starting to take off at this time and Paddy was recognised as one of the most significant emerging players. He was in great demand throughout Dublin for playing. He was recruited into the band Ceoltóirí Laighean which was largely seen as carrying on the efforts of Seán O Ríada. He eventually became the first fiddler with the 'Bothy Band' which he eventually left, becoming involved as a presenter of the hugely successful, and since much missed, RTÉ radio programme 'The Long Note'.

This career move appears to have been of fundamental importance to Paddy's subsequent history. It brought him into increased contact with his former 'Bothy Band' partner Tony McMahon who was the programme's producer. Though there would have been much basic common ground between Tony and Paddy on a simple musical level, by Paddy's own admission McMahon appears have brought about in him a massive exploration at a deeper level in his music. Paddy strongly emphasises the greatness of this impact which led him to challenge conservatism and superficiality in the music while looking to explore a total range of expression inherent in the music. This questioning approach was also significantly re-enforced by his association with Colm O Briain when Paddy was subsequently appointed as the first Traditional Arts Officer to the Arts Council. It must be said that in the latter capacity, like his father's pioneering work in developing Donegal music,

Paddy also played a critical role in the formulation of a 'Donegal Fiddlers Guild' along with the then Donegal Arts Officer Michael McMullen. This movement in many ways acted as a precursor to 'Cairdeas na bhFidléirí'. Having left the Arts Council to work as a radio producer and subsequently as a presenter of the television programme 'The Pure Drop' in RTE, Paddy now is best known as a solo performer, often accompanied by Dónal Lunny. His deep, rich tone and bowing have become somewhat of hallmarks in his playing. He has been very successful in his journey to establish a range of expression. His music ranges from subtle to clear and straightforward to defiantly aggressive. The last two decades have seen him as one of the most impacting musicians in Irish music.

Séamus Glackin is now in his early thirties. He started to play music at the age of six on the piano accordian under the direction of Tom McKenna, a then retired violinist with the RTÉ Orchestra. Tom called to the Glackin home and would take the children in individual fifteen minute sessions concentrating on technique and general musicianship. At the age of ten Séamus made the move to the fiddle and came under the direct influence of his father. By this time the Doherty influence was also present on his playing as the private tapes of John were a regular feature in the home. Séamus recalls the adventure and excitement of holidays in Donegal which included the mandatory seeking out of John Doherty. During one of these sojourns John was located in Teelin and recorded his LP on the Comhaltas label using Séamus' Hofner fiddle. By his early teens Séamus had already developed into a player of significance. He was active in competitions and had an advantage in being able to access Paddy's now refined playing approach which he admired greatly. By his late teens he was open to a wide variety of musical influences from the like of Seán McGuire and The Four Star Quartet to Stefán Grapelli and Django Rheinhardt to Seán Keane and Willie Hunter. Séamus, to me, appears to be the most natural musician of the brothers and as such, possibly the most adventurist. A facet which he appears to have inherited from his father is his ability to teach fiddle music in a most effective and lucid manner. In my years of observing teachers I have never seen one to surpass Séamus Glackin.

The youngest of the three brothers, Kevin, is also in his early thirties. He started playing at the age of six and again, the most important influence on his music was his father and John Doherty.

He also received lessons from Tom McKenna. Other early influences on Kevin were the recordings of Seán Keane, Denis Murphy and Julia Clifford as well as Bobby Casey. Fiddle playing for Kevin was to some extent a routine family affair until he started to venture out to Comhaltas sessions as a young teenager. There, he came into contact with other players of his own age group and this seems to have brought a positive change in his drive to play. He found a growing degree of fun and enjoyment in the social side of fiddle playing. Since that time he has continued to grow to a player of major importance. He has worked closely with Séamus to develop a highly spirited duet. Kevin is a consummate fiddler and my view would be that of the three brothers Kevin's playing appears to be the most aggressive.

There is a distinct commonality in the playing of the Glackin brothers arising primarily from the influence of their father, and to a lesser degree through Paddy who would have passed on some of his own approaches by coaching his younger brothers in preparation for underage competitions. Despite this, each maintains his individual approach to the music. Though Séamus and Kevin have increasingly combined to perform as a duet appearances by the brothers as a trio have been all too rare. Recently as part of the proceedings of the 'Annual Fiddlers Meeting' in Glenties Paddy, Séamus and Kevin performed in connection with a tribute to the contribution of their late father. The five sets which they played that autumn evening was for me the most superb combined fiddle playing I have ever experienced. While the players had the ability to achieve such a level of excellence there was no doubting that that particular playing was further fuelled by their deep feelings for their father.

Modern communication has permitted the rapid flow back into Donegal of the music simmering in Dublin. As a result, the impact that the Glackin family have made in Donegal is considerable. Their music has been followed with intense interest and many of the younger players in Donegal have enthusiastically adopted a variety of their musical directions. The older generation also looked on them as players to be respected and considered them very much their own.

Gweedore is not remembered as being a stronghold of fiddle-playing in the first half of this century, and many have pointed to the activities of the famous Father James McFadden by way of explanation. Father McFadden left a somewhat schizophrenic legacy in this part of the county. He is justly remembered as the heroic defender of tenants' land rights and as the conqueror of the oppressive tactics of the landlords of the area. At the same time he is held directly responsible for the almost mass destruction of fiddles in the parish, and the premature decline of the house-dances. Fr. McFadden, like many of his colleagues of that period in rural Ireland, held the belief that house-dances and dancing in general were the travelling partners of drink and promiscuous behaviour. His response was to undertake a concerted effort to eliminate all house-dances and destroy as many fiddles as was deemed necessary to put a stop to the practice.

In his book 'History of Landlordism in Donegal'[19] Proinnsías O'Gallchóbhair tells of Father McFadden's later years:

> In June, 1901, Canon McFadden bade goodbye to the parish of Gweedore, and took up abode in Glenties as pastor of the ancient and historic parish of Inishkeel. Though appointed to a progressive, well equipped parish, he found an ample field for construction, and improvements. He brought all the great qualities which had endeared him to his former parishioners with him to Glenties. He saw on his arrival there that steps would have to be taken to mitigate the dangers arising from indiscriminate dancing in country houses. He also saw it would not be feasible to suppress a form of amusement which had such a grip on the people. Instead of suppressing it, the Canon decided to control it and with that end in view he reconstructed the Market Hall which had been acquired by the people of the parish from the Marquis of Conyngham some years previously. In this hall dancing was permitted under conditions which were more conducive to the welfare of young people than those which might otherwise obtain.

While his activities no doubt had a deleterious effect on the musical development of the Gweedore and Inishkeel parishes, it must be seen as an ironic twist that the annual meeting of Donegal fiddlers now takes place in the Highlands Hotel, Glenties, directly across the street from the Market Hall in which Father McFadden so fervently hoped to control the expression and enjoyment of Donegal fiddle music.

Whatever about the mixed fortunes of fiddle playing in Gweedore in the early part of this century, the latter half has seen an explosion of energetic playing. All of this is due to the herculean efforts of one man, Proinsías O Maonaigh. He was born in the 1920s and spent his young life at Coisclaidigh, Gweedore. Music was at his disposal from an early age as his mother Rose O'Donnell, or Rósíe Bheag Rósie Móire as she known locally, was a well-known musician. Though she started to play music on a borrowed concertina, she eventually moved to the melodeon becoming an accomplished performer who had often played with the Píobaire Mór. Indeed, many of the latter's simple dance tunes have come into Proinsías' repertoire from his mother.

Proinsías was enthusiastic about music from an early age and quickly sought to play the fiddle. By the time he was in secondary school he was already an accomplished player and in demand for local dances. Johnnie Doherty, who we have already seen was for a period a fellow student with Danny O Donnell in Killybegs, spent his adult life running his shoe shop in Middletown, Gweedore. Proinsías, who knew him well, remembers that he gave up fiddle playing in the early 1940s with the advent of the jazz era. At this time he started to play the piano and accordeon and performed at céilís and dances, later forming a band. Proinsías, who played his first céilí with Johnnie recalls that he was a very good fiddler and accomplished sight reader. He is also of the opinion that had Johnnie continued with the fiddle he would certainly have become one of the best known players in the area. Johnnie died in 1991.

Eventually the opportunity to attend teacher-training college gave him scope to travel in a wider circle and enhance his playing. During this time he was a regular performer at céilís in a band comprised largely of his fellow pupils. From 1952 to 1957 he was based in Ramelton where there were increased demands for his playing.

In 1957 he was offered a teaching post in his native Gweedore and on returning, he began to radically expand his commitment to playing. He was receiving requests from parents for fiddle and tin whistle tuition for their children. Such were the demands that he found the need to form a number of classes. His reputation as an extraordinary teacher grew and amongst the beneficiaries of his efforts were his own children. A small band based on Prionsias and Joe Jack O Cuireann was formed through his efforts, which would eventually grow to become Ceoltóirí Altan, and ultimately give rise to the now renowned traditional group Altan.

At last, during the 1970s, traditional music entered its modern golden age. One enigmatic phenomenon of this development was the joyous discovery of traditional music by young, often urban-based, people throughout the Ulster counties, most of whom had little or no previous direct exposure to the music. While there was some interest from this new generation of players in piping, the majority opted for the flute or especially the fiddle. Gweedore became a mecca for the legions seeking to learn and expand their abilities, and at the centre of this whirlwind of musical enthusiasm was Proinsías. His home, at times, became a virtual junction for music followers who might be travelling from the south, Scotland, London, America or anywhere fiddle music was appreciated.

Over the past decade and a half, Proinsías' playing has gone from strength to strength. While he is still sought out for performances and as a source of new material, his huge contribution to Donegal fiddle music lies in his almost unparalleled achievement in the local development of Donegal fiddling. He has taught two generations of accomplished fiddlers from the Gortahork - Gweedore - Dungloe area. A significant and pioneering development arising in no small degree from his teaching accomplishments has been the formation of 'Scoil Cheoil Ailigh' which provides tuition in traditional music on a number of instruments with the fiddle being in greatest demand. Pupils in their young adult years who owe the development of their gift of playing to Proinsías include Hugh Hiúidaí Bheag O Gallchóbhair, Paula, Róisín and Aoife Doohan, Brendan Galway, Geraldine Boyle and Jason Philbin. No doubt there is special joy afforded to Proinsías in seeing his grandson Ciarán O Maonaigh grow into a fiddler. Besides these are vast numbers of players who informally sought him out to learn both tunes and technique, and who have all been obliged by this abundantly gifted fiddler.

Máireád Ní Mhaonaigh is now in her early thirties. Around the age of nine years she travelled to Dublin to compete in an Irish singing competition. Following that she found herself sitting next to Cavan fiddler Tony Smith in a session. Máiréad was utterly taken by his playing and fixed her intentions on fiddle playing. She came under the guidance of her father in his classes at home and with his help and that of her brother, Gearóid, she progressed rapidly into an accomplished player. At this time Gaoth Dóbhair was becoming an important musical meeting place. A regular visitor was Dinny McLaughlin and he made a further impression on her. His technical ability held a great attraction for Máiréad and this increased her desire to play. Another regular playing partner at this time was Ballyshannon fiddler, Terry McIntyre, who along with herself and her father formed the fiddle nucleus of Ceoltóirí Altan. By her mid-teens she had become one of the most gifted players in Donegal.

Her style from her earliest days has been one marked by a vibrant enthusiasm and attack. She has embraced the influences of the Dohertys, Tommy Peoples and in more later years, the fiddlers of the central and southwestern areas of the county. She holds a special appreciation for the music of Danny O'Donnell. Her father's admiration for the playing of Neillidh Boyle has meant that she is well versed in his approach to playing.

In her late teens she travelled to College in Dublin. Her arrival there was somewhat like Tommy Peoples a number of years previous. The whirlwind of her playing impacted with great force there. Máiréad has amassed a repertoire of astounding breadth. She has added to this by composing a number of significant pieces herself. For more than a decade now she has also been indirectly opened to the repertoire of Fermanagh and Leitrim through her long established and exhilarating duets with her gifted flute playing husband Frankie Kennedy.

Máiréad's style is a highly aggressive one much related to her bowing technique. Her grip is well up the shaft of the bow and her triplets are rapid and energetic. This dynamism appears to directly transfer itself into the playing both at a basic and a deeper level. Along with Frankie Kennedy, Máiréad formed the now famous band Altan. Over the past number of years this band has grown to be one of the most influential groups playing Irish music at the international level. Their influence has been such that Donegal music has benefited immensely in terms of growing popularity. At this stage there is almost a direct correlation between Altan tours and floods of applications seeking to book places on the Donegal

Fiddlers' Summer School in Glencolumbcille.

Mairéad Ni Mhaonaigh has exhibited a strong personal commitment to the development of Donegal fiddle playing. She has given freely of her time and art on a regular basis to teach and foster Donegal fiddle playing, particularly amongst younger players. She will be a seminal influence on future generations of Donegal style fiddlers both at home and across the globe.

TARLACH Mac SUIBHNE, AN PÍOBAIRE MÓR

On September 4th, 1835 during the course of his Ordinance Survey work in Donegal, while John O'Donovan was being ferried across the narrow entry of Mulroy Bay he spotted a family walking on the strand. He enquired about them and was told by his ferryman that they were the dispossessed Mac Suibhne na dTuath. By his own account[20], O'Donovan's imagination was fired by the riches to rags misfortune of the once noble family and arranged to meet the patriarch, Eamonn Ruaidh, to gather information on his family history.

It is certain that his family had been dispossessed of ancestral McSweeney lands and Horn Head House, in particular, in north Donegal during the Ulster Plantation. At that time Eamonn Ruaidh, an uilleann piper as was his father, claimed to be sixty-one years, thus born in 1774. O'Donovan also noted:

> On entering the house my eyes were astonished at the sight of two able-bodied men (with thighs as thick as those of two fat bullocks) playing with deafening sound, the one upon the Bagpipes, the other upon the Fiddle. On enquiry I learned that these were two sons of Mac Sweeny who had been for the last month employed in Captain Hart's house.

O'Donovan recorded the following family lineage from Eamonn Ruaidh which extended to one of the last known Mac Suibhne Chieftains of Doe, Maol Mhuire an Bhata Bhuí:

> Sir Malmurry, the father of Donogh More, father of Morogh, father of Donogh Óge, father of Torlogh, father of Emon (Eamonn Ruaidh), now the senior aged 61, Donogh and Torlogh.

The last two individuals in this lineage are to be read as sons of

Eamonn Ruadh, namely Donnacha and Tarlach, the Píobaire Mór, and almost certainly are the two noted by O'Donovan as playing the fiddle and pipes respectively. The names Donnacha and Tarlach were common christian names in the Doe chieftain lineage and as such, were fitting choices for the two brothers. Eamonn Ruaidh, who lived to be 96 years, came to settle in Lunnaigh in Gweedore where Tarlach, apart from seasonal forays to Scotland, lived out his life. There is some degree of confusion concerning the lineage offered by Eamonn Ruaidh. He indicates his father was Torlogh, whereas in a lineage provided by An Píobaire Mór[21], he indicates his grandfather was named Eamonn and not Torlogh. There is some evidence to support this as based on information provided by An Píobaire Mór, C.P. Meehan tells us Eman Mac Swine, grandfather of the piper (in this case, Tarlach), lived to the age of ninety six, and, two days before his death, staggered to the door of his cabin to see the hounds pass[22]. It may indicate the level of confusion on this issue that this Eman and Tarlach's father, Eamonn Ruaidh, both died at the age of ninety six.

Tarlach Mac Suibhne, as we have already seen, was one of the most intriguing of musicians during the last century. While he is best remembered as a piper, he, along with his brothers Pádraig and Donnacha, was also a fiddle player. As with almost all facets of his life, the circumstances of his birth are also a mystery. The tombstone erected by his daughter's children at his grave cites his age at death as being 98 years, thus indicating that he was born in 1818 (when his father would have been forty-four years). Francis O'Neill[23], on the other hand, indicates that he was born in 1829 (Eamonn Ruaidh would have been fifty-five years).

Tarlach, himself was visited in 1909 by a writer from the Weekly Irish Times[24] and in discussion informed the correspondent he was seventy-eight years of age. This would have him born in 1831 when his father would have been fifty-seven years old. This latter date would appear highly unlikely as he could not have been the person identified in John O'Donovan's visit. It is also worth noting in relation to this article that a family lineage supplied by Tarlach conflicts with the one given by his father to John O'Donovan at Tarlach's grandfather's generation and at least one other generation. Considering the intense family pride in their forefathers this is surprising to say the least. Taking into account the combined evidence of O'Donovan's description of meeting two fine, strapping lads in 1835 and the range of ages of Eamonn Ruaidh at the birth of his son, the date of 1818 for the birth of Tarlach appears by far the most likely.

The Píobaire Mór is also popularly believed to have been born in Glenfin. Seán O Gallchóir[25] provides evidence from the late Doochary seanchaí, Pat O Canáinn, that he was born in the townland of Árd Leathan, in the parish of Glenfin and his people moved to the townland Doire na Coradh, then to Mountcharles and onto Doe before settling in Lunniagh, Gweedore.

As a child he learned music from Master Mac Giolla Easbuic of the National School in Gortahork. It is almost certain that the instrument he was learning at this time was the fiddle since the finger span required on his flat set of pipes was grossly in excess of that which could be covered by a young boy's hand. It is also clear that as part of his early studies he acquired the ability to read music and three incomplete scraps of his music manuscripts from this period of tuition can be found in his pipes case which is held by the Donegal Historical Society. He also obtained a very rare copy of 'O'Farrell's Collection of National Irish Music for the Union Pipes' published about 1804, which almost certainly originally belonged to his father. He valued the book tremendously. It was customary at that time that lineages and occasions of family importance were recorded in the family Bible. New births, baptisms, marriages and deaths would all be chronicled in the revered book. So strong was Tarlach's respect for this music collection that on page four we can see him recording the event of his marriage with the words "CHARLES SWEENY MARRIED TO SARAH CROSBY ON 24TH ..." (the remainder of the date is now illegible).

In light of this it is almost certain he incorporated some of the 62 tunes in the publication into his repertoire. One firm piece of evidence indicating his absorption of the O'Farrell material is seen in the appearance of the unusually titled tune *Nanny Wilt Thou Gang With Me.* Many of Tarlach's tunes were passed down through the repertoire of the Dohertys and during a private recording made by Fr. Eoghan O Colm, John Doherty can be heard to introduce this tune under the mixed language title *Nanny an bhFuil Tú ag Dul a' Gang Wi' Me.* It is almost certain that this tune arrived with John via family connections to the Píobaire Mór and ultimately from O'Farrell's collection. It is less certain how much of an influence the sixteen pages of instructional text on uilleann piping techniques had on his playing.

Tarlach grew into a six-foot intensely strong-minded man who liberally mixed facts about himself and his music with faerie lore. Much against the social trend of the time he married Sarah Crosby, daughter of the Protestant Minister Alexander Crosby, and it is reputed that he inherited a set of pipes from her father. There is an inaccurate account that his pipes had been handed down through the Mac Suibhne Clan via Seán a' Díomáis O Neill and this may have lent itself to the confusion. Local folklore recalls that Sarah (or Sally Mhór as she became known) immediately fell in love upon first seeing the Píobaire Mór. She very quickly proposed marriage to him. His response was reputed to walk her along the road commanding the well-dressed, well-bred woman to throw her shoes and cloak into a raging river. All her personal valuables were then thrown along the roadside. After she had fulfilled this test of trust she was told that to be his wife would mean the loss of all worldly goods but a matching with royal blood.

Tarlach and Sarah had six children, sons Seán and Eamonn and four daughters Sorcha, Ann Jane (who emigrated to Philadelphia where she married into the McManus family and died there on July 22, 1929, aged 66 years), Sinéad and another whose name has since been forgotten. Francis O'Neill tells us that the children scattered over the world with only one, a girl, showing an interest in the pipes while nothing is mentioned as regards fiddle playing.

A good description of Tarlach and his mannerisms appears in O'Neill's 'Irish Minstrels and Musicians'[26] and there are some further fragments of information in his other work, 'Irish Music a Fascinating Hobby'[27]. From O'Neill's writings we learn that the third part of the now popular four-part *Derry Hornpipe* was collected from the Píobaire Mór during his six month visit to Chicago to perform at the World's Columbian Exhibition in 1893. Other tunes which are strongly associated with his playing are *The Wild Irishman,* which was his favourite reel, the jig *Cherish the Ladies, Carolan's Farewell to Music,* the reels *Toss the Feathers* and *Down the Broom* as well as the air *Seán O Duibhir a' Ghleanna.*

Included in the reference material in their book 'The Piping of Patsy Touhey'[28], Pat Mitchell and Jackie Small quote a correspondence from piper John Egan in the Chicago Citizen relating to Tarlach's visit to Chicago. Dated October 21st, 1893 Egan began by praising the standard of pipers at the 'World's Columbian Exhibition' continuing on to state: "Mr. McSweeney, (he was invariably referred to as Charles McSweeney in America) who was brought from the old country by Mrs. Hart to the Donegal Village, is a perfect type of the old Irish piper. He is a fine musician and plays some grand old Irish pieces that are now almost obsolete..." Egan then goes on to praise Patsy Touhey as a perfect master of the instrument. This favouring of Touhey over Mac Suibhne would seem to have been the overall verdict of the Chicago music fraternity and is echoed again in the writings of Francis O'Neill when he describes Mac Suibhne as having "fittingly represented an antiquated and oppressed Ireland" while noting Touhey's "expert manipulation of a great set of Taylor pipes made him the centre of attraction".

One of the most consistent pieces of folklore concerning Tarlach's numerous eccentricities was that he won the World Piping Competition during his sojourn in Chicago[29]. The story goes throughout west Donegal folklore that the competition came down to himself and the renowned Patsy Touhey, and having both battled it out Mac Suibhne eventually won the contest with a highland *Dúlamán na Binne Buí* which is said to have been composed by him. It is worthwhile noting that this same format with the same winning tune is mentioned by Róise Rua Nic Ghríanna[30] in her autobiography but in this instance about the Arranmore warpiper Mící Mhícheál Bhig O Dónaill. This setting of the story mimics the standard folklore motif of the music contest, where the winner is pushed to playing his last tune and then wins with another which he composes on the spot.

The idea of a world piping championship in Chicago being held at all is rather suspect. It is curious that Francis O'Neill, a clear piping enthusiast, who records the main events of Tarlach's trip to America, does not mention such a contest. It is also unlikely that, if such a competition were held, it would have been set in the format of a play-off to the final tune. This, no doubt, is the influence of folklore and, considering the central character, was almost assuredly created and encouraged by Tarlach himself.

The overwhelming body of evidence indicates that no world piping competition took place in Chicago. Firstly, the event in Chicago was not a World's Fair as is popularly recounted but was correctly titled the World's Columbian Exhibition. Furthermore, O'Neill, who had such a fervent interest in the pipes makes no mention of a competition which would normally be expected to have proven fertile ground for his attentions. The one shred of evidence which might have confirmed the story was alluded to by Pádraig Mac Sheáin, when discussing the Píobaire Mór in a broader article on the MacSweeney Clan in 'Bealoideas' in 1964[31]. He notes that a certificate confirming Tarlach's winning the world title was kept with his famous copy of O'Farrell in his pipes case. Thanks to the kind assistance of Lucius Emerson of the Donegal Historical Society, who now holds Mac Suibhne's pipes case and papers since both, along with his pipes were generously entrusted to the Society by Dermot McShane, (Pádraig's son) I was able to examine Tarlach's papers. I can confirm that the certificate which accompanies the rare music book is that which was awarded to him on winning the Unpublished Airs competition at the first Feis Ceoil piping competition held in Dublin on a May morning in 1897. As a matter of record, Tarlach took second place later the same evening in Dublin to Robert Thompson of Cork in the open competition.

To completely unravel this mystery we must now look at the proceedings of the piping competition held by the Feis Ceoil Society in 1897. In relation to the development of the folklore of Tarlach's world title, it would be reasonable to believe that this competition, the first of its kind, could be construed as a world championship, and considering his fondness of *Dúlamán na Binne Buí,* he may well have played it at the gathering, thus furnishing the bones of the story. This explanation, which sees Tarlach not as winner of a world piping title but having captured one of the first Feis Ceoil titles becomes much more reasonable when the all the evidence and the association between a world title and the Feis Ceoil Certificate is taken into account.

From the strength and consistency of folklore it would appear that whether he composed *Dúlamán na Binne Buí* or not, it was surely one of his favourite pieces. So strongly is this tune associated with Tarlach and the famous competition lore that there are at least ten different highlands which have been played by many of the legendary fiddlers of the last generation, all of which were firmly identified as *Dúlamán na Binne Buí* and all of which were equally strongly claimed as being the tune which won Mac Suibhne the world title. Oddly enough it is now impossible to discern which one was the highland associated with the Píobaire Mór, as even John and Mickey Doherty, who directly inherited much of his music, played totally different highlands (in Mickey's case the highland is a version of the Scottish tune *Cutting Ferns*) which they claimed were his *Dúlamán na Binne Buí*.

Tarlach travelled the north of Ireland and Scotland widely playing both fiddle and pipes. It must be said, however, that of the two the pipes were his chosen instrument. He was acutely aware of his powerful ancestry, directly through to Maolmuire an Bhata Bhuí of Doe Castle. The downfall of the Mc Sweeney clan with the loss of lands and power clearly left an angry mark on him which he appeared to balance with an exaggerated, intense sense of pride. Indeed, pride and a direct manner are the traits most commonly attributed to him. The following is a brief and typical reference to him which appears in the short story 'Eibhlín Ní Bhrían agus an Chéad Saighdiúir Dúbh' by Seán Bán Mac Meanman[32]. In this account, which no doubt has a good basis in fact, we are told of the excitement prior to a house-dance at which the Píobaire Mór was engaged to play. The following description of the man himself is given (my translation):

> Around by the walls the seating was laid out nicely: chairs, stools, planks and empty boxes. The Píobaire Mór was sitting regally in the corner, one leg crossed over the other, the pipes on his knee, one eye closed and humming and crooning under his breath. It is said that he is a very proud man.

Tarlach would not play for just anyone and he conducted his house playing professionally. He had to be booked to play and in this process fees, which were always in excess of other local players, were clearly set out. His directness of character and the tremendous value placed on his music afforded him the ability to gain the upper hand in confrontations with Father McFadden. The priest, who as we have seen, was extremely zealous in breaking up house-dances ran into the Píobaire Mór during some of the latter's engagements. When this occurred Father McFadden would send the attendants fleeing from the house. Mac Suibhne would steadfastly refuse to move, claiming that he had been engaged to play and would not leave until he had been paid his agreed fee. To shift the musician and ensure that there would be no more music in the house, the priest was forced to settle the reckoning with the piper out of his own pocket.

Each summer the Píobaire Mór would be contracted for one week to play for Lord Leitrim's guests. He was able to demand a hefty fee and attentions equal to those afforded the landlord's personal guests. While playing for the descendants of those who brought about his clan's downfall must have greatly annoyed him, he was able to wreak revenge psychologically. Having played for the gentry for the week his final act before parting was to go out into the Lord's fields and play with increased vigour for his cattle! We also know from O'Donovan's account that both Tarlach and Donnacha hired to Captain Hart of Doe to play during the summer.

More suitable company for Tarlach would have been Pádraig Pearse. An account in 'An Claidheamh Solais'[33] from 1906 shows that Pearse was in the area to deliver a lecture at Cloch an Fhaoilidh College to be followed by a céilídh. Tarlach regularly played for these gatherings. Pearse was met at Creeslough by a party of students where he was transported by horse and car to Marble Hill. Tarlach sat next to Pearse in the car and played along the journey. They also had a discussion in which he tried to argue that the biblical ancient Methuselah was in fact identical to the Irish legendary, Fionntáin.

Tarlach Mac Suibhne died on July 13th, 1916 at the apparent age of 98 years while his wife, Sarah, died on November 29, 1920, aged 82 years. He is buried against the eastern boundary wall in the old cemetery in Magheragallen, Gweedore where, as individualistic and defiant as he was in life, he remains so in eternal rest - all headstones in this cemetery face the sheltered east while his alone faces oceanwards, to the wind gusting west. His uilleann pipes, fiddle and manuscripts are now in the possession of the 'Donegal Historical Society', and the two instruments are on public display in their museum in the Franciscan Friary, Rossnowlagh.

Interestingly, these pipes strongly reflect the intrigue of their owner. Tarlach led some observers[34] to believe that his pipes or alternatively the chanter[35] came into his possession from the princely O'Neill's of Shane's Castle, County Antrim and were once the possession of Seán a' Díomas himself. The connection with Seán a' Díomas could not have been possible on age grounds alone.

Just as Tarlach himself was gifted by the faeries with music, so too he maintained were his pipes enchanted. Francis O'Neill[36] tells us that when Mac Suibhne arrived in Chicago in 1893, his instrument from age and disuse was entirely unfit for the service required; and had it not been for the kind helpfulness of Seagt. James Early it would have been scarcely possible for him to fulfil his mission. Noting O'Neill's comments, and comparing the pipes in the photographic portrait taken in Chicago[37] with those known to be his, it is certain that the Chicago set were borrowed for the occasion of the photograph. When the set in the portrait is examined and compared with that held by James Early in a picture taken with John McFadden[38], there is a strong similarity in all but the chanters. The chanter held by Tarlach in the Chicago portrait is remarkably like his own, so it would appear that he may have used the body of Early's pipes in conjunction with his own chanter. Short of being able to play his own set this would have been a sensible approach for him to take as he would have had a natural affinity for his own chanter. Again, judging from the length of Early's chanter they would appear to have been a flat set and may well have been pitched in tune with Tarlach's chanter allowing him the full range of use of the instrument.

Photographs of him as a fresh, but mature man and almost certainly pre-dating his trip to America are included in 'Songs of Uladh'[39] as well as The Donegal Annual[40]. In each he is posing with his own set of pipes and the bass drone slide is clearly missing indicating their loss prior to travelling to Chicago. In discussions with Proinsías O Maonaigh, I have come to be convinced of his belief that the loss of the slide may well have given rise to the story recounted from Tarlach in O'Neill[41] where he first encounters the faeries and, in fright, runs home with the parts falling one-by-one off the pipes. Collecting the pieces, he then has to retrace his way to the faerie rath of Gweedore in the morning.

A photo of a much older Tarlach, certainly post-dating his American trip was recently discovered by Belfast fiddler, Andy Dixon, and appears in Ciarán Carson's 'Irish Traditional Music'[42]. In this case, the Píobaire Mór is seated in front of a wall with his warpipes at his side and playing his own set of pipes. This photograph again shows the missing bass drone slide. Tarlach appears to be satisfied enough to pose and most likely play his instrument despite O'Neill's earlier confirmation of their poor state. It is also interesting to note that it was almost certainly this deteriorating set which he used four years after his Chicago journey to play at the Feis Ceoil in Dublin!

Several of the Píobaire Mor's tunes have been passed on to the present generation through the Dohertys, as well as Proinsías O'Maonaigh via his mother. These include *Bean ag Baint Dilsc (The Connachtman's Rambles), Mac Suibhne's Reel, Mac Suibhne's Lament and Mac Suibhne's Jig or Rí na bPíobairí* . The latter is one of three Donegal jigs under this title and refers to Tarlach's status as a piper. It is identical to that recorded by Paddy Glackin along with *Arthur Darley's Jig* otherwise known as *Bruckless Shore.* Sadly, no other information exists about Donnacha and there is only a tune or two associated with his other brother Pádraig as noted in 'Songs of Uladh'.

Other fiddlers of the northwest who have left their mark on the local fiddle tradition include the late Alec Murphy a noted hornpipe player of Maghery, Séamus Mac Fhionnlaigh of Tory Island, Dónal Bhell O Baoill, a noted member of the Mac Grianna family which included writers Seosamh (Máire) and Seán Bán, the latter of whom was also a good fiddler. There was also Jimmy Mhicheál Boyle of the Rosses and Micheál Logue Boyle of Lettermacaward who had some lessons from Neillidh Boyle. Currently Arranmore Island is undergoing a dynamic resurgence in fiddle playing. Islanders actively involved in fiddling in the past were Johnny Gallagher and Anton Frank Gallagher of Aphort, Paddy Dhónail O'Donnell of Labrannagh, as well as the late Féilimí O'Baoill of Laidhb Ghairbh. The late Neil Neddy Bhain of Maghery returned from America during the Depression years and re-established himself as a major player for house-dances. Neil Duffy of Meenacarn, Lettermacaward was also a well known player and died in his seventies in the 1960s. His son Patrick still lives in the family home and plays the fiddle. Lastly, the late Patrick Bonnar, of Doochary, was the main player for house dances in and around that village.

REFERENCES

1 Arthur O'Neill. *Memoirs of Arthur O'Neill in Annals of the Irish Harpers,* Charlotte Milligan Fox, John Murray, London, 1911, pp 150-151.

2 Mici Mac Gabhann. *Rotha Mór an tSaoil* (ed. Seán O hEochaidh), Foilseacháin Naisiúnta Tta., Baile Átha Cliath, 1959, pp. 89 - 97.

3 Undated, in papers of the *Cairdeas na bhFidléirí collection,* Gleann Cholm Cille.

4 *The Moving Clouds, The Enchanted Music of Ireland,* Folktracks Cassettes, FSA-60-170.

5 Major-General Joseph A. Sweeney. *Donegal and the War of Independence. The Capuchian Annual,* 1970, p 428.Sg31

6 Op. Cit. Capuchian Annual

7 *Amhráin Chúige Uladh.* Gilbert Dalton, Skerries, County Dublin, 1977 (reprint of 1927 edition with additional research by the new editor - Colm O Baoill).

8 J. N. Hamilton. *The Irish of Tory Island.* Institute of Irish Studies, Queens' University, Belfast, 1974.

9 *The Moving Clouds,* op. cit.

10 Undated, in papers of the *Cairdeas na bhFidléirí collection,* Gleann Cholm Cille.

11 Undated, in papers of the *Cairdeas na bhFidléirí collection,* Gleann Cholm Cille.

12 *The Moving Clouds,* op.cit.

13 *Irish Press,* August 8th, 1932.

14 Undated, in papers of the Cairdeas na bhFidléirí collection, Gleann Cholm Cille.

15 Séamus Ennis radio script, Irish Folklore Commission Collection, UCG.

16 Danny O'Donnell, pers. comm., 21/1/93

17 Michael O'Riordan. *Connolly Column.* New Books, Dublin, 1979. pp. 73, 162.

18 Breandán Breathnach. *Ceol Rince na hÉireann Cuid a Do.* Oifig an tSolatháir, Baile Átha Cliath, 1976.

19 Proinnsías O Gallchóbhair. *The History of Landlordism in Donegal.* The Donegal Democrat, Ballyshannon, 1975 p.187.

20 John O' Donovan. *Ordinance Survey Letters.* Fr. Micheál Flanagan (ed.), Bray, 1927, pp 29-30.

21 Anon. *Irish Weekly Times.* April 24,1909.

22 Rev. C.P. Meehan. *The Fate and Fortunes of the Earls of Tyrone and Tyrconnell.* Dublin, 1886, p. 371.

23 Francis O'Neill. *Irish Minstrels and Musicians.* EP Publishers, Yorkshire, 1973 (facsimile reprint) pp. 289 - 295.

24 Anon. *Irish Weekly Times.* April 24,1909, Op. Cit.

25 Seán O Gallchóir. *Tarlach Mac Suibhne, An Píobaire Mór.* The Donegal Annual, 1979, pp 245-252.

26 Francis O'Neill. *Irish Minstrels and Musicians*. Op. Cit.

27 Francis O'Neill. *Irish Music - a Fascinating Hobby*. Norwood, Darby Pa., 1973 (facsimile reprint).

28 Pat Mitchell and Jackie Small. *The Piping of Patsy Touhy*. Na Píobairí Uilleann, Dublin, 1986.

29 Dónall P. O Baoill. *Seanchas agus Dinnseanchas i nGaoth Dóbhair*. Scathalan, Irish Chumann Stair agus Seanchais Ghaoth Dóbhair, Uimhir 3, pp 61-62.

30 Róise Rua Nic Ghríanna. *Róise Rua*. (Pádraig Ua Cnáimhsi, eagarthóir), Sairséal - O Marcaigh, Baile Átha Cliath, 1985.

31 Pádraig Mac Sheáin. *Seanachas fa Chlann tSuibhne agus fa Tharlach Mac Suibhne, An Píobaire Mór*. Bealoideas, Baile Átha Cliath. 1964, pp. 71-84.

32 Seán Bán Mac Meanman. *Eibhlín Ní Bhrían agus an Chéad Saighdiúir Dúbh*, in *An Chéad Mham*, Coiscéim, Baile Átha Cliath, 1990, pp.151 - 163.

33 Anon. *An Claidheamh Solais*. Oct. 6th, 1906.

34 Matthew O'Flanagan. *Turlough MacSweeney - the Celebrated Piper*. *The Evening Telegraph*. October 18th, 1915.

35 Pádraig Mac Sheáin. Op. Cit.

36 Francis O'Neill. *Irish Minstrels and Musicians*. Op. Cit.

37 Francis O'Neill. *Irish Minstrels and Musicians*. Op. Cit. p. 291.

38 Francis O'Neill, *Irish Minstrels and Musicians*. Op. cit. p. 309.

39 Pádraig Mac Aodh O Neill and Seosamh Mac Cathmhaoil. *Songs of Uladh*. Belfast, 1904, p. 15.

40 *Donegal Annual*, Letterkenny, 1977.

41 Francis O'Neill. *Irish Minstrels and Musicians*. Op. cit., pp. 289 - 290.

42 Ciarán Carson. *Irish Traditional Music*. Appletree Press, Belfast. 1986, p. 6.

CHAPTER EIGHT

NORTH DONEGAL

The northern portion of the county can be generally considered as being comprised of that area west of Lough Swilly to the Derryveagh Mountains and Glenna River and between the sea to the north and a line connecting Letterkenny and Dungloe to the south. Within this district lies the Horn Head, Rosguill and Fanad peninsulas, and amongst others, the coastal towns of Gortahork, Falcarragh, Dunfanaghy and Creeslough.

As we have already noted in Chapter Five, a great deal of information on the fiddlers of this area arose from the work at the start of this century by the members of The Irish Folk Song Society, London through its associated Journal of the same title. Unlike the majority of the collectors in the first two decades of this century who focused their activities on Munster and Connacht, there was a good representation of Ulster material in the London society's efforts, particularly from Pádraig Mac Aodh O'Neill (sometimes writing under an English form of his name, Herbert Hughes) and Charlotte Milligan Fox of Omagh, County Tyrone. Through their work we are introduced to several fiddlers from this area who, without the accounts in the 'Journal of the Irish Folk Song Society, London' and 'Songs of Uladh', would almost certainly have gone unrecorded.

PROINSEAS Mac SUIBHNE

The most noted player of the area at the turn of the century would almost certainly have been Mac Aodh O Neill's main source, Proinseas Mac Suibhne (sometimes referred to in an English form of his name, Frank Sweeney). He would appear to have been a native of Fawans, Kilmacrennan where Mac Aodh O Neill notes his mother, Cáit (Ní Dúbhthaigh), and sister, Cáitlín, both noted singers, were living. Mac Suibhne made a conscious effort over the years to meet the older players of his locality and learn their versions of tunes. Judging by some of the ages of his sources, it would appear that much of what he contributed to Mac Aodh O Neill's collecting originated from the first quarter of the last century and probably before that Mac Aodh O'Neill describes him as follows[1]:

> Proinseas Mac Suibhne, farmer, fidiler and philomath (he was also the headmaster of the National School at Losaid, Gartan) - a clansman of the mic Suibhne of Fanad. To Proinseas is due much credit for his efforts to obtain and preserve all the tunes known in his locality. He has done this for years past in his leisure hours, often procuring other airs unfamiliar in his own parish from wandering musicians; and with a natural talent for music and an exceptionally retentive memory (which through continued practice he has cultivated to a high degree), he has been able to learn by heart hundreds of different melodies - principally the old dance music of the country. This he has accomplished without any knowledge whatever of the science of modern music. Many of the tunes thus learned he has heard played or sung by older musicians, who have since died; and not a few of these tunes are unknown at the present time to the younger folks living in the actual townlands from which they were obtained. The old music was fast dying out - music, indeed, it could be called, of a bygone generation. From him I took down nearly half of what appears in this book...

Through Mac Suibhne's playing and Mac Aodh O'Neill's astuteness in ensuring he recorded their sources, we are further introduced to other important fiddlers of the locality. We learn of Seán Mac Giolla Carr of Fanad, who died just prior to 1903 having lived well into his eighties. He had given Mac Suibhne *March of the Clan Suibhne* and on the basis of the transcription, both Proinseas and Mac Giolla Carr were familiar with piping imitation. In Proinseas Mac Suibhne's folk account of the origin of the *Fairy Reel* we are told of the existence of a good fiddler, Mac Fhionnlaoich, from Falcarragh.

Mac Suibhne also noted that he had learned from Nabla Ní hAnluain, a fiddler, who was then quite elderly and living in the workhouse at Dunfanaghy having been evicted from the Olphert Estate. Dónal An Taillúir Mór Mac Lochlainn is another fiddler who supplied tunes to Mac Suibhne and from whom Mac Aodh O'Neill collected directly. He was elderly at the time of the collector's visit in 1904 and had himself learned one of the tunes some forty years previously from Séamus O Dómhnaill, then an old fiddler, from Cluain Cille, Tearmon.

Séamus Óg Mac Fhionnlaoich, a young boatman and fiddler from Port na Bláth, supplied Mac Aodh O'Neill with an old air from the area while taking him on a visit to Tory Island aboard the Saint Ambrose. Robert Sproule, a fiddler from Dromore, Kilmacrennan, gave Mac Suibhne a jig, *The Humours of Baile na Féad*. Other fiddlers who supplied Mac Suibhne with tunes were Aodh Gordon, an old fiddler from Ceis Lionain, Kilmacrennan who could play in position; Antoine Mac Suibhne, a young player also capable of position playing, from near Bearnas Gap, Tearmon, and Uilliam Ua Curthainn an old fiddler from Glenswilly.

We also learn of Dómhnaill O hArcáin of Ramelton who played the piping air *Céad Bliadhain ó Shin*. He learned this from Pádraig Mac Suibhne, the fiddler and brother of Tarlach, 'An Píobaire Mór', who had died prior to 1903. The tune appears to form the introduction to a longer descriptive piece *Brian Boroimhe's March.* Lastly from this body of work we learn of the existence of Dómhnaill O Gallchóbhair, the Dark Fiddler of Fanad.

NEIL AND JOHN COLL

One of the local fiddlers to have excelled in the second half of the last century was Neil Coll. He became famous throughout the locality earning his living by combining farming, fiddle playing and as master of a number of dancing schools in his district.

The story which recalls Neil Coll's most prestigious performance relates to the wedding of one of the local gentry. Sir Peter Bam was the local landlord and lived in what is now Ards Friary. Bam apparently married late in life a woman many years his junior. To celebrate his good fortune he hosted a massive post-nuptual reception to which one member from each house in the locality was invited. This event was attended by Hannah Ward the mother of Danny McCarry, (the well known Donegal fiddler, now in his late seventies), when she was a young woman. She held vivid memories of the occasion and often recalled it to Danny. The story, in Danny's words is as follows:

> He (Bam) was so delighted to get a younger woman that he asked all the tenants. The two of them (Danny's parents) couldn't go so me mother opted to go... There was a big room especially for the guests, the upper-crust crowd I suppose you'd call them. And the crowd not so important were back in a big room by themselves. So, the Belfast

> fiddler was playing away for the upper crust and Neil Coll was playing for the ordinary people. After a while, some of them (the upper crust) maybe had a better ear for music than they got credit for. Some of the big fellows listened in and they came into the room. And then a few got curious to see what was happening and they came in. And the next thing, the whole lot came in. So the big fellow himself wondered what was happening and he had to investigate. And he came in and listened to the fiddler Neil Coll a while. And he said 'play me the *Flowers of Edinburgh*' and he danced it! And when he finished dancing it he put his hand in his pocket and he gave him a guinea. I suppose it would be a gold guinea. And he said 'Here, you're the best fiddler in the British Isles', he said. Me mother saw that happening and that's no hearsay you know.

Neil Coll died towards the end of the last century. His fiddling prowess, however, was passed onto his son. John Coll took on the mantle of the first choice dance player and fiddle teacher as well dancing master in the area. John's life-span overlapped with Andy McIntyre and the two struck up a close friendship with Andy noting down some of his tunes.

An anonymous article in 'The Tírchonaill Tribune' recalls some of the circumstances of John Coll's funeral and typifies the admiration in which he was held by his friends, Andy McIntyre, in particular. The following is an extract from the article[2]:

> Neil Coll had a son called Johnnie, a noted fiddler and he taught the fiddle to many of the young men of the parish. When he died, some of his past pupils bought a wreath to place on his grave in Doe. Andrew McIntyre, another noted fiddler and poet, paid a poetic tribute to him and attached it to the wreath. It went:
>
> *Here's from one who strove to drink*
> *from the sweet sounds you shed*
> *with tender care this votive verse*
> *on thy lone grave is laid*
> *but if 'midst all through cold neglect*
> *remembrance should pall*
> *I weave this chaplet to enshrine*
> *your memory Johnnie Coll*

If Proinseas Mac Suibhne was Pádraig Mac Aodh O'Neill's philomath, Andrew McIntyre (also known as Alastruim Mac Antire in 'Songs of Uladh' and Andy MacAteer as he is still sometimes referred to in his native area), was to prove his polymath. He was born in 1877 at Ballymore, half-way between Creeslough and Dunfanaghy. His mother, Letitia Collins, came from a very musical family and she particularly encouraged Andy's interest in music. He attended primary school in Ballymore where he was noted as a very attentive student. On leaving school, he served for eleven years as an auxiliary postman at the Derryreel Post Office. During this time he engaged in a relentless pursuit of self-education. Indeed, during this period he often placed a candle on his chest to permit him to read in bed well into the night. This practice resulted in a severe burning when he fell asleep without quenching the candle.

In early 1910 he returned home to work on the farm and in September of 1914 was appointed Master of Dunfanaghy Workhouse where he may have become acquainted with the fiddler, Nabla Ní hAnluain, noted above. On October 31 1916 he married Mary Martin, of Derryreel, whom he had met during his days at the post office and who also worked with him in Dunfanaghy. Mary was a native Irish speaker and Andy's familiarity with the local dialect and his passion for languages led him to become fluent in the language. Irish was the commonly used language between Mary and Andy. The Dunfanaghy Workhouse closed on March 31st, 1917 and he took up similar duties in the workhouse in Milford. In 1918 he accepted the post of School Attendance Officer of Clondehorkey Parish.

At the end of 1921 McIntyre's big break came when he secured the post of Assistant Librarian under Sam Maguire (not of footballing fame) who, through the foresight of the Carnegie Institute, held the post of County Donegal's Head Librarian. In March 1923 Maguire moved onto Coleraine and the post of County Librarian was filled by his assistant, Andy. Shortly after his promotion Andy was summoned by the Carnegie Trust to attend a librarians' conference in London. He crossed from Belfast to Liverpool and onto his final destination. This trip is briefly recalled in Frank

O'Connor's autobiography[3]. During the journey Andy remained in close contact with O'Connor arising from the latter's ability to speak Irish. Despite some reservations about him, O'Connor, on the basis of his meeting with McIntyre concluded "Ulstermen are the nicest people in the world except in the matter of religion and dialect."

During his early period in the library he came into contact with the Englishman, Arthur Fowweather, who had come to teach in the Prior School, Lifford, in the 1920s. In his memoir, 'One Small Head', Fowweather admiringly recalls Andy McIntyre as follows[4]:

> My brief experience in the North West of Ireland had already loaded my eager mind with numberless impressions of the rich variety of individuals to be met with there, but through the Carnegie Library I met one of the most memorable of them all. When Maguire's work assumed such proportions that Dublin headquarters decided he needed an Assistant Librarian for Donegal, Andrew McIntyre arrived from remote Dunfanaghy on the northern coast to fill the position. One day I wandered in customary fashion into the Library after school and met him. Anything less like the conventional Librarian I could not hope to imagine.
>
> Andy McIntyre was a shortish man with sparse sandy hair and pebble glasses. He was around forty and dressed in rough home-spun tweed. He was excessively short-sighted and inelegant to a degree. Andy was a mountainy man who was almost a caricature of the ignorant Irish peasant. It did not take me long, even at the first meeting, to find that here was a man with startling breadth of scholarship and a knowledge of and reverence for English Literature surpassing anyone I had ever known. Later I found that he was almost entirely self-educated. A few years at the National School constituted his formal education. Hugh Law, a member of the Westminster Parliament, had discovered the boy's intellect and had given him the free run of his extensive library in the Old Rectory at Dunfanaghy. Andy read in Mr. Law's house and took more books home to read. There he had often only the help of a rush light as lamp or candles were out of his family's financial reach, and he had ruined his eyesight with long night hours of reading. However he had been enabled to be a postman, then Workhouse Master in Dunfanaghy and now, an answer to a prayer if ever I knew one, a real curator of books and book learning. Now he could live all the time with his beloved literature, have a nice little house in the Barrack Square, Lifford, with his adored wife, and browse among books to his heart's content. If Maguire was the administrator, then McIntyre was the scholar. He had something that meant more than his own satisfaction to him, for now he had a chance to bring books and

learning to his own dear Donegal. He was the kindest and gentlest of men who opened further the eyes of at least one lad (Fowweather) to the richness and beauty of English literature, and who, without realising it, taught that same young fellow something of humanity as well.

During this time Andy became very close friends with Peadar O'Donnell who was also living in Lifford. While their similar interests in literature would have, no doubt, brought them together, O'Donnell's exposure to and appreciation for Donegal fiddle music through his own family would further facilitate a kinship. McIntyre took a strong interest in cultural matters and was active in participating and playing at Gaelic League functions in Lifford.

His writing was also running at a high level of output and his interest in poetry led him to become acquainted with George Russell (AE), Percy French, G.K. Chesterton, Stephen Gwynn, W.B. Yeats and Frank Cousins. He continued in his capacity as County Librarian until his retirement in 1948. Twenty years later he would be succeeded by his son, Eddie, making this the only instance of both a father and son having held such a post in Ireland.

Concerning his musical exploits, Andy was in his playing heyday in the first decade of this century where he was extremely popular for providing music for house dances and convoys. He was not adverse to turning his literary talents to writing lyrics. As we find in 'Songs of Uladh'[5], he composed the words to the song *The Maids of Bearnas Gap* and offered an alternative version of the air from that which Mac Aodh O'Neill obtained from Cáit Ní Suibhne. Like his acquaintance, Proinsias Mac Suibhne, Andy made a concerted effort to learn and collect tunes from older players within his locality. No doubt through his familiarity with Pádraig Mac Aodh O'Neill, he saw the 'Journal of Irish Folk Song, London' as an outlet for his own collecting pursuits and contributed a brief entry in 1905[6]. In this material we can see he included a piece from his close friend, John Coll, as well as one from Pádraic Glacan whom he described as a well-known fiddler from his own parish having flourished in the 1870's. In a 1904[7] volume of the 'Journal of the Irish Folk Song Society, London', Mac Aodh O'Neill (writing as Herbert Hughes) includes a reel from Andy entitled *The Letterkenny Frolic* which he notes was very well known all over Donegal. This tune is hardly played today.

Andy spent thirty-six years in Lifford but his heart never left

Ballymore. Summers saw the family being relocated to the area for their holidays and Andy's search for old musical outlets. His musical stimulation received a significant boost during the Thirties with the emergence of the broadcasting career of Neillidh Boyle. The latter would often travel to Dublin by train and this meant a round trip from Strabane. Neillidh would often stay in Lifford with Andy the night before departure and also on returning from Dublin. These meetings inevitably resulted in night-long sessions. Such visits were seen as a testimony to Andy's stature as a player since around this time Neillidh was at the height of his powers and was known to have a very low tolerance for anyone other than what he considered an outstanding player.

Likewise at this time, Andy became friendly with the Ballyshannon fiddler, Harry Carey, who was then working as an agricultural adviser based in the County Offices in Lifford. A photograph of Andy has survived and a copy was recently donated to the Donegal Fiddle Archive in Glencolumcille by Harry Carey's daughter, Eithne Vallely. It is a group photograph of the local Gaelic League members taken outside the Lifford Courthouse. McIntyre is at the extreme left of the picture with his fiddle under his right arm. He is a well-dressed, portly man with a moustache, conforming very closely to the description recorded by Fowweather.

Andy's frequency of playing appears to have decreased approaching the Forties with a corresponding interest in sourcing his music from the wireless. Following the radio coverage of the Eucharistic Congress he became fascinated by the medium and read books on the theory of radio transmission and reception. Based on this, he was able to make a crystal set which was one of the first in the Lifford area. He regularly listened to BBC Northern Ireland and had little appreciation for the material broadcast by Radio Éireann. He enthusiastically bought commercial recordings from across the spectrum of musical tastes amassing a collection of approximately three hundred discs. By the Fifties, his fiddling dropped off considerably and following the death of his wife in 1957 he stopped playing. Andy loved literature and clearly revelled in his work but there is no doubt that his passion lay with traditional fiddle music and particular, that music of his own Ballymore area. Andy McIntyre died in 1959 and is buried in Lifford.

THE EXTENDED McCARRY FAMILY

Michael McCarry was born in the latter half of the last century in Kildarragh, at the foot of Muckish Mountain. He was a competent fiddler despite being hindered by an persistent whitlow in the index finger of his left hand. This condition had the effect of reducing his playing greatly and he ultimately lost power in the finger. For a while he continued on and played with three fingers. Michael worked most of his adult life as a migrant labourer often spending long spells away from home in Scotland. While away, he maintained an interest in the fiddle and brought home many Scottish tunes with him resulting in a considerable mixed repertoire of old local and Scottish pieces. Michael's younger brother, Neil, also played and is known to have lived out his adult life in Ballybofey.

Michael married Hannah Ward of Magherameena, Dunfanaghy who played melodeon. Her father Charles was also a fiddler. Her brother, Manus, was an excellent fiddler and played professionally in Scotland before emigrating to America. Another brother, Daniel, was exceedingly good and a very regular visitor to his sister's house. Three of his most requested tunes were *The Scholar, The Salamanca* and a very nice three part version of the hornpipe now usually called *The Black Swan.*

Michael and Hannah McCarry had seven sons and four daughters at the family home in Kildarragh. Of these children, Patrick, Johnnie, Mick, Francis, Rita and Theresa became proficient fiddlers before moving away from the area. Another son, Danny, who has continued to farm at the family home, however, excelled in playing.

Danny McCarry was born at Kildarragh on June 10th 1917. He cannot remember when he first started to learn the fiddle but it is certain he was making attempts to play before he was ten years. His uncle, Daniel Ward, after whom he was named, had a very significant early impact on Danny's playing. He was very impressed by Daniel and strove to be able to play to his uncle's standard. It was not too long before he surpassed him and was receiving significant recognition for his prowess.

His passion for music seemed all-consuming and he can remember often walking away in the middle of ploughing to check a variation in a tune on the fiddle. Every moment of his spare time was devoted to either playing or teaching himself to read music and this drive resulted in him absorbing a huge repertoire from his father, his uncle Daniel as well as the majority of other local players. Danny remembers the areas old repertoire was dominated by highlands and barndances. *The Old Grey Goose* was always played for the cotillon and *The Petticoats Loose,* which he learned from his father, was always played for the Irish National Reel.

Fameoutside his locality came when he travelled to compete at Feis Clonliegh in Lifford which he easily won, defeating Andy McIntyre who gave a great rendering of *The Daisy Fields.* Andy took pleasure in the success of someone from his home place, ensuring that a good session and abundant hospitality were shown to what was obviously a major emerging talent. Following this and other successes in competitions and public performances, Danny was prevailed upon to broadcast and his reputation was further enhanced.

By the Forties and into the Fifties, his mentor, Daniel Ward, had come to be greatly impressed by the playing of Seán McGuire. He strongly urged Danny to study McGuire's playing as well as that of the recordings of Michael Coleman. Danny absorbed these influences readily and adapted what he had learned to fit in with his own style of playing.

During the early Sixties he travelled to Glasgow where a friend took him to meet Neillidh Boyle shortly before his death. Neillidh played a couple of hornpipes in flat keys for Danny hoping to impress him. Danny replied with a number of similarly challenging tunes and the two fiddlers struck up a mutual respect. Danny also remembers meeting Frank Cassidy when he travelled to Carrick to play in Frank's dance hall. Frank was very impressed with Danny's playing and requested him to play some tunes. Danny obliged and Frank returned the compliment by playing *The Mathematician* hornpipe brilliantly. Frank was very pleasant and took time to teach Danny some technique, stressing that all bowing of triplets should be staccato. He further demonstrated this by teaching him *Blanche's Hornpipe.* Later in life, he briefly met John Doherty and John Gallagher of Ardara both of whose playing particularly impressed him.

Today, Danny McCarry is one of Donegal's most astounding fiddle exponents. In his late seventies and despite the effects of a hard mountain sheep-farming life which has left his hands looking ravaged he plays in a style which may be temptingly compared with Neillidh Boyle. His fiddling is very rapid with an overt, aggressive, attacking vigour. The demands of such a style are considerable, yet so mastered are his bowing and fingering techniques that Danny is ever able for the challenge. His comprehensive skills open the full range of the fiddle and he readily avails of both positions as well as playing in flat keys. Danny McCarry, almost in defiance of his age and the demands of his hardworking life, may well be viewed as the embodiment of all that is good in Donegal fiddling. With his single-minded determined playing he maintains a deep respect for the repertoire in which he has become a consummate master.

An older local player who Danny remembers from his youth was Hughie Harkin who played on a copy of a Stainer fiddle which was very much sought after by the local players as its tone was lovely. Danny paid close attention to him when he was very young as he was impressed by his playing. Hughie was very humorous and good natured, noted for his rendering of *The Templehouse Reel.* He regularly played for house dances with Andy McIntyre. A very elderly player was nearby neighbour Danny Sweeney. As a very young man Danny first met him when going out to play with mummers. Sweeney was particularly enamoured with Danny's setting of *The Rights of Man.* Lastly, other older players Danny remembers from his youth were Jimmy Doherty from Kilmacrennan and Frank McHugh.

THE MILLER FAMILY

The Millers were travellers who came to settle in Dunfanaghy. Joe Miller, the father, was a steady player who was very enthusiastic about fiddling and encouraged it amongst his sons. Kevin eventually grew up like his father becoming a good player and having a great interest in playing. He actively sought out tunes from the players of the district. It was another son, Eugene, however, who became the most accomplished player in the family. Eugene died as a young man from pulmonary tuberculosis. A limited number of tunes from Eugene were fortunately recorded shortly before his death by Danny Doherty and these reveal a player of accomplished skill. Stylistically, they show a mixture of influences from both Michael Coleman and Seán McGuire, both of whose recordings he studied.

ANDY KING

Andy was a contemporary of Eugene King and both regularly played in and around Dunfanaghy. He was well known to Danny McCarry who considers him a good player and representative of the older style of fiddlers from the district. Andy was likewise recorded around the same time as Eugene. These few tunes again confirm a player of great skill with a less ornamented, more direct style.

Lastly, a fiddler who was popular for house dances around the Falcarragh-Gortahork area was Dan Doherty. Dan was an enthusiastic player and knew Danny McCarry as well as the fiddlers in both the King and Miller families. His repertoire was strongly based on his house dance tunes and have been passed down to the current generation by his son Danny Doherty who is an active melodeon player in Gortahork. Dan died recently having lived well into his eighties.

CARRIGART FIDDLERS

Until recently a significant body of fiddlers lived around Carrigart and following the decline in house dances centered their activities on the Glen Bar. Charlie Bayers, who died about five years ago, from the High Glen had a great partnersip with Patrick Boyce of Carrick, Carrigart. Other players included Hughie Duffy of Carrick, JohnMcBride of Gleneheragh, brothers Jim and Ned Duffy of Glencheo, Manus Herrity of Downings, Mandy Gallagher of Tullagh and Jimmy Mhíchéal O'Donnell of Derryscleigh. Tom O'Donnell of Glenmeenagh is remembered as a particularly good fiddler. The tradition is kept alive today in the playing of Andy McFadden of Devlinreagh, Carrigart.

REFERENCES

1 Pádraig Mac Aodh O'Neill and Seosamh Mac Cathmhaoil. *Songs of Uladh*. William Mullan Publishers, Belfast,1904.
2 Anon. *The Duck Street Boys From Cashelmore*. The Tírchonaill Tribune. August, 1993.
3 Frank O'Connor. *My Father's Son*. Blackstaff Press, Belfast, 1994, pp 17-19.
4 Arthur Fowweather. *One Small Head*. Down Recorder, Downpatrick, 1980, pp 96 - 97.
5 Pádraig Mac Aodh O'Neill and Seosamh Mac Cathmhaoil. Op Cit., p 48.
6 Andrew McIntyre, *Journal of the Irish Folk Song Society*, London, Volume 2, nos. 1+2, 1905, p 13.
7 Herbert Hughes, *Journal of the Irish Folk Song Society*, London, Volume 1, nos. 2+3, 1904.

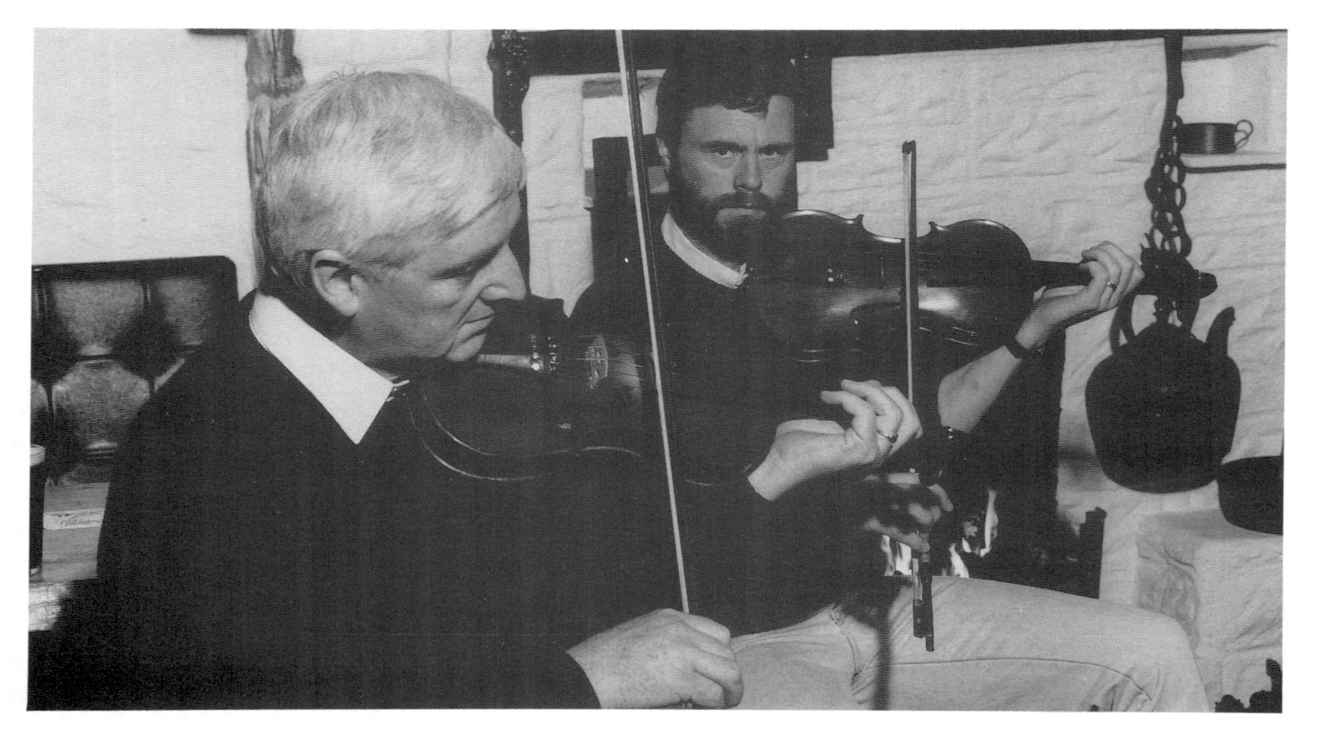

Tom Mac Intyre left and Caoimhín Mac Aoidh, Ballyshannon

Tom Glackin of Maghery
(photo courtesy of Glackin family)

Kathleen McGinley of Raphoe playing at home in November, 1993

Paddy (the elder) Kelly – 'The Man From Bundoran'– winner of the first All Ireland senior fiddle competition.

Jimmy Lyons of Teelin

Attendants at the first annual meeting of Cairdeas na bhFidléirí in the Highlands Hotel, Glenties, October, 1983

Pupils of the first annual meeting of Cairdeas na bhFidléirí Summer School, in the Highlands Hotel, Glenties, August , 1986 (photo courtesy of Frankie Kennedy)

Columba Campbell and his father Peter, at home in the Croaghs

Columba Mac a'Bhaird playing a tin fiddle made by Mickey Doherty

Vincent Campbell of the Croaghs

Presentations of water-colours by Máiréad Ní Mhaonaigh at the Annual Meeting of Cairdeas in Glenties 1991, in honour of the contribution to Donegal music of Tommy Peoples and the late Tom Glackin. From Left: Tommy Peoples, Kevin Glackin, Caoimhín Mac Aoidh, Paddy & Seamus Glackin.

CHAPTER NINE

INISHOWEN

Inishowen is probably the most easily identified cultural catchment in Donegal. Being a peninsula only its southern extent needs marking. This is usually taken along an east-west line passing through Newtoncunningham and Derry. The heart of Inishowen is dominated by beautiful, rugged mountains with most of the population congregating in the well known towns near the coastline.

One of the best insights to fiddle playing in Inishowen in past generations is probably afforded from accounts appearing in 'The Last of the Name'[1], the autobiography of Charles McGlinchey, a native of Meentiagh Glen between Buncrana and Ballyliffin, who came to settle in nearby Cluainte, Clonmany. McGlinchey, a weaver and tailor, was born in 1861 and lived into his early nineties. In the years immediately prior to McGlinchey's death in 1954, Patrick Kavanagh, the principal teacher of Gaddyduff National School, was a regular visitor to his home transcribing the accounts of his life and his community's history. This work is a significant one as it affords us an accurate account of the lifestyles and customs of the people of Inishowen which extend well into the last century when McGlinchey's inherited memories are taken into account. Concerning his ability to put an Inishowen perspective on matters, it is well worth noting that he only left the peninsula twice during his lifetime; once while in his early thirties to spend a season of farm labouring in Scotland and secondly to attend the Eucharistic Congress in Dublin in 1932.

A very good indication of the role of music at lint production gatherings is given by McGlinchey in the following passage. It is interesting to note how similar this these circumstances are to those known to Francie Dearg O'Byrne in Kilcar. McGlinchey recounts[2]:

"The people long ago had gatherings for a night's scutching or cloving of lint. There would be twenty or thirty at a gathering. They did the work in the barn or some outhouse, and other times in the kitchen. They had a dance after the work was done. Someone would be got to play the fiddle, or two or three women would lilt. They had gatherings, too, for making quilts... At a lint cloving or gathering like that, some people could take right music out of a reed by putting a piece of paper on it and blowing on the paper. Children do it yet with a coarse comb".

He goes on to recall the atmosphere of a house dance and introduce the fiddler, Neil McColgan, who based on the account given, must have been one of the formidable players of his day in Inishowen. Like Patrick McGill's fiddler, Willie The Duck[3], and obviously with much greater success, Neil provided entertainment on the somewhat lucrative ferries to Scotland. Furthermore, judging from his description it would appear that there were more fiddlers in the extended McColgan family than Neil [4]:

"At Christmas-time people went to visit their relations if they lived a bit away and would maybe stay the night. If it was a girl who was visiting, the people of the house got up a dance, and all the neighbours attended. There was always great run on a strange girl about a place. For the dance somebody was got to play the fiddle. Neil McColgan was the best fiddler in my time. He was a blind fiddler from Ballyliffin and was in great demand for all the dances. They made a collection at the dance of a penny a head, and that was how he made his living. He played on the boat, too, from Derry to Moville for people who would be out pleasuring on the Foyle in the summer-time. And he used to play on the boats too going to Scotland. He got his keep on board the boats, too, for he would draw trade to whatever boat he was on.

Neil was a noted singer and poet too. He would not sing sitting down. He always got to the middle of the floor and put the fiddle under his chin and sang the song and played at the same time. One night before Christmas in the year 1852 he was going in Urris and arranged with two lads by the name of Friel to go across with them to Fanad next day. But Neil slept in and they went on without him. Coming back again they brought over a young man, Hugh Friel, from Fanad, who had come over to see a girl he had married a short time before. She was the name of McDonald, and was called the "Star of Dunaff". The boat struck a rock and all three were drowned. Neil McColgan made a song about the drowning - *In the year of 52, in the month of December.* I have heard it sung many a time but I haven't the words of it. The McColgans were a breed of people there was great music in. Music is a thing that follows tribes of people.

Another fiddler is noted in McGlinchey's succession list of his parish's priests. Father William O'Donnell served as curate there between 1841 and 1868. During this period McGlinchey maintained[5]:

> All the noted singers were in the choir at that time. They had no harmonium and the music they had was on fiddles and flutes ... Billy Andy Porter of Gaddyduff used to play the fiddle.

PAT MULHEARNE

Without a doubt today's most important link in the Inishowen fiddle tradition is provided by the playing and memories of Pat Mulhearne of Falask, Drumfries. Pat was born there on Saint Patrick's Day, 1900 and now in his ninety-fourth year is still a very lively player. Neither of his parents played the fiddle but both were good singers. Their cottage was a well known céilídhing house with singers, musicians and dancers calling nightly to pass the evenings. In this setting, Pat was exposed to local music from his earliest years. By the age of ten he was anxious to play music and recalls seeing Paddy McDonald playing on the street during the fair day in Buncrana. Paddy regularly played fiddle on the streets in Derry and the towns of Inishowen. He also played at emigration boats on the quayside in Derry. The meeting at Buncrana fair seemed to have a great effect on Pat and consolidated his desire to play the fiddle. He can remember that throughout the day he followed McDonald from one place to another to hear as much of the music as he could. Soon after this event Pat started to play.

His early efforts were largely through teaching himself and he remembers that fiddlers were not too common at this time. By his early teens, however, he was well able to play for dancing in his house and had become recognised by his neighbours as a fiddler. Around the age of sixteen he was referred to Johnnie Graham for lessons. Johnnie did not come from Donegal but was a native of Ulster and born around 1876. He worked on the local railway and at the time of first coming into contact with Pat lived in the station house in Drumfries. Pat regarded him as a player of great note with a very friendly personality. He was also a talented teacher who managed to bring Pat along very quickly on the fiddle. During these lessons he learned to read music and was soon availing of tunes through O'Neill's works as well as studying technique by reading violin tutors.

Pat continued to play for gatherings in his parents' house where the dances were mostly Lancers, for which the jig *Father O'Flynn* was played, highlands, polkas, hornpipes and quadrilles. Being raised in a céilídh house in the early decades of this century has bestowed on Pat a wide store of tunes, songs and recitations which were the mainstay of home entertainment in this setting.

By his early twenties Pat had joined a small group of players to provide music for céilídhs which were then moving from the houses to some of the larger local halls. Transport at this time for most people was restricted still to walking or bicycles. As a result, the group did not travel widely but the few large céilídhs each year were big events and playing for them generated great excitement. The mainstay of the group at this time was Pat Mulhearne and Joe McLaughlin, an accordion player from Cleenagh, Ballymagan.

Pat continued to play for dancing mainly during his twenties and thirties though this activity extended on well into his fifties. By his early thirties Pat had become an extremely accomplished player whose recognition as such was increasing. During this decade he was invited to play on the national radio station. He broadcast from both the Dublin and Athlone transmitters as well as the BBC in Belfast. He also started to play in regular local competitions such as the Derry, Carndonagh and Letterkenny Feiseanna. As a young man he did occasionally travel to Scotland to attend weddings of friends and relations but his stays were always short and he did not meet any Scottish fiddlers.

Pat's playing, even to this day, is typified by an extraordinary control of volume and tone. His technical standard is highly accomplished and his style is marked by a distinctly dotted rhythm. His repertoire is very wide representing four main sources of tunes. First amongst these is his old house dance repertoire which was gathered from his earliest years of playing at home and with Johnnie Graham. The next are his tunes sourced from collections. The third element of his repertoire are tunes which he learned from commercial recordings most notably of James Scott Skinner and Michael Coleman both of whom he admired. Lastly are the more recent acquisitions to his repertoire through his continued participation in the music over the last thirty years. It must be noted that whatever the source of a tune, Pat plays consistently in his own strong style. Having absorbed a tune he places his stylistic stamp on it.

Other fiddlers Pat recalls include his uncle, James McLaughlin who was a good player and in great demand around Buncrana to play for gatherings. Like Paddy McDonald, James commonly played at the quayside in Derry for emigrant ships. McLaughlin had learned from Neil and Pat McKenny of Drumfries who were extremely good players. Another fiddle playing relation of Pat's was his second cousin, Johnnie O'Donnell of Buncrana. Also, Jimmy Durnian of Inch Island was an accomplished fiddler with whom Pat was fond of playing.

DINNY McLAUGHLIN

Pat Mulhearne has played a pivotal role in the fiddle tradition in Inishowen as his excellent playing acted as an inspiration to many of the younger generations aspiring to play. One of his pupils, Dinny McLaughlin, flourished under him and has gone on to greatly foster the growth in playing in the peninsula. Dinny, or Dinny White Harra, as he is locally known due the abundance of McLaughlins in the locality, was born at Shandrum near to Pat's house in Falask. Writing in the local magazine, Inis Eoghain, he described his first meeting with Pat who was coming to play for a gathering in Dinny's father's house and the impression it left on him. At the time of the event Dinny was about six[6]

> My father was busy all evening getting dry clods for the fire. My mother, Mary, was baking and all hands cleaning up the house for this big event. It must have been a summer's evening, for it was still clear when Pat arrived. My father walked up and down the floor for an hour or more waiting on Pat. My brother was the eldest and was questioned many times as to the message he delivered: the day, the date, the time: to make sure that Pat got the proper message. I couldn't help but notice my father pacing the floor and wondered who the man could be that was so important.
>
> Someone at the door said, 'There's Pat coming now.' I rushed to the door to satisfy my curiosity, and there was an ordinary man with a case under his oxter. He was greeted with very friendly hand-shakes from all and seemed a very nice man. All hands spoke to Pat and made him very welcome. He sat on a stool close to the big fire and opened the case and out came the fiddle. I was amazed at its beautiful shape. When he hit the strings with his thumb it seemed like magic. I didn't leave Pat's side during that night. And from then on I was determined to get a fiddle.

Dinny's father, James, was a fiddler as was *his* father before him.

Pre-occupied with running a farm and raising a family, James did not get much time to play and his fiddle fell into disrepair. Dinny's ambition to play continued and at the age of around fourteen he was given the loan of a fiddle during a visit from an old playing partner, Eddie Kavanagh, from Drumfries. Eddie was a regular player who at this time was in his declining years. The next day Dinny attended Pat Mulhearne for lessons. The old céilídh house traditions which were so strong with Pat were obviously passed onto his pupil. Dinny took a great interest in dancing, singing and recitations. More importantly he grew to become a fiddler of considerable skill making at least one solo recording and two others as part of the group Aileach which he founded. During his younger days Dinny struck up a close playing association with the Derry fiddler, Eugene O'Donnell, who subsequently emigrated to Philadelphia.

Dinny re-invested his energies for a considerable number of years in teaching music throughout the peninsula. His excellence as a teacher is confirmed in the output of highly accomplished pupils. These include the late Jimmy McBride, originally from Greysteele, County Derry who had a long association with Inishowen.

JIMMY McBRIDE

Jimmy studied under Dinny for a number of years and even adopted Dinny's technique of grasping the bow by the top of the shaft and with his thumb under the frog. He developed rapidly into a player of great ability and towards the close of his teenage years came distinctly under the influence of the playing of Antrim fiddler Jim McKillop. His reputation grew and he started to receive demands for playing throughout Ireland and Britain. After returning home from a brief spell in England he travelled to play at a function in Raphoe. He died tragically in a car accident returning home. Sadly his great potential and promise were never realised.

CÍARÁN TOURISH

Cíarán Tourish, is now in his late twenties. He started to learn the fiddle at a very early age from Dinny McLaughlin. His father, George, has always been interested in Irish music as is his mother, Rosaleen, who plays the piano. Cíarán improved rapidly as a fiddler. By his earliest teenage years he was highly respected as a player and has been in great demand throughout the county ever since. Trips to the Rosses and Gweedore areas during his formative years played a significant role in his development as it introduced him to a wider circle of players particularly amongst his own age group. During these early years and through to the present he has enjoyed a great playing relationship with Pat Mulhearne whom he views as a player of considerable significance. Towards his late teens he came into contact with the players of central and southwest Donegal such as the Campbells, James Byrne and Con Cassidy. This resulted in him broadening not only his repertoire but also expanding his stylistic influences.

Cíarán has developed into one of Ireland's leading fiddlers. At the time of writing he is living in Dublin and playing professionally with the band Altan. Over the past decade he has continued to improve his playing and has opened himself to a broader range of musical influences. Ciarán has played in numerous band line-ups including Connailigh, The Pyrotechnics and The Gooseberries. He has, however, firmly maintained the central importance of his Donegal background.

Cíarán's style is marked by an extraordinary level of technical accomplishment allowing the most difficult of passages to be executed with ease. His mastery of exciting variation is almost uncanny while his command of reversing has been particularly admired by the older, accomplished generation of fiddlers in the county.

THE HARRIGANS

Róisín and Damian Harrigan from Burnfoot are now in their early twenties and mid-teens respectively. Each started out under the guidance of Dinny McLaughlin and Damian, in particular, was strongly influenced at an early stage by the playing of Tommy Peoples. They have since developed an affinity for the playing style of the southwest of the county. Over the past six years they have formed a strong playing relationship with James Byrne and his influence is clearly evident in their playing. Their repertoire and bowing styles denote their exposure to the playing in the southwest of the county. Their duets are highly intricate and have now become highlights of Donegal fiddle gatherings. Despite their relative youth, their fiddle playing already has a mature, accomplished hallmark. It is certain that Róisín and Damien will contribute to the Donegal fiddle tradition by becoming seminal players for their peers and the next generation.

LIZ DOHERTY

Liz Doherty, also of Buncrana and in her mid-twenties, has occasionally partnered the Harrigans and likewise started out with Dinny McLaughlin. Having grown to become an accomplished player she went on to complete a degree in the Department of Music, University College Cork under the guidance of Micheál O Suilleabháin. She has developed an interest in the related tradition of Cape Breton fiddle playing and lived there briefly. She is now lecturing in music at U.C.C.

THE O'DONNELL'S

The O'Donnell family of Buncrana are noted fiddlers in the peninsula. Johnnie O'Donnell was a near contemporary of Pat Mulhearne and is remembered as having been a good player. He was a mechanic who emigrated for a time to America and eventually came home to Buncrana. After returning he was known locally as Johnnie "Broadway" as he opened the well known "Broadway Ballroom" which was located in what is now the top floor of Hegarty's Furniture shop. With the demise of the showband era in the sixties he closed his business.

His son, P. V. O'Donnell, a contemporary of Dinny McLaughlin, showed great ability on the fiddle from an early age. He has gone on to become a very talented player who prior to emigrating became highly regarded throughout the country. Choosing to follow a career in music he eventually left for North America and is well known in musical circles along the east coast. He currently lives in Canada playing with the band Barley Bree with whom he has recorded. One solo track of his playing is the reel *The Cup of Tea* which gives a good indication of his abilities. P.V. continues to make occasional visits home where he plays with his younger brother, Oliver, also a fiddler.

SÉAMUS GRANT

Séamus Grant from Clonmany is now in his late sixties. For some time now he has been the most influential fiddler in north Inishowen. He is noted particularly for his clear, highly dotted rhythm style of playing which shows very distinct similarities with that of Pat Mulhearne. This common occurrence between two of the more senior players of the area tends to confirm the strength of the Scottish fiddling connection in Inishowen. The strong volume and tone of these players, coupled with a distinct, almost syncopated rhythm, certainly had origins in the seasonal migrations between Inishowen and Scotland.

OTHER INISHOWEN FIDDLERS

Other Inishowen fiddlers include Jimmy Clingan and Peter Clarke who played with the Donagh Dance Band in Carndonagh. Jimmy also played the banjo-mandolin with the band. Fred Anderson of Hollymount, Carndonagh was also a noted fiddler. These three players are documented in photographs appearing in Maura Harkin and Sheila McCarroll's book Carndonagh[7]. John McCracken, who has a particular respect for the Shetland fiddlers also plays and has for years been influenced by Pat Mulhearne.

REFERENCES

1 Charles McGlinchey. *The Last of the Name*. The Blackstaff Press, Belfast, 1986. Patrick Kavanagh (editor).
2 Charles McGlinchey. *The Last of the Name.* Op. Cit. pp 36-37, 40.
3 Patrick McGill. *The Rat Pit.* Brandon Press, Dingle. 1982.
4 Charles McGlinchey. *The Last of the Name.* Op Cit. pp.137-138.
5 Charles McGlinchey. *The Last of the Name.* Op. Cit. p. 79.
6 Dinny McLaughlin. *Memories of Pat Mulhearne.* Inis Eoghain, The Inishowen Community Development Group, Carndonagh. pp. 22-23.
7 Maura Harkin and Sheila McCarroll. *Carndonagh.* Carndonagh. 1984.

CHAPTER TEN

EAST DONEGAL
AND
THE LAGAN

The eastern portion of County Donegal is a large and once relatively prosperous area of the county. Along with Inishowen it shared the centre of the textile industry and in addition good farming land. It also includes the area commonly referred to by the migrant farm workers of west Donegal as The Lagan[1]. Though this name was in vernacular use, it's exact borders and geographic extent can be quite misleading. When surviving migrant workers talk of the The Lagan and contemporaneous accounts are read, it is clear that it was a large area in east Donegal as well as parts of west Derry and Tyrone.

This chapter covers the district east of the Derryveagh and Croaghs Mountains, south of Inishowen and encompassing the Finn, Swilly, and Foyle river valleys. It also includes the towns of Letterkenny, Ballybofey/Stranorlar, Raphoe, Carrigans, St Johnston, Castlefin, Convoy, Killygordon etc.

Unlike the western seaboard and central portion of the county which held a great reputation for fiddle playing from the early decades of this century, this district has been less popularly appreciated. As noted already, this is certainly a direct result of the concentration by collectors in the middle decades of this century, on the areas where Irish was spoken, to the detriment of East Donegal. The eastern portion of the county has thus received little external musical attention and except in the case of a few players was assumed to be an unproductive area for fiddling. This view, though widely held, is grossly incorrect.

There was, and is still, a strong tradition of fiddle playing in this district. It is characterised in much the same way as the southwest of the county where the tradition has concentrated in a number of family dynasties and local nests. In contrast, however, while the great names of the southwest style flourished in the first half of this century, east Donegal has produced it's array of geniuses in the second half.

THE EXTENDED PEOPLES FAMILY

The Peoples family contains a significant number of players as well as singers, many of whom, both in the past and through to today, have proven to be extremely influential at both local and national level. They have centred around the village of St. Johnston. Overall, the members of this extended family reached exhilarating heights of playing and in the past were much more skilled at reading music than most local players. The latter ability never impinged on the traditional approach of their music and served solely to expand repertoire. Their style is generally remembered as being a steady dance-based one but with a strong dotted rhythm which many associate with Scottish influences. This latter feature shows many similarities with the playing of Pat Mulhearne. Highlands and strathspeys, often executed with great technical accomplishment, were numerous.

Jimmy, or as he was sometimes known, Jamie, was the father of Mattha and Tom Peoples and through to today is considered the most significant player of the locality during his time. He regularly played for house dances and social functions in local halls and is remembered as a particularly sweet fiddler. In his younger days he travelled as far as Derry for opportunities to play. Older people recall that on summer evenings those working locally in fields could take delight in hearing him play some distance away in a local hilltop hall as his volume was strong enough to make the music carry. In his adult life he formed a playing partnership with Sarah Ponsonby and to some extent with her husband John.

The occasion of their first meeting bears some humour. Jimmy had heard of Mrs. Ponsonby's ability as a player and went to seek her out. He travelled in by Letterkenny enquiring for her and eventually found her house by the Dry Arch. Jimmy went to the door and, after knocking, got a less than favourable reception. A resident of the asylum in the town had escaped that day and locals were warned to be cautious of strangers. Mrs. Ponsonby was convinced that Jimmy was the said man and the very friendly partnership that developed was nearly doomed from the start. A rare photograph of Jimmy Peoples now in the possession of his grandson, Tommy, pictures him as a tall, thin, mustached, elderly man. He is standing and playing the fiddle in a field.

Mattha, known more widely as Matt, was a well known handyman in the area and fixed bicycles and light machinery. His skills sometimes meant that he was also called upon to mend fiddles. He was a daily visitor to his brother Tom's house where he usually carried out his work and sometimes played there to pass the day. Mattha had a very unusual repertoire and today he is remembered as a very tidy player. At least three of his tunes have been preserved in the playing of his nephew, Tommy. These are two reels which bear his name and were commercially recorded by Tommy in duet with Matt Molloy as well as a highland.

Tom was known to have learned some tunes from his father but is best remembered as a fife player in the local band. His fifing was abandoned earlier than he would have liked when he was stricken with persistent and chronic bronchitis. This illness was aggravated by a working life spent in flax mills and quarries where dust was a constant problem. His daughters, Monica and Mary Ellen, both picked up some fiddling from him but it was his son, Tommy, who went on to captivate the imagination of his own and subsequent generations of players. Tom died on December 31st, 1977 and is buried in St. Johnston.

Bob, a cousin of Tom Peoples, was a native of St Johnston. He is remembered as having been a very good player with a particularly rich highland repertoire. He was in popular demand for house dances. Bob is enthusiastically described by Kathleen McGinley as "very tuneful". He was well capable of reading staff notation and had a good grasp of musical theory. He used this to his advantage by becoming a respected teacher in the locality. One of his pupils was Bob Doogan and eventually he took on the latter's younger sister, Kathleen (Kathleen McGinley), to whom he taught her first reel, a local version of *The Tarbolton.* He was regularly partnered for dances by Tommy McMenamin. Tommy was a good player and a dry wit. One night soon after buying one of the first cars in the area he drove off with Bob to play. Having gotten lost on the way home the car finished upside-down in a field. McMenamin got out of the car, freed Bob and then declared "home at last"! Bob was married to Nellie Glackin whose father came from Dungloe and appears to have been a relation of Tom Glackin of Maghery.

George, a native of St Johnston, was born in 1908. He was another cousin of Mattha and Tom Peoples. George's young days were typified by playing at house dances where he was very popular. Again, like Pat Mulhearne, he picked up an interest in singing from those he heard at the dances. Whereas fiddlers who have maintained a link with singing have become scarcer with the decline of the house dance, George Peoples saw himself as much a singer as a fiddler. In terms of fiddle style, George played straight melody to a marked dotted rhythm with staccato bowing and minimal left hand ornamentation. George's reputation as a player of note spread to wider circles and he was eventually pressed upon to perform on national radio. He agreed and broadcast from Athlone.

Unfortunately few recordings exist of George's playing[2]. These are quite representative and confirm his staccato, dotted rhythm style of playing. In general, his rhythm was more accented than that of Bob Peoples. George Peoples died on August 16th, 1988 and like Bob he is buried in St Johnston.

Jimmy Peoples daughter, Maggie, was the mother of Joe Cassidy. He learned his fiddling largely from his grandfather, Jimmy. In many ways Joe appears to be much like his Teelin name-sake, Frank Cassidy. During the last decade, he has played only rarely arising from problems with arthritis. Yet, those that remember him well from his younger days rave about his abilities and the sweetness of his tone. Sadly, no recordings appear to exist of his playing. Though a shy player by nature, Joe clearly brought fiddle playing in this area to its zenith by the 1950s. Like his relation, Bob Peoples, he had an excellent grasp of reading music and used this to expand his repertoire. He was the most sought after player for dances and functions in the locality and was the regular player for Nelly Sweeney's Irish dancing classes. Mrs. Sweeney made the weekly trip from Derry to hold her classes, primarily for young girls, in Raphoe. It was there that Kathleen Mc Ginley first came into contact with him and through repeated exposure learned three of his tunes which she still plays with great flair. These are the jig *Haste to the Wedding*, the slip jig *Barney Brallaghan* and an outstanding hornpipe in the true Peoples melodic mould which locally is known as *Joe Cassidy's Hornpipe*. It is a very close version of O'Neill's *The Humours of Castle Bernard*[3] and shows some similarities with James Hill's composition *The High Level Bridge* hornpipe.

TOMMY PEOPLES

The status of fiddle playing in the St Johnston area was declining during the post-Emergency era. The players in the Peoples family were ageing somewhat and the frequency of house dances as well as other social outlets for fiddlers were drying up. Mattha, Bob Peoples and Joe Cassidy rarely performed outside their own houses preferring to play solely for their personal entertainment. The one exception was George Peoples. He was extremely close to his wife and sometime after her death George sought a greater social contact through playing. Indeed, he often felt his village needed a good awakening with fiddle music. It was at the end of this period of decline that Tommy Peoples started to make his first strides at playing.

Tommy was born in Letterkenny in September 1948. While his earliest exposure to fiddle playing came from his father, Tom, who helped him figure out tunes, it was his elder cousin, Joe Cassidy, who formally taught him. Lessons with Joe started at the age of seven and continued on for a couple of years. These consisted of going to Joe's house and playing tunes and learning new ones. Joe placed an emphasis on strict staccato bowing and passed on his ability to read to Tommy. These Sunday trips to his cousin's house were always anxiously awaited by Tommy as the absence of any form of sporting outlets meant that young persons in the area had precious little to do with their free time. In this way, a trip to Joe Cassidy's was tantamount to an adventure.

From his earliest memories, Tommy recalls an ever-present desire to hear and play music. This urge once led to consternation when as a young boy Tommy had learned that Dinny McLaughlin was to play one evening in a nearby house. Unable to resist the temptation to hear him, Tommy sneaked away and sat outside where Dinny was playing. Listening to tune after tune, he did not notice the time passing and eventually returned home to "face the music" with his parents.

He was certainly a gifted pupil and by his early teenage years had already become an accomplished player. Kathleen McGinley recalls her first meeting with him around this time. They happened to be both paying a visit to Pat McGill's house in Glentown. Pat was a cousin of Tom Peoples and married to Mary Peoples, a sister of Bob Peoples. Though still a teenager, Tommy played that day with a mastery that Kathleen had rarely heard. He was blossoming in his ability and increasing his repertoire. At this stage he remembers playing with a more staccato style than that which he plays today.

A major satisfaction for his strong drive to play and develop as a fiddler arose through being allowed to attend the monthly Comhaltas sessions organised by Hughie McGovern in The Institute, Letterkenny. These provided two playing outlets. There was the formal, almost performance, setting of the official session as well as breakaway informal gatherings which usually took place in a back room. Preferring the back room setting, young Tommy came into contact with Vincent Campbell, Frank Kelly, Charlie Patton and Jimmy Hueston. Tommy acknowledges these players had a crucial influence on him at this stage. Another fiddler whom he remembers being particularly impressed with from these sessions was Tony O'Donnell from Brocagh. His technical ability seemed to signal to Tommy some of the wider capabilities of the instrument. Tommy can remember appearing at National School early on the mornings following such sessions to receive tuition in preparation for a scholarship (which he eventually won) to Saint Eunan's in Letterkenny with the music ringing in his ears as if it was still being played live in the play sheds. Around this time he was seriously concentrating on the accuracy of his playing and starting to work on a system of bowing which varied from the staccato bowing he had picked up from Joe Cassidy. In an effort to crispen his triplets he found that the vast majority of fiddlers played the normal two lead-in notes and then started the triplet on an up bow. He felt that this was a lighter stroke and did not emphasise the triplet sufficiently. He altered his bowing so that his triplets always began on a firmer down bow. This pattern is interestingly associated with James F. Dickie in Scotland as well as Michael Coleman and Hugh Gillespie in Irish tradition. Tommy continued to work strongly on this and soon developed his diagnostic crisp, snapping triplet. His playing since this time contains two types of triplets, a normal bowed one starting on a down bow as well as the snapping triplet which he uses interchangeably to astounding effect.

Tommy went as a boarder to Saint Eunan's College, Letterkenny. Dr. Kirwin, the Principal, was to later note he was one of the cleverest students to attend the school. Tommy admittedly found his passion for playing much greater than that for the books. He had no fiddle with him at first so his only recourse was to avail of one kept in the house of Pa Butler. Pa and his wife, Ma, ran a small newsagent and sweet shop near the college and were affectionately seen as father and mother figures to many of the boarders at Saint Eunan's. Pa played a bit on the fiddle and loved the music. He was highly impressed by Tommy and offered him the use of his fiddle whenever he wanted it. Tommy would almost nightly escape from the residence hall and make his way to Pa's to play for hours before scaling the walls to return to the residence hall.

Though an able student, Tommy realised that his future did not lie in academic pursuits. After a short period at home he headed for Dublin where he worked in the Carmelite Friary in Aungier Street for a couple of months. He had very little musical contacts at first and in his free time during the day he would window shop. Once, he found a small shop with tin whistles on display. Having left his fiddle at home he decided that he might make a whistle player and went in and bought one. During the transaction he fell into conversation with the owners. The shop was The Horseshoe, at the top of Capel Street, and the owner none other than John Kelly. John put Tommy on the track of the sessions in Dublin, particularly those in Thomas Street and Church Street, which at this time would have been the nerve-centre of activity. He started to attend these, but, there were some complications. The Friary locked its doors at eleven o'clock sharp requiring Tommy to frequently exercise all the wall scaling skills he had perfected at Saint Eunan's.

Eventually Tommy became more familiar with the Dublin music set up and started to venture out to a number of venues, particularly O'Donoghue's and Slattery's, where he played on the opening night of the subsequently famous Tradition Club for an Anti-Apartheid movement benefit. He came into contact with Matt Molloy who was studying in Bolton Street, Liam O'Flynn, James and Seán Keane as well as Mary Bergin. Tommy remembers that there was a great deal of goodwill extended to this group of young players by the older, established musicians at the regular venues. He was involved in the foundation of a céilídh band named *The Green Linnet* which included Tony Smith (fiddle), Johnnie McNamara (accordion), Mary Bergin (whistle) Mick Hand (flute) and Bridie Lafferty (piano).

Subsequently Tommy joined the Garda Síochána and was stationed for a period in Bray. During this time he was taking Dublin by storm with his skill and a completely fresh personal style. So unique was his approach to playing that Pearl O'Shaughnessy, herself a talented fiddler, recalls the Dublin musical fraternity being left virtually dumfounded by his ability. Demands for appearances grew rapidly. His failure to produce a single summons during his time in Bray left the Garda authorities questioning his calling in the world of law enforcement. After a brief transfer to Limerick Tommy and the Garda Síochána parted company.

He went with his good friend Gerry Scannell from west Cork to work in a furniture business in Dublin and afterwards returned to Clare to marry Maria Linnane from the musical Kilfenora family. At this time, he was working in Shannon and often met with Kerry musicians Denis Doody and Dónal O'Connor who were also working locally. Demands for playing increased. Tommy based himself in Dublin to meet the calls for performances as well as for more lucrative daytime work. For an extended period he was lodging in accommodation at the Brazen Head and during this time was inspired to compose a significant number of tunes. In 1974 he briefly performed with an informal group which made at least one tour of Brittany and recorded there under the name '1691'.

In the same year The Bothy Band was formed around a group of friends who had been touring the folk club circuit of the country appearing under various names and line-ups. Soon after their first public appearance in a small, underground lecture theatre in University College Dublin the group's fiddler, Paddy Glackin, left and was replaced by Tommy. Though on a crest of popularity at this time, traditional music soared even higher with this scintillating combination of Tommy, with Matt Molloy on flute and Paddy Keenan on pipes backed by the string and keyboards of Donal Lunny, Mícheál O Dómhnaill and Tríona Ní Dhómhnaill. The sole commercial recording of this line up was issued in 1975 and clearly belies the Donegal fiddle influences of both Tommy and Paddy Glackin on the band as a whole.

Tommy eventually left the band and concentrated on playing around his home base of Kilfenora and later in Toonagh, County Clare. His time in Kilfenora saw him playing with the Kilfenora Céilídh Band which sometimes entailed travelling as far as north Leitrim. This period seems to have been a musically happy one for Tommy as his nervousness with public solo playing was cancelled out by performing in a large, stable group. The line-up included many local musicians Tommy had come to admire and the fun atmosphere generated by the dancing tended to lift the music.

Throughout the late Seventies and into the Nineties, Tommy's fiddling has continued to develop within his unique personal style. For a very brief period, he was away from the instrument following an injury to his left little finger which, at the time, appeared to threaten his ability to play. By using a shoulder rest and with dedicated work on adapting his fingering he managed to completely overcome the difficulty to the point where his playing fully recovered.

The evolution of Tommy's music appears to strongly mirror his personal growth. His early playing was fast and powerfully impassioned. It reverberated with the recklessness of youth while still managing to hold incredible control within the playing. Even at this stage, though, it generally did not contain much of the hallmarks of the local style such as the strong dotted rhythm. The major exception to this, however, is Tommy's playing of strathspeys. Worth noting is, Shetland fiddler, Aly Bain's opinion[4] that for years he was of the belief that Irish fiddlers were unable to interpret this rhythm within its natural context until he heard Tommy's playing. This completely changed his view. Overall, his playing was more in line with a distinct, personally developed style, yet, exhibiting an overt sense of attack which was far more characteristic of the Donegal fiddlers than the more rhythmic and fluid styles of the remainder of the western seaboard.

As the years moved on and life became much more settled for

Tommy, these changes became reflected in his music. His latter recordings and present playing have certainly lost the urgency of his Sixties and Seventies performances. Tommy's fiddling now exhibits a more moderate pace matched by a greatly enhanced melodic imagination and challenge. In musical matters Tommy is accommodating to others almost to a fault. On a broader, personal level he is a warm gentleman and certainly a deep thinker. It is not surprising that the renowned Dublin fiddler, Tommie Potts, noted that the person he felt the greatest kinship with as a traditional musician was Tommy Peoples. Thankfully, this depth of personality has expressed itself increasingly over the years through composition and his considerable number of imaginative tunes appear in various rhythms such as highlands, strathspeys, airs, reels, jigs, hornpipes etc.

Tommy's extraordinary talents also extend into the area of teaching to very high standards. Before leaving Donegal he had done some teaching with John Douglas, who is close to Tommy's own age. John is a son of Paddy Douglas, now in his late sixties. Both Paddy and John are highly respected players in their own right. Paddy's father and maternal uncle were also players and the latter made some fiddles. Tommy Peoples greatest imprint, however, has been on his daughters, Siobhán and Gráinne, as well as his nephew, Séamus Gibson.

Already in life Tommy Peoples has contributed richly to the Irish fiddle tradition. His playing has easily matched, and most would freely argue, soared above that of the great players of previous generations. While he will no doubt continue to enhance the tradition for years to come, Donegal fiddlers are extremely proud of, and inspired by, his considerable achievements.

Though born and raised in Clare just over twenty years ago, Siobhán Peoples' enduring exposure to her father's music has left its distinct mark on her playing. Her style, while certainly containing influences of her native area, has all the Donegal elements present in Tommy's music. Siobhán's familiarity with Donegal music and fiddlers is extensive. Through her family relations she is well known to the fiddlers of the eastern end of the county. The past few years have allowed her to become more mobile and she is a frequent and very welcome visitor in southwest Donegal. Through these trips she has forged great playing partnerships and won the admiration of players such as James Byrne, the late Con Cassidy and Vincent Campbell amongst numerous others.

An accomplished player and performer in her own right, Siobhán has also inherited her father's qualities as a talented teacher and now enjoys a constant demand for general classes and more advanced teaching.

Séamus Gibson, now in his mid-twenties, is a native of Castletown, St. Johnston and grew up in a very musical environment. His mother, Monica, is a daughter of Tom Peoples while his father, Eddie, plays the melodeon as well as the flute and the tin whistle. From a very early age Séamus took an interest in the fiddle and tightly focused his interests on his uncle Tommy's style of playing. Séamus has rapidly grown into a player of extreme accomplishment. His style of playing is remarkably in the spirit of his uncle. Unlike the legion of fiddlers who strove to ape the likes of Michael Coleman on the release of his recordings, Séamus has managed to attain a fidelity to Tommy's style of playing while critically avoiding the pitfalls of mindless imitation. He has studied well the bowing, left and right hand ornamentation techniques as well as the melodic variation approach in Tommy's playing. As a result, Séamus' playing demonstrates an uncanny oneness with the overall style of his uncle, yet, he has put his stamp on tunes by the clever use of his own interpretations of the feel of pieces as well as ornamentation and melodic variations. He is able to take these skills into new found territory such as, into tunes not played by his uncle and apply them at his ease to exciting effect.

Like Tommy Peoples, he has inherited the ability to compose beautiful tunes which have found great popularity amongst Donegal players. Two reels, in particular, which he has named after Joe Cassidy and George Peoples have been enthusiastically received far beyond Donegal. Séamus is a player of tremendous promise and looks like keeping fiddle playing in east Donegal at a lofty standard for many years to come.

A native of the countryside between Raphoe and St Johnston, Kathleen McGinley started to learn the fiddle around the age of ten years. At that time, her second eldest brother, Bob Doogan, had a fiddle and was taking lessons from Bob Peoples. It was through her brother's practising that Kathleen took a great interest in the fiddle. She regularly borrowed his instrument and tried to pick up as many tunes as she could working by herself and with some help from her brother. After a while, it became apparent that she was making good progress and was sent to Bob Peoples for lessons. Her lessons continued until she went to the Convent of Mercy secondary school in Strabane. There she took lessons, which included some elements of classical playing, from Cathleen Brogan. After a year Miss Brogan became ill and Kathleen took lessons from Barney Connolly of Strabane whom she remembers as being a good player.

Besides her brother and Bob Peoples, her earliest influences also included her mother's brother, Fred McDaid, Charlie Carr as well as Tommy McMenamin, noted above. Her maternal grandfather, Paddy McDaid, who lived to be ninety two years, had a local céidhling house. He also acted as a source of tunes through his lilting and singing. She remembers her repertoire at this time as having a good element of strathspeys and highlands.

Kathleen continued to play, particularly enjoying local sessions, until the time she was married. At this stage, she gave up playing and concentrated on making a home and eventually rearing a family. Her eldest son, Martin, took up the fiddle in 1969. Though never having lost an infectious enthusiasm for fiddle playing, this development seemed to draw her closer to playing again. As Martin improved in his playing, Kathleen appears to have become more directly involved with his development. Finally, in 1975, after a gap of approximately twenty-five years, Kathleen started to play the fiddle again with genuine conviction. This return to active playing meant that she started to travel to fleadhs and areas with a strong fiddle playing tradition. She started to win back all her old tunes and through regular playing with Martin has accomplished a highly developed duet.

Soon after returning to active playing she met Danny O'Donnell which made an immediate impact on her. In his fiddling, she was able to instantly identify with his old house dance repertoire while at the same time, the execution of his style in unfamiliar tunes was immensely appealing to her. As such, Danny O'Donnell's repertoire and playing has left a significant imprint on her. She has also been a long admirer of Andy McGann's music and more recently has come to show a great appreciation for the repertoire and style of her friends, Tyrone fiddlers Pat and Rose McKenna.

Kathleen's repertoire includes a considerable amount of material which she can recall from her early days of playing. It also contains a notable amount of material she would have picked up in her wider travels after returning to playing. Her style has a very sweet tone matched by an extremely accomplished technical ability. She adopts a perfectionist approach to her learning and playing with the influence of Danny O'Donnell often readily apparent.

Kathleen's love for fiddle playing has extended beyond informally meeting and playing with other fiddlers. She has taken an active role in the development of fiddling in the Raphoe area. Following a once-off session in the early 1980s to mark the occasion of the ordination of Fr. Oliver McCrossan who was soon to leave for the missions, she decided to ensure that players met more often. As a result, she was to the forefront in organising a regular session in The Central Hotel, Raphoe. These sessions acted as the main outlet for local fiddlers and soon the older players who had been out of circulation started to play publicly again. Noted musicians from much wider localities heard of the great atmosphere of these small, comfortable sessions and made a point to travel to them. Through much of her efforts, fiddle playing in east Donegal has grown to its current lofty status.

Martin was born on January 9th,1961 and came under the early influence of Kathleen. By the mid-1970s he was an accomplished player on both fiddle and banjo. He left the latter instrument to ultimately concentrate on the fiddle. Local players to have influenced him by this time also include George Peoples, Jimmy Hueston and Charlie Patton as well as his contemporaries Bríd Harper and Séamus Gibson. By the late 1970s he had become greatly influenced by the playing of Tommy Peoples. During the early Eighties Martin had reached such a level of playing expertise that he was in constant demand for performances. Though still firmly focused on the traditional idiom, his playing was expanding and including other musical styles. His versatility allowed him to play with a variety of bands which incorporated popular, blues and country-rock forms. He also formed an all too-shortlived duet with the gifted Leitrim flute player, Seán Lee. This pair's playing was scintillating with an uncanny ability to match each others melodic approach to their tunes. Martin also played with the more traditional bands, Howden's Leap, White Island and Dervish which reflected his growing exposure to the Fermanagh and Sligo styles.

During the past number of years he has been based in Belfast though in regular contact with players throughout Donegal. While his solo playing is in great demand, his duets with his mother have a unique appeal. Martin is one of the most important fiddlers to grow within the Donegal tradition over the past two decades and has, like Kathleen, been active in efforts to re-invest his talents in the development of fiddling amongst the younger generation of players. He has taught a number of local pupils and is a regular teacher at the Scoil Fhidléireacht Thír Chonaill in Glencolumcille as well as at various workshops for young Donegal fiddlers.

THE EXTENDED GILLESPIE FAMILY

Hughie Gillespie was born at Drennan, Ballybofey in September 1906[5]. At the age of three years he was taken to live with his maternal grandfather, Hugh McElwee, near Brocagh. This practice of fostering with grandparents was a regular feature of Irish life at that time as the need to earn a living typically demanded extensive working hours. Couples striving to improve the lot of their families subsequently fostered some or all of their children with their own parents when possible. Hughie was introduced to the fiddle at the age of seven years through his cousin, Eddie McMonagle, who brought an instrument back with him when returning from seasonal work in Scotland. While his father was a good player, it was his uncle, Johnnie, one of the area's best fiddlers who made a lasting impact on him. Soon Hugh was in demand for playing at house dances while he continued to grow in ability.

Hughie's young life was dominated by sheep farming and on February 4, 1928 at the age of twenty-three years he boarded the Athena from Moville and emigrated to America in pursuit of richer rewards. His landing in America coincided with the Wall Street Crash and hard times for the natives meant harder times for the emigrant. Hugh was a personable character and became involved in selling a wide range of goods, including poitín, which had a prized value during this era of prohibition.

He was staying with an uncle and came into contact with Neil Smith who also lived in the same building. Neil was a member of Packie Dolan's highly successful band and through Smith, Hughie was introduced to the recordings of Michael Coleman. Having been greatly impressed by Hugh, Neil took him around to meet Coleman and by all accounts the meeting was a significant one for the two fiddlers. After hearing Hughie play, Michael is remembered as extending to him the offer of on-going tuition. This was quickly snapped up and the two began what was to become a close, lifelong friendship. Michael recalled travelling to Sligo Town one night as a young man noting the lights shining on the sea from the coastal towns in Donegal. With this happy memory in mind he nicknamed Hughie "Donegal Bay".

Coleman's fame soared and demands for public appearances, radio broadcasts and commercial recordings flooded in. It is a great testimony to Hugh's ability that at this time, Michael consistently sought him as a playing partner for his public and radio performances. For his recording sessions, Coleman always made sure Hughie came along to keep an eye on how things were progressing.

During the mid-Thirties Michael Coleman moved in with Hugh and his family. At this time Hughie received intensive tuition on bowing technique from his friend and the Sligo influence had clearly dominated his playing.[6] Through this impressive network of contacts Hugh had become a member of the Musicians' Union and was making a good living playing with dance bands such as The Star of Erin Orchestra and his cousin, Jim Gillespie's Four Provinces Orchestra.

In May of 1937 Michael Coleman was recording and again asked Hughie to join him at the session to supervise matters. While talking with the studio manager Michael remarked on Hugh's great ability and secured him an audition. All went well and over the next two years Hugh went on to record some of the best commercially released records of that time. Unlike his Sligo counterparts Killoran, Coleman and Morrison, Hughie was fortunate in being accompanied by sympathetic guitarists. His recordings are clearly in the Sligo idiom with flowing, articulate bowing, a wide range of ornamentation and the use of accidentals (sharps and flats not associated with the key signature) to create subtle shades in melodic variation. In the absence of restricting pianos his music pulsates with an infectious drive. The repertoire similarly shows a strong Sligo influence, though *The Irish Mazurka* as well as the reels *The Donegal Traveller* and *Miss Montgomery* are more than likely sourced from his early playing days at home.

He realised his dream of returning to live in Donegal in 1964 and settled in Carrickmagrath, Ballybofey. Hugh continued active playing and formed close partnerships with Frank Kelly as well as Cathal and young Paddy Tunney. The Tunney brothers are both fiddlers noted for their sweet tone. Cathal is now living in Canada and makes regular visits home while Paddy is based in Letterkenny and still associates with many of the players of east and south Donegal. Hugh's daughter, Rosemary, also picked up the fiddle from him. Hughie saw out his final years at his home in Carrickmagrath. His death on Halloween night, 1986 brought to a close the final chapter in the golden era of roaring reels on 78's. When Hugh went to his grave, he took his fiddle with him, no doubt in anticipation of a re-union with the Sligo Triumvirate.

Good fiddle playing in the Gillespie family did not stop with Hughie. His brothers Mickey and Jim were also accomplished fiddlers. Like their brother, they were influenced by their father but their aspirations were directed at their uncle Johnnie's talents. They played locally at house dances and eventually joined the Seán Mac Cumhaill Céilídh Band featuring with another local fiddler James Quinn of McRory's Brae near the eastern slope of Barnes Mór Gap. James, along with his brother Johnnie, was also a noted step dancer. The brothers travelled all over the northwest playing with the band between the two wars.

FRANK KELLY

Frank was born just over fifty-five years ago in the townland of Mullaghinery near Killygordon. Though his parents did not play he was raised in a extremely musical household. Fiddlers visiting his home were Lawrence and Alice McGoldrick (now Mrs. Kelly in Donegal Town) as well as John Dan McLaughlin who called on an almost daily basis. These players were to have a very strong early influence on Frank as did Mick Kelly who played mouth organ and John Callaghan, a lilter and singer.

Frank started to play at the age of eight or nine years. His brother, Eddie had bought a tin fiddle that had been made by Mickey Mór Doherty. He made early attempts to play on this instrument and eventually his father, Bernard, who was a great enthusiast made a fiddle for Frank out of an old blackening box. This was to be his first and much cherished instrument.

Given the céilídh house nature of his early days, it is not surprising that his original repertoire was comprised of house dance tunes including highlands and germans etc. These seem to have come mostly from John Dan who showed him how to play them on the fiddle as well as John Callaghan who patiently lilted the tunes for him until he had them correctly. Callaghan was a great lover of the house dances and anxious to assist Frank in progressing on the fiddle as he felt the need for a fiddler was an important one. Another visitor to the Kelly house at this time was Simi (Stranorlar) Doherty who lodged with the Kellys as a night's playing often went into the morning. One memory Frank has of Simi was that as rosin was in short supply at that time, Simi would use the resin from the fir trees at the back his house for his bow. Another trick that the Dohertys had in this respect was when a bow was getting thin on hairs or they had no rosin they would cut a sally (willow) rod the length of the bow about two hours before playing. The sap in the rod would rise, becoming sticky and ready for use as a bow by the time playing would start.

Frank quickly developed into an accomplished fiddler. He was aware that through his grandmother, Mrs. McElwee from Glenfin, he had relations who were noted fiddlers. These were none other than the Gillespie brothers. He came to know and admire the playing of Jim and Mickey. In an effort to expand his musical horizons he started listening to the American-made 78s of Hugh. In these recordings he discovered the wonder of musical imagination and brilliance of tone. He strove to match the playing but considering the instruments he had at his disposal it was fruitless. Eventually, around the age of twelve, word came from America that Hugh Gillespie was returning for a visit. Frank was taken to Hugh's mother's house to meet his famous relation and remembers the excitement of meeting Hughie as being on the scale of having an audience with the Pope!

Rather than playing for the young fiddler, Hugh began by asking Frank for a tune. He launched into *Master Crowley's Reels* as he had tried to pick them up from Hugh's recording. Hugh was pleased by the playing and offered to work through the tune with Frank until he had gotten Hugh's full version. This close attention from Hugh heightened Frank's enthusiasm and commitment to fiddle playing. He tried to absorb as much music from Hugh as he could during his short stay. Not long after this, Hugh returned permanently. This provided Frank with the opportunity to play with Hugh and the duet was exercised three or four times per week for years. During this time Frank came to be well acquainted with the intricacies of Hugh's playing to the point of being fully conversant with his approach to variation and ornamentation of tunes. He also came to note and admire Hugh's ability to "back treble" (starting a triplet on a down bow) which was a hallmark of the Coleman bowing style absorbed by Hugh.

By the late Sixties Frank had built a considerable reputation as a fiddler. He was highly active in Comhaltas, particularly attending the sessions in the east of the county. His respect for the organisation's efforts leads him to conclude today that if it was not for Comhaltas activities, he would not be playing today. Frank attended numerous fleadhs with several competitive successes culminating in capturing the All-Ireland competition at the Buncrana fleadh in 1979. With Comhaltas he came to meet a wider variety of fiddlers when touring America and Canada. Frank also played fiddle along with Jimmy Heuston and Oliver Thomas in the Crossroads Tírchonaill Céilídh Band.

In more recent years, Frank has continued to play quite actively supporting the various musical functions in the county. He has a detailed knowledge of the older style of the east of the county and is highly appreciative of that played by Mickey Doherty. Through his long association with Hugh Gillespie, he is happy to conclude that Sligo has the best body of music, but Donegal has the best fiddlers.

THE HARPER FAMILY

Three brothers, Stephen, Barney and Pat Harper, born around the first decade of this century formed one of the strongest and best remembered playing units in east Donegal. Natives of Castlefin they were renowned throughout the area as great house dance players. Stephen, in particular, shone out amongst his fiddling associates. He played for a while in a band with the Molloy brothers, Patsy and Joe from the border village of Clady. Their music consisted of popular tunes mixed with house dance music featuring Stephen. Barney and Pat emigrated to Scotland, where another generation of the family has taken up fiddle playing.

Stephen, on the other hand, eventually emigrated to Hendon, London where he spent about thirty-five years before returning to Castlefin in November, 1987. After coming home, he continued to play but with advancing age and failing health occasions became rarer. He did, however, have the opportunity to savour some of the best music ever to come out of east Donegal as his son, Packo, married Susan Kelly, a sister of Frank Kelly and they raised a very musical family. Amongst them are two fiddlers, Bríd and Siobhán. Stephen Harper died on September 8th, 1993 and is buried in Castlefin.

Bríd Harper, now in her late twenties, was born in Castlefin. She started to play the tin whistle just after her eighth birthday attending local classes with the Ballyshannon fiddler Cyril Curran and later Pat McCabe the accordionist from Clones, County Monaghan. These were organised by her uncle, Frank Kelly. Around this time she was also getting some help learning to read music from Patsy Molloy. After a number of months playing the whistle she took to the fiddle. Another one of her teachers at this time was Mary Smith, a fiddle player from the west of Ireland who came to live in Castlefin for a short period. By her tenth year Bríd had already become a player of tremendous promise. It is worth recounting that around this time I can remember seeing Bríd play music of great power. She was sitting on a chair at a session in Gortahork. The depth of the music belied her age as she tapped time with her feet in mid-air. Her legs were not long enough to reach the floor!

Her influences at this stage were the regular visitors to her home including her uncle, Frank Kelly, Patsy Molloy, Peter McConnell, Vincent Devanney, from Castlefin, Seán McCosker, a box-player from Dromore and the duet of Charlie Patton and Danny O'Donnell. Bríd rapidly expanded her playing by learning from books and recordings. With the exception of Joe Burke her interests were centred on the commercial and some private recordings of the fiddlers Paddy Glackin, Brendan McGlinchey, John Doherty, Vincent Campbell, Seán McGuire and Michael Coleman.

Bríd played with her sisters in the family céilidh band The Golden Harp which was very popular throughout the county. She was an annual attender of various fleadhs and a successful competitor at the highest level. Arising from capturing provincial titles she often attended the weekly classes at the annual Scoil Éigse. There she came into direct contact with players such as Paddy Glackin and Paddy Ryan. Her meetings with Paddy Glackin would appear to have been important ones for Bríd as her style of playing exhibits many of the finest characteristics of Paddy's playing. Her fiddling is very adventurous with an exceptional tone and clarity underlain by solid timing. In her adult years Bríd travelled widely and has come into contact with players of various traditions and styles. Her playing continues to mature and provide an inspiration for younger fiddlers. She is married and although living in Tyrone, keeps frequent contact within the musical circles of Donegal.

Like her sister, Siobhán Harper has also grown up with an enviable musical exposure. She developed into a player of similar talent and has been involved in musical tours on numerous occasions. Living in Sligo now, her playing is all too frequently heard.

JIMMY HUESTON

Jimmy Heuston was born in 1919 within a mile of the Tyrone border near Castlederg. Though born in Donegal, for convenience sake he attended primary school in County Tyrone. Though his parents did not play, his maternal grandmother's brother, Patrick Doherty, was one of the area's noted players of his day. He emigrated to America where he lived to see his one hundred and tenth birthday. Jimmy started to learn the fiddle at the age of fourteen. At this time he became familiar with the previously mentioned Joe Molloy and his brother. Their music astounded him and he lobbied hard to learn the fiddle. Not having an instrument of his own, the Molloys were happy to lend him their instruments to get him started. Joe, was well known for his playing of the jig *The Girls of Banbridge*. Other players he remembers from that period include John James McGlinchey and his son who lived within a mile of his own home. They were, in Jimmy's opinion, very good fiddlers. He also came into contact with the well known fiddlers Johnnie Crampsie and Tommy Keenan of Aghyaran.

As a young man he came more frequently into contact with the Harpers of Castlefin, Stephen, Barney and Pat. Jimmy has great praise for these fiddlers and singles Stephen out as being the most exceptionally talented player of his generation. In 1952 he moved to Lettermore, Drumkeen to take up a post with the Donegal County Council. This move gave him a firm base to develop contacts with the fiddlers of the Drumkeen catchment. He started to meet more regularly with the Harpers, Charlie Patton, George Peoples and Frank Kelly. Jimmy became a regular attender at the Crossroads, Letterkenny and Drumkeen Comhaltas sessions as well as the Raphoe sessions. He also met John and Mickey Doherty on a routine basis and formed a particular affection for Mickey's playing.

Despite recent illnesses, Jimmy's playing continues to demonstrate his exceptional ability. His style is largely staccato in bowing but he is highly regarded for his clarity of tone and pitch. He plays with an unusually deft triplet which reflects to some degree the pattern played by Tommy Peoples. Having played for house dances and for solo dancing competitions throughout his life he has a great sense of rhythm and timing. His hornpipe playing is particularly measured. Jimmy's talents have been thankfully passed on to his daughter who is a similarly gifted player, but unfortunately all too rarely heard.

Mary Ann McPhelimy was born into a musical family living outside Castlederg, County Tyrone in 1905. Her two brothers were good fiddlers and her mother played the concertina. After marrying, she came to live on her husband's farm at Ballinacor, Killygordon. There she came into contact with a lively nest of fiddlers and was one of the most popular players in the area. She could recall that there was an abundance of players in the locality when she settled there. A Miss Young, who had some tutorial duties with the landlords, the Johnson family, also taught music locally and made a significant impact by showing many of the fiddlers how to read music. This resulted in a rapid opening of repertoire to the players of the district.

Some of the fiddlers Mary Ann regularly played with at house dances and remembered with respect include Robert Brady who emigrated to America, and cousins Peter, Jim and Vincent McConnell from Killygordon. The latter were extremely talented fiddlers who were in tremendous demand for house dance playing. They were initially taught by Patrick Connaghan, who often partnered them. They eventually came to learn to read from Miss Young. Eddie Sweeney, also from Crossroads, was another player who was noted for his sweet tone and considered the best player of his age group.

Mary Ann's passion in life was fiddle playing and she was much in demand for house dances which flourished during her adulthood. Unlike other women of her generation, she does not appear to have given up playing altogether during her child rearing years. Mary Ann Patton continued to play throughout her life up until her final years. She passed away in her eight-eighth year on August 25th, 1993.

Her son, Charlie Patton, is now in his early sixties. He is a lifelong player and one of the most enthusiastic and dedicated followers of fiddle music in the county. When he was about six years of age, he was taken to a dance in Aghyaran Parochial Hall. There he heard Eddie Lynch playing and was greatly impressed by his music. Eddie was a very good player from Carrycaughan, Killeter. This meeting appears to have left a significant impression on him.

One of the main movers behind the development of traditional music in Letterkenny has been Hugh McGovern. Hugh was born in Swanlinbar, County Cavan, and took to fiddle playing at an early age. He moved to Letterkenny when he was fifteen years old and continued to enthusiastically pursue fiddling. For years he co-ordinated the local Comhaltas sessions and continues to promote playing in the town.

The rapid growth of Letterkenny over the past two decades has meant that the town has continued to benefit with the influx of fiddlers. Séamus McGuire, from Sligo, is one of the most gifted players of his generation. His partnership with Leitrim flute player Seán Lee who is also living locally has resulted in some of the most exciting music played in Ireland today. Their duet recording was one of the first commercial releases in the current decade. It's incredible level of musicianship as well as firm commitment to a marvellous local style set a standard to which all recordings to the new millennium will find hard to rise.

OTHER FIDDLERS FROM THE AREA

Michael Collins, now in his forties, is from Castlefin and a very accomplished player. He comes from a musical family and is regarded as having a deft command of technique. Over the years he has associated with Jimmy Hueston, who helped him in his early days as did the McGinleys of Raphoe. Michael is a modest player and deserves to be heard more frequently. His win in the Letterkenny Feis over his former mentor Jimmy Heuston is often recalled with great humour by the latter. George McGee of Broadpath, Convoy who died in the late 1980s was a very accomplished player and absorbed some influences from the recordings of Sligo players. Barney McCauley, who also died in the late 1980s having lived to over seventy years, came from St. Johnston. He was a good player and formed a great friendship with Fr. (Dr.) Gerry Cunnea, originally from Croagh, between Killybegs and Ardara who then was the parish priest of St. Johnston[7]. Fr. Cunnea and Barney often attended the Raphoe sessions. John Peoples of Ballindrait, Lifford, no relation of the St. Johnston Peoples extended family, was also a nice player and came to the Raphoe sessions along with neighbours Barney McGinley and his sister, Nancy who also played as did their father, Barney. Two fiddlers from Cloughfin who are well thought of are father and son Charlie and James Dolan respectively.

One of the musical Brown family in Drumkeen, Nora Gallagher, now lives in Stranorlar and plays regularly. Two players from Raphoe who have come to appreciate traditional fiddle music from the classical side of the instrument are Frank McCarron and Tony McGranaghan. Johnnie Murray was known to play for his own pleasure in Newtowncunningham.

Master McDermott was from the Loughagannon/Calhame area just outside of Letterkenny. He spent most of his adulthood in Newtowncunningham where he taught in the National School. He formed a highly regarded duet with the uilleann piper Hugh Devanney. Though a good all round player, Master McDermott excelled in air playing. Dan Sweeney and Willie John Bonnar were well remembered fiddlers from Killygordon.

Fiddle playing families were the Gallaghers from Glendowan and the McGinleys from Derry. One of the Gallagher boys is still playing in Roscommon where he now lives. The McGinleys have lived in both Glenswilly and Letterkenny for some time and have been active in playing in Letterkenny. As is clear from the litany of players in this area, fiddling is rich in east Donegal. Thankfully, the future is also showing much promise. Matthew McGrananghan of Cloughin, Castlefin is showing all the signs of continuing in the same mould as his near neighbours the Harpers. Matthew has yet to see his teenage years and has already reached a level of accomplishment meriting regular praise from his more senior playing partners.

REFERENCES

1 Mici Mac Gabhainn. *Rotha Mór an tSaoil.* Foilseacháin Naisiúnta Teo., Baile Atha Cliath, 1957, pp.31-58.

2 Teip George Peoples. *Cáirdeas na bhFidléiri Collection.* An Foras Cultúir Uladh, Gleann Cholm Cille.

3 Francis O'Neill. *The Dance Music of Ireland.* Walton's, Dublin, 1972, (reprint edition) No. 935.

4 Aly Bain, pers. comm.

5 Joe McGarrigle. *Donegal Profiles. The Donegal Democrat,* Ballyshannon. 1986, pp 189 - 191.

6 Harry Bradshaw. *Michael Coleman 1891 - 1945.* Viva Voce. Dublin 1991.

7 Dr. Malachy McCloskey. *Remembrances on Traditional Fiddlers and Traditional Music.* Dearcadh (Ardara Community Annual), Nollaig, 1992, pp. 102 - 103.

CHAPTER ELEVEN

TRAVELLING FIDDLERS

Up until the early decades of the present century the transport network and the mass communication media in Donegal was extremely limited. Those people who were neither emigrating nor seasonally travelling to work in other parts of Ulster or Scotland were, for the most part, confined to their locality both physically and culturally. Indeed, it was not uncommon even up to recent times to hear some elderly people say they had never left their own parish or corner of the county.

In such circumstances, news, information and influences typically had a strong local bias. In musical respects this meant that fiddlers living in a locality would have been dominantly exposed to and influenced by the players of that community. Over time, this ultimately gave rise to the emergence of local fiddle styles which, like spoken dialects, differed between sometimes quite close, yet isolated localities. There was one exception to this situation, however, and that arose from the influence of the travelling fiddler who journeyed throughout the county undertaking daytime craftwork or farm labouring and playing or teaching professionally in the evenings. Such players have in recent times been popularly associated with regular street playing or busking. It is noteworthy that in general, the Donegal travelling fiddlers considered this practice undesirable and an affront to their pride and the value of their skills. The only exception to this frame of mind appears to be playing at regular harvest and other fairs when diverse members of the local community would display their crafts or skills on the streets of the host town for money.

The travelling fiddlers served to distribute elements of musical styles as well as repertoire between what was otherwise remote communities. In Donegal, with few exceptions, these players belonged to a single extended family and where active, their impact was substantial.

Most of the children of Patrick McConnell and Mary Campbell of Ardara were to play a role in the music of Donegal. Their eldest child, Mary, a renowned singer born around 1860 would eventually marry Mickey Mór Doherty. Patrick and Mary's youngest daughter Bridget, born around 1870 would marry warpiper Húidaí Gallagher, but it was their two sons Alec and Mickey who were to make the McConnell family's greatest contribution.

Mickey and younger brother Alec, of Ardara became some of the most influential fiddlers of their day. Both centred themselves around their native village travelling south and southwest Donegal as highly skilled tinsmiths making small kitchen implements and occasional tin fiddles. They were most famous, however, for their music and had a highly developed fiddle duet. For outdoor performances they sometimes changed the format and played a fiddle and warpipe combination with Mickey taking the pipes.

Few facts are known about the McConnells' music. These come from the rare references to them from their nephews John, Mickey and Simon (Kilmacrennan) Doherty and secondly from the few older players that can still remember them. It is known that Alec was a small man with a limp. It is significant that he is consistently remembered as being by far the better player. Simon (Kilmacrennan) Doherty, who was very familiar with his uncles Alec and Mickey in his boyhood, described[1] Alec by saying "he could play for a ball (the most distinguished and demanding of dance gatherings) or anywhere", while of Mickey McConnell he noted that "he was just good enough for a country dance". Con Cassidy of Teelin could remember hearing their pipe and fiddle music travelling over the still, summer evening air as a very young child. Having seen them only rarely he described them as typical countrymen wearing grey flannel clothes. Alec never wed. Mickey married Fanny Doherty, a sister of Mickey Mór Doherty, who had been born and settled in Ardara. According to Simon (Kilmacrennan) Doherty[2], Mickey and Fanny had a very happy marriage. Such was Mickey's grief following Fanny's death that he would return to play laments at her grave for a long time after.

The McConnell brothers were obviously very close and appear to have travelled almost constantly together. From the memories of the older fiddlers it is clear that Alec and Mickey were amongst the most widely respected and highly accomplished players of their time. They were contemporaries and brothers-in-law of Mickey Mór Doherty. The Doherty and McConnell brothers played together and traded repertoire. What may have been one of the greatest sessions of Donegal fiddle playing ever is warmly remembered by Simon (Kilmacrennan) Doherty. It took place near Dooey Point, Lettermacaward, when he was a young boy starting on the fiddle. His family were camped at the time with Mickey Mór Doherty and his family. On a warm summer evening the McConnells came to stay the night and makeshift benches were built to accommodate the throng of fiddlers. As Simon remembers, it was the greatest night's music he heard in his life with up to twenty fiddlers either by the name McConnell or Doherty playing in various combinations until daylight.

As capable and comfortable as the McConnells and Dohertys were playing together, a stylistic difference existed between the two families. In general, the older players remember the McConnells as being straight, unornamented fiddlers with strong piping influences while the Dohertys were more attacking with the kind of rhythm that can be heard in the recordings of Mickey Doherty. This view appears to corroborate information from James Byrne of Glencolumcille who was told by the players of his father's generation that the Boyle family of Malinmore, who were generally known as straight fiddlers, had the McConnell style.

Simon (Kilmacrennan) Doherty, who greatly favoured the Mickey Mór Doherty style of playing over the McConnell brothers is still happy to concede that Alec McConnell was a more gifted player than Mickey Mór Doherty[3]:

> He (Alec) never met his match in Donegal. He was a small sized man, smaller nor me (Simon is approximately five feet, six inches). He says (to Mickey Mór Doherty) "you're at it" (playing). The reel he was playing was *Coppers and Brass*. And at that time Mickey (Mór) was at himself. Oh Lord Almighty, a big, tall, long-armed man and he could take that bow and he could burl (older fiddlers often use the word 'burl' to loosely mean triplet) that bow from the frog to the point. All clean work, and the reel he was at was *Coppers and Brass*. So Alec come in and he was sitting down and he was a wee bit backward (shy) and

> Mickey (Mór) carried on till he finished it. He turned the fiddle like that there to give it to Alec and said "your cow's in the pound" (beat that). "Well let me tell you" says Alec, "Mickey, she's not in the pound very much considering that you could have bowed that reel better than you've done. It's the bow tells", he says. "Well then, you play it for me" says Mickey. "I will" he says. Alec played the same reel. Well there was as much hardness between Alec and me Uncle Mickey as from here till America. Alec was the best in all Ireland! If he had of been took up to Dublin or around there, there were nothing round there could have played a reel with him! And they're good at it (in Dublin). They're good at it. I'll give them their dues. Lord his bow(ing) was sweet and nice. No tie, no holding, nor nothing at all (there were no restrictions on his bowing skill). He could go up that fingerboard there, begod, up to the bridge nearly! Great command and his fingers no thicker than a wisp. Very active; up and down; no torture at all! And he played the reel. "Now," he says. "What do you think of that?" "Ah, sure" says Mickey "that's playing" He had always to give into Alec. And he was good!

Further evidence clarifying the style of the McConnells which also confirms a general link with Scottish fiddling and piping influences came in recent years from Mickey 'Gollie' Gallagher, a well known melodeon player from Teelin who had come to meet and hear the McConnells when he was a young man.

At the 1984 Annual Meeting of Cairdeas na bhFidiléirí in Glenties one of the special attendants was Angus Grant of Fortwilliam, Scotland. Angus is considered by many to be the greatest exponent of the old Highland style of Scottish fiddle playing and piping influences are clearly evident in his music. Following on from the Annual Meeting a small session took place in the Rusty Mackeral pub in Teelin at which Angus played some requests for Mickey Gollie. The tunes were generally those which Mickey associated with the McConnells. After hearing Angus play for at least two hours Mickey was astounded at the incredible closeness of Angus Grant's playing with that which he had heard decades before from the McConnells. This information again fits in well with the view that the McConnell style was a straight one, differing from that we now associate with both Mickey Mór Doherty and his well documented son Mickey. Alec and Mickey McConnell are buried in unmarked graves in Ardara.

According to folklore, John Doherty associated the naming of the reel *The Glen Road to Carrick* with his uncles. This tune is based on the *Chorus Reel,* and is said to have had its additional parts added to it by John Mhósaí Mac Fionnlaigh. Mickey Doherty associated the story and the tune the *Fairies Slip Jig* with the McConnells and their travels in Teelin. One of their unusual waltzes is also played by John Gallagher of Ardara who learned the tune from his father, Paddy, who in turn got it from the McConnells.

THE DOHERTYS

The oldest known member of the Doherty family, Hugh Doherty, was born around Dungloe near the close of the 1700s. He played fiddle and both the uilleann and warpipes. He married Nanny Rua (red-haired) MacSweeney of Dungloe, one of the Doe Castle MacSweeneys who prior to being dispossessed of their lands were powerful figures in northwest Donegal. Her brother, Eamonn Rua, was the father of An Píobaire Mór, Tarlach MacSuibhne, discussed in detail in Chapter Seven. Hugh and Nanny had two sons, Michael and Simon.

Very little is known about Simon Doherty, otherwise Simi Mór, who was born around Lettermacaward towards the end of the first quarter of the last century. He was, like his father, a fiddler, uilleann and warpiper. His older brother, Michael was also a fiddler and warpiper who eventually based himself in the Ramelton area.

As Simi Mór died in 1899 he saw his grandson, Mickey, born in 1894, grow to be a young boy. Mickey gives us our only first hand account of Simi Mór when, as we have seen in Chapter Four, he tells us how Simi Mór came to learn the tune *Banríon na Síoga* . Simi Mór had seven children, four boys, Simon, Mickey Mór (named after Simi Mór's older brother) Charlie and Hugh, and three girls namely Bridget, Fanny and Hannah. Simon and Mickey Mór played fiddle and pipes while the other two boys both played fiddle.

MICKEY MÓR DOHERTY

The second child, Mickey Mór, born in the middle of the last century around Lettermacaward would go on to have a family which was to vastly shape the current tradition of Donegal fiddle playing. What is known to us of Mickey Mór Doherty again comes mostly from the memories of his youngest son John; then to a decreasing extent from his other sons Mickey and Simi. Three rare photographs, allegedly taken by a Donegal emigrant who after fighting with the American Army in the First World War and stopping on his way back to the United States, feature Mickey Mór. These photographs were in the possession of his grand-daughter (Mickey's daughter) the late Frances Doherty of Árd McCool, Stranorlar. Frances appears along with other children in her family and judging by her age it would seem to suggest a date around the end of the war.

In two of the pictures Mickey Mór is seated in front of a small, thatched stone byre. In the first of them, sons John (on the left) and Mickey (on the right) are seen as proud, fresh, young men. The second shows him surrounded by some of his grandchildren from Mickey's family. Although a good age, Mickey Mór looks a fit and lean individual. He is dressed in the old style wearing a hat, coat and scarf. His fiddle, a German-looking one with very wide F holes, is stood up on his knee. His expanse of beard dominates his face and while no sign of either a smile or scowl is afforded, the overall impression is one of a man who is justifiably proud and clearly portraying himself as a fiddler.

According to his son John he was a hard task-master when it came to learning the fiddle. He demanded a high standard of playing and did not suffer half-hearted efforts. As was supposed to be the case with all the Dohertys, Mickey Mór was very decided that there were tunes worth playing and others not. For those of value he was adamant that there was a right and a wrong way to play them and to choose any other option than to play them correctly was to do the music a dis-service. Under these conditions, we may take it that what we hear of the melody of the tunes in the recordings of his sons is close to that played by the father, even allowing for the stylistic changes that John would later make.

An account of the family group's appraising of tunes was given by Mickey Mór's youngest son John[4]:

> We just earned our living in our own usual way of earning a living, but yet we always, always left out so much time for to play a selection on the fiddle. And sometimes of the two fiddles. So on like that. Anything that we thought worth remembering, we never forgot it. It was always played. Any tune or hornpipe or a reel that we thought was worth keeping in memory, that tune was always kept up to the mark. But there was one thing about it. My two uncles (Alec and

Mickey McConnell), and my father's brother - my Uncle Charlie, and my father, my brother Simi and my brother Mickey and God rest my brother Hughie, they would all gather, of course on a Sunday evening. And surely there was some person would have something new to play. That was the way. Something that the rest didn't hear before. Well then, after that reel or hornpipe or whatever it would be, would be played, then it would be strictly examined by all hands to see was it fit to be passed out into the ears of listeners. Well then, that tune would just remain like that and if we thought is wasn't suitable to play for the listeners' ears at dances and parties well it would be scrapped. But the tune that was passed out by all hands for to be suitable to play in public or for the entertainment of people, well that tune was still kept in memory and there was nothing ever taken from it. It was always built up and kept as a good tune.

Mickey Mór must certainly have been one of the leading fiddlers of his day. Even when John and Mickey removed the obvious fondness of a son for his father and spoke dispassionately about him they praised is magnificent ability. His gift, according to the sons, seemed to concentrate on his bowing ability. John maintained that no man could bow a tune like Mickey Mór and that when his father was in good form in a reel his bow action was such that he could make the top of the bow whistle[5].

An interesting description of one of his great bowing performances which took place in the later years of his life is recounted again by his son John[6]:

You know what it is now a child to be listening to the father there or to be acquainted listening to a person, you know, from his childhood days on up to be a boy say of sixteen years or seventeen. Well there's many things, you know, that you'd hear so often that you mightn't pay attention to. You'd hear them so often that you'd say to yourself 'sure I've heard that before. It's no great wonder to me.' But I often heard my father playing the fiddle and, although he was very good, in the rear, I didn't pay that much attention. But there was one evening I was after coming in; I'd been away someplace and I was just after coming back. That same evening he was in great spirits. There was something pleasing his mind very much. He took down the fiddle and he began to play a reel, it's called the *Salamanca*, the *Salamanca* Reel. Well now the performance that evening was nothing more than I ever heard or saw him doing before. Of course at the time, he was getting to be an old man. His action with the bow was more than I ever knew that could be done with the bow. So I just stood up with me finger in me mouth and looking at him and listening to him. Says I "now father, since I remember, I never heard you doing the like of that before. I never heard you doing that bowing performance,' says I. 'Och, well now', he says, 'John, that's what I used to do when I has a young boy'. And I never heard him doing the same thing before or after! Now that's the truth. The bowing thon evening, right enough, it was more than I knew that a man could do with a bow.

Outside of his extended family Mickey Mór had great time for two players, John Mhósaí McGinley and Pádaí Bhillí na Rópaí Boyle. As we have seen, within the family his brothers-in-law, Alec and Mickey McConnell were also favourite playing partners. Many tunes of his were picked up and again handed on by his sons. One in particular which John always recalled was in relation to his fathers death. According to him, his father was lying very sick in bed. John went in to play a few tunes for him to raise his spirits but to his surprise and despite his considerable efforts at *McSweeney's Reel*, an old family favourite, handed down from The Píobaire Mór, his father was displeased with the playing. He called for the fiddle from John and launched into the tune. The tip of the bow started to whistle as he flailed through it. Shortly after, Mickey Mór drew his last breath and with that, his fiddle, which was hanging on the wall, burst asunder.

Even to the present, travelling families in Ireland tend to have clearly defined areas within which they journey. In Donegal the Gweebarra River was one major dividing line between travelling groups. A number of factors define the circuit of the Dohertys as north of the river. Firstly, there are the locations of the older members' birthplaces – all north of the Gweebarra; secondly the identification by Mickey of the Glendowan area as the circuit of his grandfather and lastly the marriage ties between the family and the Mac Sweeneys of Doe Castle. This was the case up till Mickey Mór's adulthood, when they began to cross the river. This decision was probably taken on economic grounds in an effort to ensure that the travelling circuits of the family were spread out over as wide an area as possible, thus avoiding overlap.

The eldest child of Mickey Mór and Mary McConnell was Fanny who married into the O'Rourkes, another travelling family with many fiddlers and pipers amongst its numbers. Next eldest, Charlie, was a fiddler. He is best remembered today through his first cousin Simon (Kilmacrennan) who credits him as being an excellent player. He also notes that he was a very tall man, in excess of six feet, who took pride in noting that he grew to be the exact same height as his father, Mickey Mór. Charlie emigrated to America for a period where he married an American girl and eventually returned home with his wife and daughter. He also brought home a fiddle which was renowned as one the best that ever came into the Dohertys' possession. He then spent a short period of time in the Meath area as well as in Dublin where he died tragically from a fall out of a second floor window. His contribution to present day Donegal fiddling lies with two tunes which he brought back from America. The first is the unusual version of *Rakish Paddy* which we know best from his younger brother John's playing and which has become popular throughout Donegal. The second, which the Dohertys christened *The American Reel*, is a very rare version of *Tom Ward's Downfall*. It is now played predominantly by Simon (Kilmacrennan) who learned it directly from Charlie shortly after his return home. Simon (Kilmacrennan) well remembers meeting Charlie's daughter a number of times and confirms she, too, was a good player with plenty of promise. It seems she and her mother returned to America following her father's death and while possibly still alive at this time, her whereabouts are unknown.

SIMON BALLINAMORE DOHERTY

Third in the family of Mickey Mór was Simon (Ballinamore) Doherty, better known as Simi, and named after his paternal grandfather from whom all the children in the family took their nickname. An interesting second-hand, yet quite reliable, account of his birth is afforded us through the memories of Lough Doon fiddler, Francie McHugh. The story was recounted to him with great consistency by his neighbour, the late Barney Boyle, on whose farm the events took place. It goes as follows[8]:

> Simon Doherty was born over by Loughfad. Aye, that was the greatest night you're talking about. It went on for a full week that! In them days there was only a room and a kitchen in the house and when the (expecting) woman got into the good, warm bed she was in no hurry to leave it. She lay down and rested and the poor man had no where to go. He was getting uneasy. (Following the birth) T'was going on there for a full week and there weren't a fiddler or a travelling body from Sligo till Inishowen point but all gathered for that week. There was great celebration. Prince Charles' (Bonnie Charlie's birth) was

> nothing to it. Prince Charles was nothing to it! They played and danced and had fires out at every bank and went round with tin fiddles and every class of fiddle you could play. There was the herring fishing then in Portnoo at the same time. And the women went away and took out big burdens of herring and began to fry them and the sparks they were like faerie lights going up into the sky. The nicest thing that ever you'd seen and that went on for a full week. So in the rear, poor Barney Boyle got fed up with the game and he sent down for Sergeant Burley who was down in the barracks and two of the men. They came up and they were in no hurry putting them away. The men fell in with the women and they were in no hurry putting them away. There was no end to the dancing and the playing!

From the few field recordings that exist of Simi his style is much closer to that of John rather than Mickey. This is surprising as his father's style was much more that which was played by Mickey and not so much that subsequently developed by John. Simon (Kilmacrennan) Doherty well remembers Simi's playing as a young man and praises him by saying[9] "you could dance to Simi from here to the Post Office. He was a strong, firm player, and could carry out firm to the morning. He was sweet and true".

In any event, one advantage of this kinship with John's style is that it lent itself to extremely tight duet playing, in fact, tighter than that which existed between John and Mickey. An RTÉ field recording of a limited number of solo performances from Simi gives us an interesting insight to the Dohertys' approach to duet playing. Simi plays the *Pigeon on the Gate* in two different keys and then explains how certain keys lend themselves to playing in octaves, making the work relatively easier for both players. Simi refers to the fiddler in the lower octave (which was normally his role when playing duet with John) as "the helper". He also calls playing in the lower octave "reversing" or "playing on the flat". The term reversing is still used by some Donegal players today and may even contribute to the confused title in Donegal of *The Reverse of Vienna* for the *Varsovienna* (otherwise *Shoe the Donkey*) which is sometimes played in octaves. He also plays *Lough Isle Castle*, which he names as *The Tullaghan Lassies* and cites his father's piping as the source for the tune.

Simi eventually settled in the railway crossing house at Ballinamore, Fintown. During his adult playing life he associated primarily with two partners, his brother John, whom he admired greatly, and Barney The Lodge Ward. He spent the last years of his life in the Railway Crossing House, Ballinamore, until he died tragically when the house burned in 1961.

MICKEY DOHERTY

The next two children in Mickey Mór's family were girls, Mary and Hannah, the latter of whom did not survive long. The next child, Mickey, was born in 1894. Throughout his boyhood he acquired his father's skills at tinsmithing. He was able to make pandais with mechanical (non-sealed) joints which because of their excellent manufacture were watertight. He was also an adept maker of tin fiddles. He could make a tin fiddle during a card session in the Croaghs and at the end of the card playing his completed instrument would be raffled[10]. Mickey would then play for a dance. One of his tin fiddles, an extremely fine instrument, still exists and is in the possession of Columba Mac a' Bhaird of Teelin while another is in the possession of Peter Oliver of Ardara.

At the age of nineteen, Mickey married his wife Mary Rua and they had five sons, whom they named after each of Mickey's five brothers, and four daughters including one who died in infancy. While the children were young Mickey settled with his family in the Croaghs. When the boys grew up they emigrated and the girls tended to remain close to home going into domestic service around Ballybofey and Strabane. A photograph exists of one of his daughters in the back garden of a house in Strabane caring for a very young brother and sister. Close examination reveals the boy, at around age four, to be the gifted musician Paul Brady.

As the children left home Mickey and Mary Rua travelled a bit more and eventually came to settle in Meetinghouse Street, Ballybofey. They remained there for a number of years and then made a home in the newly built houses in Ard McCool, Stranorlar. The circumstances of this change are well recounted in Paddy Tunney's book 'The Stone Fiddle'[11]. During this time Mickey took every possible opportunity to visit Hughie Gillespie, who had recently returned from America. According to Hughie the two players got along very well with Mickey being greatly impressed by Hughie's versions of *Jenny's Welcome to Charlie* and *The Yellow Heifer.*

Mickey's musical legacy exists in two parts; in the tunes he di passed onto players with which he came into contact and secc through field recordings made in the later years of his life. Mic playing clearly differs from that of his better known brother, John, in that it is marked by much less staccato bowing and a greater dance-swing rhythm. In terms of ornamentation, Mickey favoured the bowed triplet but also had no aversion to using rolls. Those who knew Mickey well include Jimmy, Vincent, Columba and Josie Campbell and to a lesser extent Danny O'Donnell as well as others such as Peter Campbell who was acquainted with both Mickey and his father. They all are strongly in agreement that Mickey's style was very close to that of his father in contrast to John's and was based on playing for dancing.

Of the tunes which he did not record but were given to other players, the five part reel *Muileann na Maide* as played by Vincent Campbell[12] rates as one of the classic pieces of Donegal fiddling. The first part is characterised by intricate double stopped piping imitation with more exciting double stopping appearing in the remaining parts. The piping connection may indicate that the source of the tune was Mickey's father.

It was popularly believed up until recently that very little of the playing of Mickey Doherty was recorded. The primary source of material from Mickey is that collected by Caoimhín Dannachair and Seán O hEochaidh who, while working for the Irish Folklore Commission in January of 1949, collected the best bit of three hours of playing from him[13]. This material is very representative of Mickey's playing at this period of his life containing the typical elements of his repertoire. Present are the Donegal tunes which he would have been familiar with from childhood through his family. Also to be found are the later arrivals into his repertoire i.e Michael Coleman and Paddy Killoran tunes. When drawing on the Sligo recordings the rest of the country broadly favoured the absorption of the Coleman discs. In contrast, the recorded evidence and family memories confirm that Mickey strongly favoured the Killoran releases as opposed to those of either Michael Coleman or James Morrison.

Interestingly, amongst the Folklore Commission pieces is a highland he calls *DúlamáOn na Buinne Buí,* common in Scottish collections as the strathspey *Cutting Ferns*. This differs completely from the *Dúlamán na Binne Buí* played by his brother John. Mickey's version of *The Rights of Man* is certainly one of the most exciting to be heard. It is played relatively quickly for a hornpipe and marked by a torrent of scalar runs which make all other versions I have heard pale in comparison. The recording standard of this material was just about the best available in its day for field recordings and therefore affords us an excellent opportunity to hear the tonal quality which Mickey could produce in his playing.

A limited number of pieces were collected by the BBC in Belfast. These include a powerful performance of *The Boyne Hunt* which he consistently associated with the folk tale of the Twisting of the Rope. This piece is rendered in a pipe-imitation style using extensive double stopping in the first part of the tune and is a firm testament to his rhythmic and technical prowess. Other material was recorded by Ciarán Mac Mathúna of RTÉ with significant assistance from Dr. Malachy McCloskey. Breandán Breathnach, working in association with Tom Glackin also collected from Mickey and some transcriptions of this material appear in 'Ceol Rince na hÉireann, Cuid a Do'[15]. Some material was also collected from Mickey by Peter Kennedy then working for the BBC in London[16]. A great deal of the latter is taken up by Mickey's unusually large store of lore on Saint Columbcille.

Thankfully a number of private recordings of Mickey Doherty have come to light in recent years which further expand his store of tunes and more importantly document his stylistic genius. Most of these recordings come from Pat Connaghan of The Forge, Doorin Line, Mountcharles. These recordings were made by Pat's father, the late John James Connaghan, in the kitchen of the family home. John James, as we will see, was himself an extremely gifted player and well known to Mickey. In the relaxed surroundings of a familiar house and playing for a fellow musician who well understood the music, Mickey flourished. John James can clearly be heard prompting Mickey to play his best tunes which he does with great vivacity. Of this material two tunes immediately strike the listener. The first is the *Morning Dew* which Mickey plays in great Donegal style and with an additional fourth part which I have never heard anyone else play. The second tune is the slip jig *Dever the Dancer* which he plays with an intricate syncopated rhythm which transforms the piece. One tune which appears on this set of recordings is of interest for historical reasons as Mickey introduces it by stating it was the first reel he ever learned, giving the title as *Last Night's Joy*. He says he picked it up as a young boy from a very old woman. He was sitting in her kitchen and she had been lilting it. As he "took a conceit on it" he was anxious to get the tune. He asked her to lilt it over and over until eventually he had the reel. With the characteristic Doherty confidence he can be heard to report that the tune could easily be five hundred years old! Mickey Doherty died at home in the company of his wife, devoted daughter Frances and brother John on May 14th, 1970 and is buried in the family grave at Fintown.

HUGH AND SIMON DOHERTY (STRANORLAR)

Following Mickey in the family was Hugh who was similarly a very talented player whose style was close to Mickey. His eldest son, Simon, was born in 1916 and only died in February, 1987. Simon spent most of his adult life around Stranorlar were he eventually came to settle near his aunt and uncle's residence in Ard McCool. Simon also practiced the family trade of tinsmithing and did make some tin fiddles. None of these however are up to the excellent standard of those of his uncles. In general, Simon chose to make simple box-shaped instruments. Musically, Simon had the basic Doherty repertoire, but was notorious for mis-matching the parts of tunes as well as keys. His style was more in line with his uncle Mickey's rather than John's. Simon's younger brother Michael now lives in Australia. During a recent visit home he played at a number of sessions. His style at that time was quite untypical of his uncles and he had heavy overtones of classical influences in his technique.

JOHN DOHERTY

Next in Mickey Mór's family was Annie, followed by the youngest child, John, who was born in Ardara[18], and not Fintown as incorrectly stated in 'The Northern Fiddler', in about 1895. He maintained in later life that he started to play around the age of sixteen or seventeen years. By this he meant playing with conviction, since it is certain he had been informally getting tunes before this age. As a young man John was extremely popular at social functions such as house dances. He was, by his twenties, already a recognised virtuoso player. The store of folklore he possessed since his earliest youth, coupled with his own humourous, good natured personality meant that he was a very welcome addition to any gathering.

John's normal routine at this period was to travel the countryside spending a week or two in a locality. During this period he would work at tinsmithing during the day as well as selling various items he might have bought in a nearby town. At night he played for dances and taught tunes. John had a more or less regular route which extended from Ballybofey up through Fintown down into Glenties, on to Ardara and into Glencolumcille heading back to Ballybofey through Carrick, Teelin and Kilcar. He very much favoured the rural areas and larger towns like Ballybofey, Killybegs and Donegal were only for passing through. He was more than a welcome guest along his route and he would not stop with just anyone. A house which could host John was an honoured one and was known to be so by the community. Though a player of tremendous stature even at this stage of his life, John was also shy about playing for persons outside of his normal travelling route. Numerous accounts exist of him hiding out in the cottages of friends along his path trying to evade collectors and broadcasters.

The early influences for John were obviously from within his immediate family as well as his uncles, the McConnells. By the 1930's he was exposed to commercial recordings ranging from James Scott Skinner to William McKenzie Murdoch in the Scottish realm to Michael Coleman, James Morrison, Hughie Gillespie and somewhat later Paddy Killoran in the Irish arena. Of these, James Scott Skinner was to make the greatest impression. As regards Irish recording influences, again it was as with Mickey, he strongly favoured Paddy Killoran rather than the other two more heralded south Sligomen or Hughie Gillespie. John certainly absorbed the melodic approaches of the recordings of Neillidh Boyle. This is evidenced in his faithful rendition of the Neillidh's recording of *The Harvest Home*. Eventually, the two men would become comfortable friends respecing each others musical ability.

From early on John appears to have adjusted his bowing style away from his father's and his brother Mickey's style to adopt the more dramatic staccato style and by almost totally ignoring the strong Scots and lesser Irish dotted rhythms. This appears to have been much closer to the old style of playing in Glencolumcille which can be heard today in the playing of James Byrne. It may well be the case that Pádaí Bhillí na Rópaí, with whom John would have met in his youth, exerted an influence on him. At any rate, through his approach, John Doherty brought fiddle playing to new heights of mastery within the Donegal context. Possibly the best clarification in the differences between John and Mickey's personal styles can be heard in their recordings of the well known reel *The Oak Tree.* Mickey's version has been confirmed by numerous players as identical with his father Mickey Mór's. In this setting, the initial two bars are completely different to those popularised today through John. There is a greater degree of swing in the rhythm and rolls are used more profusely. John's version on the other hand does not incorporate his father's opening bars and is marked by attacking, staccato bowing with even accented notes. In common, both renditions display incredibly dexterous double stopping throughout and crisp triplets in the third part of the tune.

Overall, John's style of playing is typified by almost strict, even-accented staccato bowing of highlands and jigs. His reels and hornpipes are again very dominantly played with a staccato bow and include some passages with up to three or four notes per bow. These are generally uncommon and only done to suit the note sequence of the particular portion of the tune. The only significant exception to John's staccato approach is when, like other Donegal fiddlers, he executed very long bowed pipe imitations. Normally his left hand technique had less ornamental demands due to his emphasis on bow-work. Again, the exception here is when he played double stops which, typical of John, were usually complex and imaginative without cluttering a tune.

Contrary to the stereotyped image of John's style he did play rolls, though not all that frequently. In addition he did have a special roll sequence which gave an incredible attacking sound to the note being played. Where two notes of the same pitch could be rolled, one after another, John had a preference for playing a bowed triplet on the first followed immediately by a roll on the second. The best example of this is in his version of the *Gweebarra Reel* (commonly mis-titled *Doherty's Reel*) where he starts the tune with an A note on the bottom string. He rivets the first note with a triplet then follows on with a roll on the same note making the high grace note of the roll with his little rather than the customary ring finger. Staying with the left hand, it must be said that as an untrained musician in the normal, classical education sense, John had an uncanny ability to play in either awkward keys or with difficult position work. John, like his Sligo contemporaries Killoran, Morrison and Coleman, was a fast player which undermines some of the arguments of musicians of the older generation throughout Ireland that Irish music was meant to be played at a moderate pace.

Recognition outside of his normal circles started to come for John in the late 1940's when he was sought by sound archive collectors. At this time, for a collector to come to Donegal and not record John would have been seen in the community as lunacy. His fame was taking off and in the early Fifties he travelled to Dublin to contest the Oireachtas fiddle competition which he won beating the renowned east Galway fiddler Aggie White in the process.

In subsequent years he travelled with Dr. Malachy McCloskey to some All-Ireland Fleadhs where arising from the massive demand to hear him play he was effectively holed up in a hotel room and played for specific pre-arranged groups of listeners. It was as a result of spending a night through to morning of playing rare slip jigs and unusual dance tunes for John Kelly and others that Tom Glackin was prevailed upon to arrange the famous recording session with Breandán Breathnach in the Reelin Bridge. By the 1960's John was a major force on the national scene. So strong was his influence that his style of playing was taken to be the singular, archetypal Donegal style of playing. This mis-informed view later prompted a corrective comment by Breandán Breathnach in 'Irish Folk Music and Dancesof Ireland' which stressed the error of dismissing anything that did not sound like John's style as not being Donegal style fiddle playing. It must be said though that Breathnach did incorrectly conclude that rolling is not employed by fiddle players in Donegal[19].

Around this time John was to adopt a more retired lifestyle spending a number of years in Carrick where his playing attracted musicians of note from all over the globe. His daytime work effectively disappeared and he became a fulltime musician. He suffered a brief illness which left him in the hospital for a short period. Following this he sought less demands on his playing and moved in with his sister-in-law, Mary Rua and her daughter, Frances in Mickey's house in Árd McCool, Stranorlar. To some extent, this period may mark the golden era of John Doherty's life. He was now internationally renowned as a traditional fiddler. In the capital, Paddy, Séamus and Kevin Glackin who had emerged as some of the most significant fiddlers of the maturing generation paid regular, fitting tributes to John in respect of his influence on their music. UTV had sought him for a biographical film entitled 'Fiddler on the Road' which when broadcast met with wide critical acclaim. Unlike his brothers, John realised during his lifetime the widespread fame he was due and saw the release of commercially successful recordings.

While he continued to play concerts he avoided fixed demands for regular public playing. He could perform when and where he chose. Most enjoyably of all for him at this time, however, may have been the presence of Danny O'Donnell literally down the street in Ballybofey. The two were regularly in each others company playing and comparing tunes, their origins and variations. Givens' Pub on the main street was the perfect setting for such conferences. In the back was a small snug with the acoustically ideal hard floor and walls. The Givens' were old neighbours of Danny from the Rosses who understood and appreciated the music and were protective of the fiddlers. In such surroundings John could play for a quiet, attentive audience and at the same time combine duets and chat with Danny which delighted him to no end.

These years were good ones for John but time was marching onHe eventually moved into the Rock Home in Ballyshannon where he was looked after in comfort. He had regular visitors and continued to play showing no loss of skill from the standards of his earliest field recordings. On a Monday morning in late January, 1980 I called in to see him and we parted with him flawlessly thundering out *The Black Fanad Mare* with the energy of a teenager. He died peacefully, the following Thursday. On the following freezing Saturday he was buried in Fintown Cemetery. The mass, which was especially broadcast live on Radió na Gaeltachta sent out the message that one of the greatest traditional musicians and possessors of folklore had passed on. The bitterly icy conditions made travelling an impossibility for the great numbers who wished to pay their respects at his funeral. A small group that gathered in the Welcome Inn pub outside Fintown paid suitable compliment to John. After a drink, a single fiddle was produced and given to Vincent Campbell.

He hammered out a reel in honour of John then spotted another player to whom he handed the instrument. He played a tune and then passed on the fiddle. After a while it was discovered that the only ones in the house who could not play were the barman and the three women present. Eventually fiddles appeared from under coats, beneath seats, the backs of cars and a massive musical testimony to one of the giants of Irish music ensued.

Possibly due to the difference in their personal styles there was a natural rivalry between John and his brother Mickey. Each were exceptional players who each sought to fulfil the potential of their gifts. Because of their contrasting styles each had regular followers who chose favourites between the two brothers adding to the rivalry stakes. This competition was a healthy one and certainly did not stop the brothers playing marvellous duets as their recordings for Breandán Breathnach, particularly of *Lough Isle Castle,* one of the singularly greatest performances of Donegal fiddling, testifiy. The harmlessness of the rivalry can be put into perspective by Jimmy Hueston's memory of an event at Mickey's funeral. While John acted as host to the mourners at the funeral, a declared fan of Mickey's approached him to sympathise. At this time the car was still a novelty amongst the general population and a person's importance was measured by the length of the queue of cars following the coffin to the graveyard. The Mickey devotee was heard to tell John that his brother must have been one of the greatest fiddlers ever in Ireland for never had so many mourners turned up and the equivalent of the length of the train of cars had never been seen before. John took the humorous view of the taunt. He smiled and said that all of this had for a moment been a cause of great worry for him as he thought it was himself who had died!

Looking back, John and Mickey grew up in a culture which understood and held a healthy respect for folklore and superstitions. They also took delight in adapting major storylines to suit conditions as they might arise. One well known motif in Irish folklore, often associated with Diarmúid and Gráinne, is a tree springing from the grave of a great person whose passing is much lamented. No doubt Mickey and John would find great humour in the fact that of all the graves in Fintown Cemetery a single one has borne a tree – a lone mountain ash, one of Ireland's humblest trees, which each year bears a heavy autumn fruit harvest for blackbirds thrives at the head of the Dohertys' graves.

THE O'ROURKES

Edward O'Rourke married Fanny Doherty, the eldest daughter of Mickey Mór Doherty and Mary McConnell. A native of Ardara he was a well known fiddler. His style is reputed to have been similar to the McConnells and owing to the fact that they circulated in the same small area it is reasonable to accept that they may well have had much in common. Eamonn's son Hugh, now living in Dunkineely is the best known fiddler of the family today. His style is marked by fast, very staccato bowing and would appear to show strong influences from his cousin, John Doherty, who he greatly admired. A characteristic feature of Hugh's playing is to play a tune over up to six or seven times. This is in contrast to the more typical performance amongst today's fiddlers of playing a tune three or four times at the most and then changing into another tune. Hugh's approach of sustained playing of the same tune is almost certainly a remnant of playing for dancers or alternatively playing with other fiddlers who were more used to playing for dancers than with performance playing. Another member of this family is Paddy O'Rourke, who also concentrates his playing around the Ardara area.

REFERENCES

1 *Teip Simon (Kilamcrennan) Doherty*. Cairdeas na bhFidléiri Collection, An Foras Cuiltúir Uladh, Gleann Cholm Cille.

2 *Teip Simon (Kilmacrennan) Doherty*. Op. Cit.

3 *Teip Simon (Kilmacrennan) Doherty*. Op. Cit.

4 *The Star of Donegal*. Folktrack Recordings, FSA-60-075.

5 *Teip John Simi Doherty*. Cairdeas na bhFidléiri Collection, An Foras Cuiltúir Uladh, Gleann Cholm Cille.

6 *The Star of Donegal*. Op. Cit.

8 *Teip Francie McHugh*. Cairdeas na bhFidléiri Collection, An Foras Cuiltúir Uladh, Gleann Cholm Cille.

9 *Teip Simon* (kilmacrennan) Doherty. Op. Cit.

10 *The Gravel Walks*. Comhairle Bealoideas Éireann, CBE 002.

11 Paddy Tunney. *The Stone Fiddle*. Gilbert Dalton. Skerries, County Dublin. 1979, p.149. Also see *The Derry Journal*, December,21, 1990, p.29.

12 *The Brass Fiddle*. Claddagh Records, CC44.

13 This material is now included in the Irish Folklore Commission Collection in the Department of Irish Folklore and Folk Music. Much of the material comprises the commercial release *The Gravel Walks* by Comhairle Bealoideas Éireann, CBE 002.

14 Breandán Breathnach. *Ceol Rince na hÉireann - Cuid a Do*. Oifig an tSolatháir, Baile Átha Cliath, 1976. Nos. 133, 156, 182, 199, 235, 268.

16 *The Fiddler and the Fairy*. Folktracks Cassettes FSA-60-073.

18 Lochlainn McGill. *In Conaill's Footsteps*. Brandon Books, Dingle, 1992.

19 Breandán Breathnach. *Folkmusic and Dances of Ireland*. The Educational Company of Ireland. 1971. p. 101.

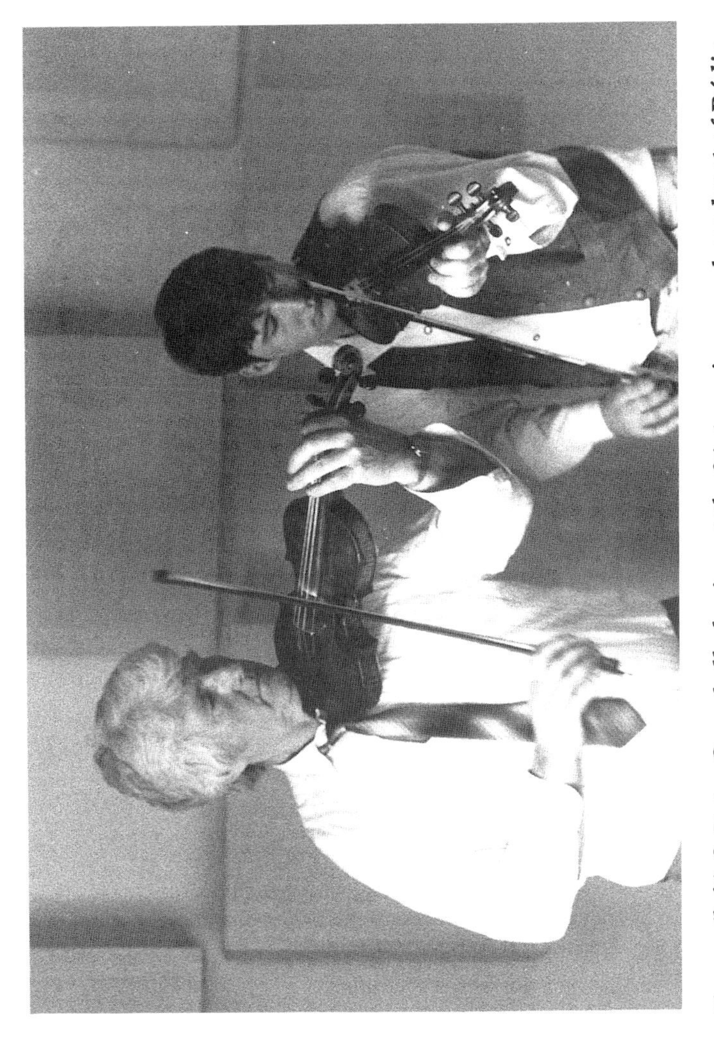

Jimmy (left) & Peter Campbell playing at the 21st anniversary broadcast of Rádio na Gaeltachta, Na Doire Beaga

Jimmy Hueston of Drumkeen

Pat (the younger) Kelly of Bundoran

Danny McCarry of Kildarragh at the foot of Mukish mountain

Pat McDermott of Kilmacrennan

Eddie Moore at his old place of Corlea

Harry Carey and his daughter of Corlea

Paddy Boyle of Cronashallog, son of Neillidh

CHAPTER 12

CENTRAL DONEGAL

At the core of Donegal lies a majestic mountain range which is traversed by a network of deep glens. The mountains are known in Irish as *Na Cruacha Gorma*, or by their English translation, The Blue Stacks. They are are also referred to in English by their inhabitants as The Croaghs, which is an anglicisation of the Irish *Cruacha* (peaks). In a cultural sense, a good portion of this general area is known as An Ghaeltacht Lar, or the central Irish speaking district. The ground here is wild, open, upland bog with small farm holdings concentrated in the glens. An excellent social history of this area, which has suffered drastic depopulation is offered by Áine Ní Dhioraí[1] as well as Séamus O Catháin[2] in their works dealing with the extremely rich folklore of the area. Fiddle playing was extensive in this region and this concentration of players was probably only rivalled by the southwest district. The Dohertys tended to settle here in their latter years and made a major impact on the playing. Their relations The McConnells were also strongly associated with this part of the county.

All that I have come to feel as being the best about Donegal seems somehow to be encapsulated in this area. The environment and scenery appear almost to compose the music heard here. Scenery/environment and music are linked in a way which defies description while the local people are gifted with great warmth and kindness. Although very capable of thriving in a modern world, they retain the distinguishing humanity of a disappearing age which marks them as a very special people.

THE GIANTS OF THE MOUNTAIN

Croveenananta is a peak which translated from the Irish may be taken as the mountain flaying meadow. It is to be found adjacent to Cruach an Airgead, or Silver Hill, in the heart of the Croaghs. It was in this area that Peter Campbell was born in 1900. His father, James, was a fiddle player and he in turn taught Peter and his brother. The house was exceptionally musical and the centre of house dancing for the local population. Most of the people in the area were able to play fiddles and a large dance repertoire consisting of highlands, germans, reels, polkas, strathspeys, jigs etc. was generated. As a young man Peter emigrated along with some of his relations to America spending time in both New York and Philadelphia. He longed for home and eventually returned, married and raised a family. During his middle age years he continued to host house dances and his home became the primary visiting spot for the Doherty brothers whenever they were in the area. The Dohertys were greatly admired for their talents and they always repaid the compliments by playing extensively and teaching their tunes. Peter regularly played for house dances in other nearby localities. On these occasions he frequently partnered Paddy The Tae Gallagher of Ardara whom he still regards as being one of the best fiddlers he ever met. Peter rarely plays now but remains a devoted enthusiast of fiddle music with an almost childlike curiosity to meet and hear new players.

Peter's sons had the tremendous fortune to be raised in what may well have been the most musical house in Ireland. Exposed to the massive dance repertoire and refined style of their father in combination with extended access to the Dohertys, particularly John and Mickey, they could be said to have been spoonfed on the cream of the tradition.

JIMMY CAMPBELL

Jimmy is now a middle aged man. His height is towering with a full head of grey hair at the top. At the sign or sound of a fiddle he shows a glowing, disarming smile as broad as his massive hands. Considering his earliest exposure to music it is not surprising that he possesses the old house dance repertoire of this area. Though over the years he has complemented this with a broader body of tunes, his playing is the most supreme example of the old house dance style I have ever heard. While maintaining a technical simplicity there is a swing in his fiddling which captures the essence of beauty in the music. The rhythm of the highland is virtually defined by Jimmy Campbell's playing of it.

While naturally attracted to the fiddle from an early age he can recall the incident which set his heart firmly at becoming a fiddler. As a very young boy he was taken down into Glenties to attend a concert of local players. Paddy Bazaar McFadden, a fiddler from Derry who sold wares at the seasonal bazaars throughout west Donegal, was one of the featured musicians. Paddy was a trick fiddler. He would put his right foot onto his left knee and place the frog of the bow into his right boot. With the bow standing straight up and the hair facing him, he would take the fiddle with his playing hand in position. Holding the base of the fiddle in his right hand, he would push the fiddle into the strings and run it up and down along the stationary bow while playing *The Boys of Blue Hill.* This display of wizardry, as he saw it, was to ensure that Jimmy Campbell would become a fiddler. He rushed home and threw himself headlong into fiddle playing. To this day, Jimmy is still capable of this contorted feat which he takes pleasure in performing for children especially. My son, Eoghan, who was around nine at the time had picked up the trick from Jimmy. We were on a visit to Arranmore Island to play and for fun he started playing *Shoe the Donkey* this way. There was a group out for the day from the Croaghs and this was spotted. They asked Eoghan would he mind coming back with them to teach it to Jimmy Campbell as he only had *The Boys of Blue Hill*! Word eventually got back to Jimmy who, true to nature, greatly enjoyed the humour of it.

Jimmy spent much of his adult life away in both Scotland and England. Most of this was in London where he worked in construction. During his time there, his amount of playing decreased due to work and family demands. He did form a very close friendship with both Danny Meehan and Brendan McGlinchey. Brendan and Paddy Conroy, a melodeon player from Connemara also played with Jimmy in a band which toured Jersey on one occasion. Since returning to live at home in the wee glen, Jimmy has been much more active in playing and his standard of fiddling has risen to that of his younger days. During a recent visit to Glenties Brendan McGlinchey was quite taken back by the playing form to

which Jimmy has returned. Jimmy's son, Peter, was rai
London and still works there. He learned directly from his
as well as from his uncles on the many visits he made to G
with his parents. He has developed into an enviable fiddler with a style markedly close to his father. If such a concept of breeding exists, it could be exemplified by Peter. Despite being reared in the urban sprawl of London, his nature and music are utterly typical of a Croaghs man. His work demands that he is too rarely heard in Glenties and his visits are always looked forward to with great anticipation.

VINCENT CAMPBELL

Excepting the grey hair, Vincent Campbell shows all the physical traits of his older brother. Vincent started to play at home, and with Jimmy involved in playing at a young age, there was a natural incentive for him to play early as well. Now in his early fifties, he has spent an active adulthood not only as the primary house dance player and performer in the Croaghs and Glenties area but also in relentless pursuit of older musicians in an attempt to capture the whole of the local repertoire. This often meant cycling miles to a player to learn a single tune which he heard the player might have. Sometimes these journeys may have been for the purposes of simply learning an unusual variation of a tune which he already had. The result of these efforts is his possessing a huge repertoire of diagnostic local tunes as well as an almost complete collection of the tunes of John and Mickey Doherty.

As a young man Vincent worked in Scotland making many associations with both Donegal and Scots fiddlers there. He moved for a number of years to County Meath where he had a farm and during this time he made regular trips into Dublin to circulate amongst its players. He eventually married and returned to take up combined farming and construction work in the big glen.

Stylistically, Vincent is incredibly accomplished, playing with a sound that is utterly unique. His bowing is short, almost unwaveringly staccato and availing of prolific double stopping droning. This latter effect, combined with a booming volume and rich tone, produces a maelstrom of impassioned music from a much older time. His technical execution is some of the most complex that exists in Irish fiddle playing. The double stopping, which appears to derive from the piping influences in the Dohertys' music, is tonally impeccable and is achieved by highly adroit left hand little fingering. To illustrate his overwhelming fingering dexterity one only has to experience his playing of either *Jackson's Reel* or the reel *Muileann na Maide*, both of which came to him via the Dohertys. In each case, with his small finger playing D on the fourth string he drones the open third and fourth strings in unison, sometimes including bowed triplets for variation. While this is taking place, he effects piping imitation by trilling the third string with his index finger and at the same time carrying the melody of the tune with his middle and ring fingers on the third string! Following on from his upbringing, this house dance music has been produced from his mind's ear and his soul. Like most Donegal fiddlers of his generation, he is unable to read music. Vincent Campbell, like his music, is larger than life. He has not only served the tradition well by his playing and collecting efforts, he has, over the past number of years, been highly active in supporting the development efforts aimed at strengthening the music. The credit for many of the successes arising from the efforts of Cairdeas na bhFidléirí lie with him.

COLUMBA CAMPBELL

Columba Campbell is another to have been nurtured in this tradition. He is rarely heard today because of the time he devotes to meeting the needs of his father as well as his second passion in life– fishing. Columba's style differs from both Jimmy and Vincent's in that it is less powerful by being more sweet and pensive in approach. His technical ability is applied with great thought while his imagination in variation is renowned. Though he does not play an instrument, the fourth musician of the Campbells is Josie. His brothers will freely admit that when they are at a loss for a tune, Josie will have it. Not only will he have the basic tune but he will be in a position to lilt each note and offer any variations required. When called on to perform the brothers do not take account of how they, themselves feel they have played. If Josie was pleased with it, then all went well. It was Josie who carved the masterfully produced stone fiddle which forms the centre piece of the Mickey Doherty memorial in Eadaninfagh.

OTHER CROAGH FIDDLERS

As already pointed out, there was a large fiddling community in this small area. An active participant at the Campbell's house dances was and remains their neighbour Cormac Quinn. He plays both fiddle and melodeon much in the style of Jimmy Campbell. He is one of the strongest enthusiasts of the music in the area. His life could be described as being consumed by the music. A number of years ago while out making hay he could hear Columba Campbell playing in the distance. Hay, sun, weather, turning etc. were all forfeited as more important duties were in need of attention. A well played tune in the right hands is as good to Cormac as a stack of hay the size of Cruach an Airgead. Pat Pheadar Mhick Mac Dabhait was another local player born about the last two decades of the last century. He taught a lot of tunes to Peter Campbell, the elder. He was one of the house dance players Peter admired most and usually topped the bill for the larger school house dances in summer. One of Peter's contemporaries was Barney Boyle who featured at house dances. A player in the age group between Vincent Campbell and his father was John na gCuinneagáin Mac a' Bhaird. As his name implies, he was raised by his relations the O Cuinneagáins. John is consistently referred to by all who remember his playing as a very talented fiddler. Another visitor was Johnnie an Fidléir Beag Molloy who came from Meenaneary to live locally after marrying a relation of Peter Campbell. It is recalled that he brought with him a wider repertoire than that found in the Croaghs. Jimmy and Andy Marley of Glassagh were also good house players as was Francie Amros (Ambrose) Given. Pádaí Bhartlaí Mc Glynn of Glenfin is remembered by all of the Campbells as being one of the greatest players ever to emerge from the area. In terms of age, he seems to fall in between the generation of Peter Campbell and that of his sons. He had a huge repertoire and could rightly be considered as important as the Dohertys in terms of spreading the music locally. Charlie Patton was also familiar with Padai Bhartlaí and considered him a player of major importance. Paddy Bazaar McFadden, referred to above, originally came into the Glenties area for visits but eventually settled in the town opening a bicycle shop on the main street where the Limelight is now located. He is still remembered as a regular player and entertainer. Another Glenfin fiddler of note is Pat Doherty. A special visitor to the Eadaninfagh area recalled by the Campbells was An Gypsy Mór. He was a traveller of great stature who came with his family specifically during the autumn to sell and repair tinware. He shaved only once a year with a cut throat razor on the night of the harvest moon. Vincent learned some of the highlands which he still plays today from him.

The extended Mac a' Luain family has become associated in international folklore circles as being the sources of some of the richest material in western Europe[3]. They also contributed a sizeable number of players to this small community. Seán John Chit of Cruach an Airgead was a noted player and associated strongly with the Campbells. He was one of the featured fiddlers at the first Annual Meeting of Cairdeas na bhFidléirí in Glenties in 1983. He was very fond of *Muileann na Maide* and the *Swallowtail Coat* reels. Seán died in 1984 and is buried locally.

The Eoghain Phadraigs of Croveenananta were exceptionally musical people and their home was a reputed venue for house dances. While he was probably the most famous dancer of the district as his name indicates, Conal a' Damhsa, Conal Eoghain Phádraig[4] was also a reasonable house dance player. His style was considered important by local fiddlers in the light of his exceptional understanding of both fiddling and dancing.

DR. MALACHY McCLOSKEY

Dr. Malachy McCloskey was born in Belfast. In 1922 with rising troubles in that city his father, a native of Croagh, Dunkineely and his mother, a native of Kilraine, Glenties decided to return to Kilraine to raise their young children[5]. As a youth Malachy showed an interest in music and his father, keen to encourage him got him a fiddle. He started to pick up local tunes by ear and subsequently took lessons which included learning to read staff notation. As he still seemed to progress faster through playing by ear the lessons were dropped.

His earliest influence was Hugh McDyer of Kilraine who lived less than a quarter of a mile away. Hugh qualified as a National School teacher at Maynooth and taught at Doobin National School. When Dr. McCloskey was about eight years old Hugh would call to the house and play while taking the time out to show Malachy the techniques of playing as well as teaching him tunes. These sessions were described as follows: "After short, preliminary chatting he would take down the fiddle which was hanging on the wall and begin to play. He played solidly until about 10 P.M. and then went home. In all, the session lasted near to four hours and covered the entire panoply of traditional music - jigs, reels, hornpipes and slow airs". Malachy was mesmerised by his reel playing at which he excelled. He was later to write "to this day I believe I never heard a better reel player than Hugh McDyer". The first reel Hugh taught him was *Miss McLeod's Reel.*

Tragically Hugh contacted pulmonary tuberculosis and spent a short time in Peamount Sanatorium. The disease continued to progress and Hugh's health declined constantly. Due to the contagious nature of the disease visitors were not permitted but Malachy was eventually given a brief chance to speak with his friend. Their discussion centred totally on fiddle playing with Hugh continuing to encourage Malachy to persist with the instrument. Dr. McCloskey remembers he died the next day aged 24 years. "I wept bitterly over his grave as I realised my mentor had gone forever. I think the year was 1924. His grave is in Kilraine graveyard". We can get some insight into the style of playing of Hugh McDyer. In recent years Dr. McCloskey has had the opportunity to meet the young Scottish player Alasdair Frazer at the Annual Meeting in Glenties. This prompted him to note: "as soon as he began to play I became transfixed for this was Hugh McDyer playing again. Even some of his mannerisms reminded me of Hugh. If I closed my eyes I was back again in the Kilraine of the 1920s listening to Hugh McDyer playing. I spent all next day at a session in The Highlands Hotel with Alasdair playing the fiddle".

Shortly after the death of Hugh McDyer, Danny and Paddy Byrne came to live in Lettermacaward. They were both accomplished fiddlers and young Malachy was mobile enough to associate with them. He also met with Con Gildea from Glenconwell who, for Malachy, had an enviable collection of old mazurkas. Now in his eighties, Con is still going well. In 1940 Dr. McCloskey was appointed as Temporary Medical Officer in Killybegs and came to associate with the Hegarty or 'The Docs' brothers as well as having occasional meetings with the famous Pádaí Bhillí na Rópaí Boyle. About a year later he went to Carrick where he integrated well with the great gathering of fiddlers there, making particular acquaintence with Frank Cassidy as well as Francie and Mickey

O'Byrne of Kilcar. In 1942 he was appointed to a dispensary in Doochary and there through his close friend, the famous step dancer whose name is remembered in a popular hornpipe, Dr. Peter Carr, was introduced to John Doherty. This meeting was a very important one as the two struck up a friendship which was firm until the latter's death in 1980. At this time John was relatively unknown outside his regular circuit. Dr. McCloskey opened many doors to the outside world for John by bringing him to various gatherings and ensuring proper consideration for him. When the word started to circulate about John's prowess Dr. McCloskey typically was called on to make contacts and introductions. Both Seán O Ríada and Ciarán Mac Mathúna depended heavily on Malachy for ensuring the success of their collecting visits to John Doherty and to Donegal in general. Arising from his close relationship with John he also came to know and associate with both Mickey and Simi (Ballinamore) Doherty.

Dr. McCloskey has reduced his duties in recent years allowing a greater freedom to enjoy his runner-up passion to community medicine. As a result, the music has benefited and he has been a tireless worker, typically behind the scenes, in helping to make the Cairdeas na bhFidléirí Annual Meeting a success in Glenties. His knowledge of and contribution towards the long term development of the music for six decades or more have yet to be accurately assessed. When that time comes all will be astounded at the scale of his achievements.

The music in Glenties has experienced some changes in recent years. Its popularity with young players has been undergoing a significant revival. Séamus Sweeney held a number of regular classes which greatly assisted in the development of players including Tara Connaghan, the McElhinney family as well as Denise and Catherine Boyle, whose parents, John and Christine, have made critical contributions to the profile of the music at both county and national level through their behind-the-scenes support.

THE SWEET CUP OF TAE

Nestled in the hollow of a ring of sweeping mountain ridges the town of Ardara acts as a major cultural crossroads. To the east is Glenties and the Croaghs, southwards lies Killybegs and Dunkineely, westwards is Kilcar, Carrick, Teelin, and Glencolumcille, while northwards opens into Dungloe. Its position at this junction made it an ideal market town attracting the buyers and sellers of goods, crafts and livestock. Amongst these vendors came musicians and on a fair day players from all of these fiddling epicentres would inevitably congregate in one house.

Séamus Ennis often played, and spoke of the meaning of the reel *The Sweet Cup of Tae*. This was a code name for tea which had been enhanced by adding either poitín or whiskey. Whatever about tea or alcohol Paddy The Tae Gallagher's house in West Port on the main street of Ardara was the focus of some of the sweetest music, past or present, in Donegal.

Paddy The Tae Gallagher was born in the early years of this century in Ardara. He started to play as a young boy having bought a tin fiddle from Simi (Ballinamore) Doherty. His earliest efforts did not leave a big impression on his father who relegated Paddy's practising to the byre. Despite this, he quickly came into demand for house dance playing. His enthusiasm for fiddling meant that he travelled the surrounding area seeking out the better players and learning from them. One such player was Neil Doherty from Doobin who was slightly older than Paddy. Neil was a tremendous fiddler to the point where he was greatly respected by all the Dohertys brothers. This is the same Neil Doherty who spent some years in Philadelphia and came to be so highly praised by the fiddler and composer Ed Reavey. He also played with another contemporary, Frainc a' Phoill of Kilraine. Frainc is remembered as a bit of a character. His mind was set solely on the fiddle and work was not a priority. As the instrument was kept near the bed he would sometimes wake in the morning, reach out for the fiddle and play away for hours sitting up in bed. His biggest tune was a complex double jig which bears his name in the Ardara area and in southwest Donegal is one of three called *Rí na bPíobairí*. Other players known to Paddy included Danny and Paddy Byrne of

Kilraine, Hugh James Harkin of Croagh, Con Gildea of Glenconwell and Jim Boyle of Strathuachtar.

Paddy The Tae gradually lost his sight by the time he was a young man. To ease the economic strain his wife opened their house during fair days serving teas. By this stage his reputation as a major player was well known and every fiddler and music enthusiast made it a point to take their tea in his house. Their home became a landmark for anyone visiting Ardara on a fair day or a day's outing. Paddy soon took on the nickname Paddy The Tae. Despite his loss of sight he was a famous creel maker and he continued throughout his life to play for house and school dances. He died in the early 1980s having led a long and very musical life.

Paddy's music thankfully did not go to the grave. His son John, known to many as John The Tae, started to attempt tunes on his father's fiddle from the age of four. He began in the upstairs room of the house playing with three fingers. The milkman, a local fiddler by the name of Breslin, heard his attempts and showed him how he could use his fourth finger. He returned the next day with a diagram of where the notes were on the fingerboard. A major hurdle was jumped and John was appearing in a concert at the request of the local parish priest at the age of five years. John The Tae absorbed the style and repertoire of his father and thus is the bearer of a rare and wonderful repertoire. The days and occasions when almost every fiddler west of the Croaghs would converge on his sitting room have stood firmly to John. He also benefited greatly from a strong association with the Dohertys based on great mutual admiration.

As a young man John played for house dances and as the halls came into effect he played with the Forthill Band which enjoyed great popularity in the area. Over the years he formed a long association with James Josie The Post McHugh who had learned both from his own father and Paddy The Tae. These duets were marvellous and very reflective of many of the Doherty partnerships. In 1956 John won the Oireachtas fiddle competition and in 1959 he won the All Ireland fiddle competition at the Fleadh in Thurles. These are fitting accolades for this player of tremendous importance in the Donegal tradition. John still plays with the vigour and strength of a man in his twenties. His technical ability is highly accomplished and his musical sense is uncanny. The drive and attack which marks much of the best of Donegal fiddle music is readily apparent in John's playing. His bowing is dominantly staccato. Though less pronounced than that of the Kilcar and Croaghs fiddlers, his use of droning injects a tremendous sense of excitement and power into his music. Following the death of James Josie McHugh, John has been playing more as a solo fiddler in Ardara. What is cause for great optimism is the fact that he has been concentrating his efforts into teaching his neighbours the four Gallagher sisters, Aoife, Eithne, Croídhe and Níamh. Though only in their teens these girls have rocketed in their standard of playing. Their association with John has been very positive as their playing exhibits a tremendous fidelity to his style and ensures a long continuation of the magic in the tunes which filled that most musical of Ardara houses. Lastly, another very promising young Ardara player is Brian McGill.

EDDIE KEENEY

Eddie Keeney was born in 1922 in Glendoan, about three miles outside Ardara. His family were noted weavers working at home for contractors in Kilcar. His father, Sonny, played fiddle and spent some time in America where he met various players and brought home tunes not known in the district. Eddie's oldest brother, Charlie, who was twenty years his senior had started to play in his youth. By the time Eddie was getting ready to play Charlie had already established himself as a good house dance player and was circulating with a large number of local fiddlers. Eddie had the advantage of getting help from Charlie as well being directly inspired by some of his playing partners. The Dohertys and the McConnells were well known to Eddie's father and brother and often visited the house. The player he most respected in his youth was Paddy The Tae Gallagher whom he describes as having "a lovely sweet touch" and who taught him some tunes.

His first instrument was a tin fiddle that had been made by Alec McConnell which Charlie bought from him for two shillings. It was very suitable for starting off but was later traded along with money for his first timber fiddle. Eddie progressed well and was soon playing in a dance band for house and school dances as well as the emerging hall dances which demanded a repertoire including popular music. This band travelled as far as Donegal Town, Dungloe, Carrick, Kilcar and Glencolumcille. During his time with the band he started to play the accordion and piano accordion as well. He also was involved in a combined music and comedy routine with Packie Manus Byrne at this time[6]. Eddie played the fiddle and composed humorous songs and sketches based on local events.

The Emergency brought hardship for the country in general but the weaving trade meant that the Keeneys had some supply of steady income. The British Army found it difficult to source production of clothing and blankets. The Kilcar contractors succeeded in securing a number of commitments for these materials and the Keeneys got some work to supplement their farming income. Eddie continued weaving at home until he moved near Newtownards towards the end of the war where he was hired in construction. In 1948 he decided to move to America. By this stage he was primarily concerned with making a living and the music was receiving little attention. He secured a post in New York as a bus driver and his fiddle playing declined. Falling back on his piano accordion, he saw a great opportunity to add to his income. He was able to get into the musician's union, Local 802, which opened up a significant supply of work on top of his day job. Offers came in for playing halls and hotels, mainly for weddings and other family functions. The work came from across the nationality spectrum and meant he had to learn the standard dancehall tunes of the Polish, German, Italian and Jewish communities on top of what he was already able to play for the Irish Americans. At one stage he was also playing with Paddy Killoran's band. Eddie was noted by his daytime employers as a highly reliable driver and frequently was offered promotions by the bus company but this work conflicted with hours for playing. By this stage the income from a good week of music bookings brought in much more than his day income and he regularly turned down the promotion offers. The steady nature of the driving job, however, dissuaded him from ever giving it up.

In the 1960s the folk music boom in America resulted in a growth in young players turning towards ethnic music. New York experienced an explosion of interest across the range of Irish music. Eddie soon started to meet players doing quite well from Irish fiddle playing. Though he had not played with any sustained commitment for a number of years he was certain that the emerging American players were not as conversant with the rhythm and style of the music. He decided to return to fiddle playing with great conviction. He re-established his high level of playing and started to make a name for himself as a player of accomplishment. He came to form a close friendship with Louis Quinn and the two often partnered each other in house sessions.

Eddie remained a member of the musician's union eventually becoming a lifetime member. While he continued to take bookings, his interests continually focused on fiddle playing. Though his repertoire has expanded to incorporate the widespread session tunes of the past twenty years, he still holds a valuable store of the old house dance tunes he learned in his youth. There is some evidence that his bowing style may have changed slightly over the years in that the old house dance tunes are typically played with a staccato bow and a very marked dance rhythm while his more recently learned tunes are played with a longer, even bow and a less pronounced swing. During my last meeting with him in 1986 he was playing with great melodic imagination and a remarkably clear, bright tone.

At that time players which Eddie recalled from his youth were Davey Cunnea from Bruckless who was born in the first few years of this century as well as John Gildea[7] from Kilraine who was a regular house player and had made a fiddle. Another player he was able to document was John Parnell Keeney, who, though a namesake, was not a relation. John Parnell, or as he is sometimes known in Irish speaking areas, Seán Parnell, was a near neighbour of Eddie's and a contemporary of his older brother Charlie. He came to get his nickname by virtue of the fact that his father had been active in local politics, particularly the land issue, and had a remarkable resemblance to Charles Stewart Parnell. All his children were known locally by their name with the Parnell addition. John Parnell travelled a good bit through the whole of the northwest of Ireland and some of his music is still extant in Glencolumcille through the repertoire of James Byrne. He was also known in Ballyshannon and North Leitrim. So strong was his association with the latter county that he was mistakenly considered a native of Leitrim.

John Boyle was born in Tullycleave, about three miles outside of Ardara on April 16, 1871. Neither of his parents played but his mother had a great love of music and was anxious to have him learn the fiddle. At that time the renowned Anthony Helferty from Inishowen was an old man and had established a house dance trail around the county with strong associations in Ardara. He took on John as a pupil and continued to teach him until about 1882 when Anthony died. John treasured all his Helferty tunes throughout his life and made a conscious effort to play in the style shown to him by Anthony. He became a well known player for all social occasions in the area and was sometimes contracted to play by the local landlord Major Johnson of Rosbeg. Indeed one of these engagements almost resulted in disaster. John was returning in a trap driven by one of Johnson's men after playing for the landlord. As they approached a small bridge very near his house the trap overturned and his fiddle fell into the river which was in spate. The horse was attended to first and then the fiddle was sought out. It was eventually found far down river and despite the raging current was completely undamaged. John Boyle lived a long and rewarding life surviving to within two months of his one hundred and second birthday.

His fiddle was passed on, as was his repertoire and style to his son John Patrick Boyle who was born around 1920 and now lives on the family farm. He was taught by his father and plays in a style which he firmly maintains is that which was learned from Anthony Helferty. This is a link of major importance as there are no other known direct connections with Helferty. John Patrick is a very musically modest man. He does not rush into playing but when he does get going his playing is very much worth listening to. His style is deeply rooted in the old house dance style with a general staccato bow, minimum left hand ornamentation and a tremendous emphasis on rhythm. John Patrick's repertoire contains many rare Anthony Helferty tunes such as the highland *Cailíní Ard a' Ratha* which is a version of the Scot's strathspey *Lord Lyndoch*. Other, more common tunes in the Donegal repertoire often surface with very rare melodic variations. Though he modestly demurs in favour of the emerging generation of players whom he deeply admires he is one of the first and most important players to whom they turn for direction, delight and inspiration.

THE WATTERS OF TULLYCLEAVE

Con Watters, or as he and his family are sometimes known by their alternative anglicised name form Whoriskey, was a contemporary of John, the elder, Boyle. Con came originally from between Ardara and Inver and married into the Tullycleave area. He regularly partnered John Boyle at local dances as well as for Major Johnson's functions. Unfortunately he did not come under the influence of Anthony Helferty as he had passed away by the time Con came to live in Tullycleave. Con had two sons who played the fiddle, Connell who was a good house dance player and emigrated to America and John. John Watters was one of the best players of his generation and was extremely popular for house dances. He was well known to the Ardara and Glenties players and played in the Forthill Band. His involvement in the band appears to have encouraged him to attempt more popular styles of music and he is sometimes remembered as an accomplished jazz player. John died around 1977.

Other players in this general area included Johnnie Gallagher who concentrated on airs and classical music, often playing for religious occasions[8]; and the O'Rourkes of Woodhill, who were discussed in Chapter Eleven . Jimmy O'Rourke was the best known player of this family in the past. He was a tinsmith and the central character for the Walt Disney film Darby O'Gill and the Little People was based on him[9]. Brendan McHugh from the Glenties side of Frosses was a regular local player and particular enjoyed house dances. A quiet and gentle man he died suddenly within the last few years.

FRANCIE McHUGH

Francie, from the shores of Lough Doon was born on June 9th, 1906. For as long as he can remember he had an interest in music. At five years he was learning to lilt the tunes of his maternal grandmother, Kate Sweeney, from Meenmore, Dungloe. She played the melodeon and was then in her one hundred and fourth year. Both of his parents played the fiddle and melodeon and under their guidance he rapidly grew to become a proficient player. By the age of fourteen he was in demand for house dances and local concerts. Francie's playing is particularly sweet and direct. His repertoire is comprised of the typical house dances tunes which would have been popular during his young adulthood. He has a vast array of highlands and germans and having played them regularly at convoys where the atmosphere was convivial he has salvaged a considerable store of locally composed humorous words to his dance tunes.

Francie does exhibit some influences of the Dohertys' music and the result of the process by which Scottish strathspeys are transformed into Donegal highlands is marvellously displayed in his playing. A tune such as *Peter Ballie* takes on a melodically rounder structure and flowing rhythm to emerge as *The Brown-Sailed Boat* in the hands of such a master. This very gentle man who is widely known as the boatman who ferried thousands of visitors over to the beautiful island fort at his door is showing every sign of continuing his family tradition of playing well into his second century.

An interesting account from the early part of this century concerning a dance at Portnoo shows the kind of performance settings into which Francie would eventually mature as a player. It goes as follows[10]:

> I was talking with a fiddler the other evening in a house where there was a dance, up by Portnoo. I happened to mention the name of another fiddler I had heard playing a night or two before in Ardara. 'Him, is it?' put in my friend. 'Why he's no fiddler at all. He's only an old stroller. He doesn't even know the differs between "*Kyrie Eleison*" and "*The Devil's Dreams*"!' He became very indignant. I interrupted once or twice, trying to turn the conversation, but all to no purpose; he still went on. Finally, to quiet him, I asked him could he play "*The Sally Gardens*". He stopped to think for a while, fondling the strings of his instrument lovingly with his rough hands; he then said that he didn't know the tune by that name, but if I'd lilt or whistle the first few bars of it, it might come to him. I whistled them. 'Oh', says he, "that's "*The Maids of Mourne Shore*". That's the name we give it in these parts. He played the tune for me quite beautifully. Then there was a call from the man of the house for "*The Fairy Reel*", and the dancers took to the floor again. The fiddlers in Donegal are 'all sorts', as they say - farmers, blacksmiths, fisher boys, who play for the love of the thing, and strollers (usually blind men) who wander about from house to house and from fair to fair playing for money. When they are playing I notice they catch the bow in a curious way with their thumbs between horsehair and the stick. At a dance it is no uncommon thing to see a "bench" of seven or eight of them. They join in the applause at the end of each item, rasping their bows together on the strings and stamping vigorously with their feet.

REFERENCES

1 Áine Ní Dhioraí. *Na Cruacha Scéalta agus Seanchas*. An Chlóchomhar. Baile Átha Cliath. 1985.
2 Séamas O Catháin. *Uair an Chloig Cois Teallaigh*. Comhairle Béaloideas Éireann. Baile Átha Cliath. 1985.
3 Séamas O Catháin. Op. Cit. 1985.
4 Séamas O Catháin. *The Bedside Book of Irish Folklore*. Mercier. Cork.1980. pp 98 - 101.
5 Dr. Malachy McCloskey. *Reminiscences on Traditional Fiddlers and Traditional Music*. Dearcadh - The Ardara Review. Nollaig. 1992. pp 102 - 103.
6 Packie Manus Byrne. *Recollections of a Donegal Man*. Roger Millington, Dyfed. 1989. p. 121.
7 Packie Manus Byrne. Op. Cit. pp. 80 - 89.
8 Lochlainn McGill. *In Conal's Footsteps*. Brandon Press. Dingle. 1993.
9 Lochlainn Mc Gill. Op. Cit. p. 249.
10 *Useful Hints to Donegal Tourists*. 1911. pp 36 - 37.

CHAPTER THIRTEEN

SOUTHWEST DONEGAL

More so than any other district in County Donegal, the southwest has seen a series of family-based fiddling dynasties. Almost every village had one and in some districts most townlands. While the Dohertys were not permanently established here, they were regular visitors in this area and here they arguably left their strongest mark. The repertoire of this area is highly diagnostic and diverse. Highlands, germans, mazurkas, polkas, waltzes as well as the more familiar rhythms exist in numbers not found elsewhere in Donegal. In places, the history of playing here seems to go back to the very roots of the music.

THE MacFHIONNLAIOCHS OF LOCH INSE

Possibly the earliest established of the local fiddle dynasties was that of the intriguing Mac Fhionnlaiochs, or McGinleys of Loch Inse, an elevated townland to the west of the road between Carrick and Glencolumcille. Moses Mac Fhionnlaioch was probably born in the first decade of the last century and was most likely from the Glencolumcille/Carrick area. Very little is known about him other than the fact that he was a blacksmith, played the fiddle and had ten children. Some of these were to become the best players of their generation in the county, if not the country. Although the house and forge have long since fallen down, the byre of the family home still stands.

Moses' children were all labelled, as was the custom, with their father's christian name, Mosaí, which is pronounced as Wosey in it's Irish form. The music of the Mhosaí's, as they are collectively known today, comes down to the present generation through five sources. A few tunes and stories have remained in the repertoire of the Dohertys and the O'Byrnes (Deargs) of Kilcar while a good amount of both has been passed on to James Byrne by his father, John, and the throng of fiddlers in Glencolumcille. The chief source of music and information on the Mhosaís lies with Paddy O'Gara of Min a' Mhucra, now living in Manchester, whose father was a pupil of Moses son, Paddy Mhosaí and who was well acquainted with another, John Mhosaí. Lastly, the State Papers lend us some factual information concerning another son, Maurice Mhosaí.

The eldest of the ten children, Maurice Mhosaí, is the best documented. He enlisted into the Royal Irish Constabulary at the age of 24 on the eighteenth of September, 1854. Documents in the State Papers show that Maurice Mhosaí was born in 1830 and was five feet eight and one half inches in height as well as single at the time of his recruitment. He was recommended to the force, as was the norm, by the local Protestant Minister, the Reverend J.M. Staples. Prior to joining he was listed as having been a labourer.

After a brief seven month period of probation in the Depot, Phoenix Park, he was transferred to County Monaghan. On the first of May, 1855, he was promoted to Sub-Constable. A transfer to County Louth followed on the first of October 1863 and he was subsequently promoted to Acting Constable, today's equivalent of Sergeant, on the first of November, 1873. While stationed in County Louth he married a County Monaghan girl on the third of December, 1868.

Records of his service indicate that Maurice's life in the RIC was a subdued one as he received no distinctions and was cited for minor punishments only three times during the late 1850s. He retired at the age of 49 on November 10th, 1879 with an annual pension of £53 per year after serving twenty five years and one month.

Not surprisingly, no record of the birth exists for his brother John Mhosaí. An estimate for the period can be made on the basis of the factual records concerning Maurice Mhosaí. Families during this era tended to be large with minimal spacing between children. As he was the youngest of the children, it is safe to say that John Mhosaí was born approximately in the mid-1840s, possibly in the height of the Famine. He spent his youth and middle age as a seasonal traveller across the northern counties of Ireland and going as far as Scotland. He is remembered selling clothes and when in south and west Donegal dealing in fish. He complemented his income by playing fiddle at house dances and other social gatherings. Folklore about him in southwest Donegal is rich and always reports him travelling with a white horse.

As was sometimes the case in the past with large families whose children spread over the globe, unusual meetings occurred between the elder and the tailings of the family. Con Cassidy recalls such a reputed meeting between John and Maurice Mhosaí:

> John Doherty always said that his father was the best fiddle player he ever heard and that John Mhosaí was the best fiddle player that his father ever heard. So he must have been good!
>
> He won a big prize at some Feis between Cork and here. He happened to be in that area at the time and he heard of the Feis. It was an open air affair. In those days I think the average people didn't attend these places. It was only all upper class. John wasn't dressed as a gentleman you know. He had just his working clothes on and he had the fiddle. They were going to stone him out of it! 'To hell with him! What does this down and out know about fiddles?'
>
> Some man was sensible enough to give him a chance they picked up stones and bits of sods going to stone him out of the place. When he drew the bow a few times and started on a tune there were no sods thrown. And he won the first prize! But he must have been good you know. He was bound to be a great fiddle player!

This story has several versions. Usually Maurice is patrolling the streets and as soon as John starts to play Maurice immediately recognises the style from his home place. He brings John back to the barracks to enquire about him and on investigation discovers the brother he left behind as a very young boy.

Although John Mhosaí travelled quite a bit it would appear he did not spend concentrated periods of time in different musical communities in Donegal. For example, in the Croaghs, where folk memory is extremely strong and accurate, the most reliable sources available do not remember him as a visitor to the area. Peter Campbell, now in his mid-nineties, recalls him only through the stories of John Doherty.

Peter's son, Vincent, tells a story he heard from John concerning one of several versions of the first meeting of Mickey Mór Doherty and John Mhosaí. Considering John Doherty's age at the time of the meeting it is quite likely that there is some truth in the story. Further evidence supporting the basic thread of truth in the tale is the accuracy of the geographic locations. The event took place at a time when the Doherty family was stopping at The Blowing Rock, or as it is known in Irish Carraig a' Phudair, near Churchill. At the time John reckoned he was about five or six years of age. This would have put John Mhosaí in his late fifties or early sixties.

Mickey Mór Doherty went out one afternoon to a nearby pub along with his young sons. He was sitting playing away and all inside were enchanted with his music. After a while in came a man who had been into Letterkenny selling fish from a white pony and trap. He sat near the Dohertys and took a keen but quiet interest in the music. By this stage, Mickey Mór and the boys suspected he was a musician and hoped he might play. The fishmonger eventually spoke up asking Mickey Mór if he could play a reel. Mickey Mór played the tune with great life and enthusiasm. After a short while the stranger pointed out that there was another part to the tune which Mickey Mór had not played. Mickey Mór asked the fishmonger to play it as he and the boys would be interested in hearing it. The gentleman took up the fiddle and played the tune including the extra part in a way which thrilled the Dohertys. Mickey Mór shook the fishmonger's hand exclaiming that he could be only one man, the great John Mhosaí from Glencolumcille.

The music took off at a great rate and the lone fiddle was passed around for hours. The local RIC patrolman was out on his rounds and heard the music and called into the pub. He was fond of music and stayed. He was eventually missed at the barracks and another man was sent to locate him. When the second man found his quarry he, too, stayed on to listen. This process continued until the only man left in the barracks was the local seargeant. Fearing an ambush he rushed out, leaving the barracks door wide open. He eventually found his men and joined them in the pub. That day is remembered to today as the day the barracks was abandoned.

Today John Mhosaí remains the main focus of both musical folklore and history in the area. It is true to say that in the area leading into Glencolumcille from Carrick and in the glen itself he made the dominant impact on the local style and this can still be heard today. John was a strong volume player with a brilliant, attacking, short bow. He taught many of the local players during his winter seasons at home. He was also a noted composer. Paddy O'Gara recalls an account from his father which testifies to one of his compositions. Here is Paddy's account:

> Now it was Paddy Mhosaí that taught my father. He was a brother of John and many's a time I heard him say he used to go regularly as a young fella to him. It was there that he learned. This night, in particular, he was coming close to the gate of the house he heard music in the distance. Well, he said to himself, is it the faeries or what is it? He just didn't know. But finally it came closer and closer so he realised then that it was fiddling music. Then he could hear a horse as if a horse was walking or trotting and who was it but John Mhosaí. He used to keep a horse but John lived in Glencolumcille in the village there and his horse used to known the ways and wander at will in and out to his home place. My father asked him, he said 'well that's a very nice tune. I never heard it before. What is it?' 'Well, I just composed that now on my way out. I have terrible trouble with this horse. I cannot keep him. He's neither in my home place nor he won't stop in my own place. But anyway, I am just composing a tune now and I am calling it *The Rambling Pony*.

Several tunes of John Mhosaí's are still played in the area, mainly through James Byrne. He has been credited with composing the piece best known as *The Glen Road to Carrick* or alternatively titled *On the Road from Glen to Carrick,* which was to commemorate the location of his family home. This tune is primarily a version of the *Chorus Reel,* but it may well be possible that the additional parts played in Donegal are from the work of John. Another is the reel *Tobaca Daor* which as Francie Dearg O'Byrne maintained referred to a trip made by John on his white pony into a pub in Glencolumcille to purchase tobacco. John Mhosaí became involved in a card game and had to return home penniless and with the loan of a plug of tobacco. Another one of his tunes appears to be the reel *Gealach na gCoinleach.*

Paddy O'Gara recalls an interesting family connection which he had heard from his father. As he remembered it, John Mhosaí's wife was a sister of Anthony Helferty another famous fiddler associated with Ardara. John Mhosaí appears to have died in the second decade of this century and is buried in the cemetery in Glencolumcille.

His brother Padaí Mhosaí apparently lived a more settled life and did not travel much outside the area. He was a noted player though never regarded as highly as John. Importantly, however, he did have as comprehensive a repertoire as his brother and very fortunately this has been passed to even the younger players of today in direct succession. One of Padaí Mhosaí's best pupils was the father of Paddy O'Gara from the neighbouring townland, now sadly deserted, of Min a' Mhucra. Paddy O'Gara was born there in 1929 and quickly absorbed the music of his father. He has a vast and valuable selection of tunes which he has been very active in passing on. Having the advantage of living almost exactly half way between Carrick and Glencolmcille, Paddy had the opportunity to become familiar with the players of Carrick, Teelin and Kilcar to the south and the legions of fiddlers in Glencolmcille to the north. His genial nature and tremendous enthusiasm facilitated his meetings with these players and he was very popular at any musical venue. He played for some time with the dance band in Teelin and became a very close friend of Mickey Gallagher.

He was fortunate in being the first cousin of Patrick Doherty and a second cousin of Johnnie Boyle of Braade. These two players were some of the most active and skilled in the glen. The homes of both these players were particular favourite stopping places with the McConnell brothers. They left many of their tunes and a great deal of their stylistic influences with Johnnie and Paddy. Paddy O'Gara describes this relationship as follows:

> Yes there were two fiddle players here at one time. They were called the McConnells - Alec McConnell and Mickey McConnell. They spent a lot of their time in about Glencolmcille. Now there was a second cousin of mine, he lived in Braade. He was called Johnnie Boyle and any fella that came to Glen they would always spend their time with him and he learned a lot of their music. Now it was through him that I got a lot of the music that I have. I also had a first cousin of mine and he was called Patrick Doherty. He was a very good fiddle player. Sad to say, he is dead now, but I spent many happy nights with him playing and he learned a lot of his music from the McConnells too.

Paddy O'Gara eventually emigrated to Manchester where he has lived for a considerable portion of his adulthood. Over the past few years, however, he has made regular extended visits home. He has spent much time playing with the younger enthusiasts and ensuring his music is passed on. He has also established a strong partnership with James Byrne. The rare repertoire gathered from the Mhosaís through his father, the Teelin and Kilcar tunes as well as the McConnell material from his cousins, have been treated with the height of respect by Paddy. He is a player of considerable ability. The preservation actions of this open and friendly man have ensured that a major portion of the musical heritage not only of the southwest but of Donegal as a whole have been made safe and available to future generations.

Whatever about fiddle playing in Glencolmcille, the music in Teelin was said to be extremely basic at the turn of the present century. This style was characterised by straight, staccato playing with no infusion or rhythmic inflections and an almost total absence of ornamentation. In short, it was the simplest form of music for house dancing. Players of this music included Jim Phat James Byrne, Paddy Barron and a blind fiddler named MacLochlainn who lived near Sliabh Liag. This was all to change dramatically with the combined effect of two dynamic forces, the power of the Dohertys and the McConnells as well as the genius of three brothers and their cousin.

During the early decades of this century the McConnell brothers and the Doherty family were regularly visiting the southwest and their advanced level of performance was causing the local players to re-think their approaches to playing. There was a considerable number of fiddlers living in this small community and emerging in their midst were the enlightened Cassidy brothers Paddy, Johnnie and Frank, along with their cousin, Con.

THE CASSIDYS

The Cassidy brothers were noted for their brightness as well as their astuteness in business. Following the end of The First World War Paddy and Frank travelled to Finner Camp outside Bundoran and bought a number of surplus bicycles as well as a large marquee tent. They opened a bicycle shop in Carrick which was quite successful. With the tent the brothers started to promote concerts and dances. Many of the leading names in traditional music today still fondly recall playing in Frank's hall.

Musically, they combined to form one of the most incredible forces in Irish music this century. They achieved a level of fiddle playing as well as developing a particular style as diagnostic as a thumb print. Paddy Cassidy is now the least known of the three brothers. He was very mechanically minded being involved in watch repairs and working with photography as it developed in the early 1900s. He is remembered as a very good, steady house dance player and thrived in combination with his brothers. Johnnie, who was approximately ten years older than Frank was the main player amongst the brothers for years. It appears the influence of the Dohertys moved him to try to attain a higher standard of playing. He worked hard at developing a personal style and soon was the primary player in the area. Like Paddy, he was very mechanically minded and noted the tinsmith's craft of making tin fiddles. In the 1920s a large brass drum was recovered from the sea by fishermen at the foot of Sliabh Liag. Johnnie and Frank got some pieces of it and they went on to make what many consider to be the tangible symbol of the Donegal fiddle tradition, the brass fiddle, now in the possession of the Cassidy's nephew, Charlie McDevitt of Kilcar.

All of this time the youngest, Frank, was developing in the shadow of his two older brothers. By the Thirties, however, he had grown to a player of incredible proportion. He had perfected the stylistic aspirations of Johnnie. Frank was now playing with what has become recognised as the archetypal Teelin style. He had achieved a sweetness of tone which was one of his hallmarks. Fiddlers who survived Frank have debated for years whether it was by a particular tension of the bow or alternatively the closeness to the bridge where he bowed which contributed to his tonal quality, but, all are in agreement that such a sound was never produced before or since Frank Cassidy.

In terms of sources for his music Frank certainly availed of the local repertoire as well as having picked up tunes from the Dohertys and the McConnells. He also was known to have been greatly attracted to the music which was coming into the area on 78 RPM discs. This included traditional fiddle playing as well as classical music. He was reputed to be able to replay full classical pieces on hearing them only twice. Such recordings apparently are the source for the waltzes which are quite numerous in the local repertoire. During the period of Army recruitment at the start of the First World War a number of militia bands visited the area to attract volunteers. These bands would parade and play for quite some time. Many of the brass band tunes were picked up by Frank and his brothers and have survived to present day players through the transmission of Con Cassidy.

The extant recordings of Frank Cassidy consist of those made for RTÉ and the Irish Folklore Commission in the late 1940s as well as a limited number privately recorded in the family hall in Carrick by An tAthair Liam Mac an tSagairt and others by Cathal McConnell. The duet material from the Forties with John Doherty shows Frank to be totally conversant with the Doherty approach. It is fast, attacking and aggressive. The two play tunes and airs largely associated with the Dohertys and engage in reversing. The solo pieces, however, show the more reflective Frank Cassidy approach. The bowing is longer than that normally associated with Donegal music, ornamentation such as rolls are liberally applied and abundant use is made of accidentals. This latter device appears to be a characteristic of the Teelin style developed by Frank and enthusiastically adopted by his admirers.

One of the privately made recordings has Frank playing the well known double jig *The Lark on the Strand.* In the second part of the tune he demonstrates his technical ingenuity by playing repeated F sharps on the first string using a technique commonly employed by American flat picking guitarists called 'pulling off'. This very effective sound which Frank must have developed in isolation as, to my knowledge, it has never been employed elsewhere in Irish fiddle music. His dynamic ability is amply demonstrated in his execution of *The Wedding Jig* with its combined demands of complex fingering, double stopping pipe imitation and bowing. Frank's version of the well known *Tuam na Farraige* runs counter to the general playing with the complexion of the tune totally changed by the subtle nuances of melodic variation.

To put all this in context, from the time when the renowned musician and collector Séamus Ennis first met Frank on September 9th, 1943 he noted that Frank Cassidy was the best traditional fiddler by far he had ever met in his travels. Unknown to many, Séamus was an accomplished fiddler and when in the humour to play regularly resorted not only to the tunes he collected from Frank, but consciously played them in his specific settings. Séamus absorbed Frank's version of *An Londubh* which he had in turn learned from the lilting of John Lyons. This was passed on by Séamus to Tommie Potts and can be heard on the latter's historic recording. Séamus also recorded Frank's *Cronan a' Mháthair* for Gael Linn.

Frank had thrived in playing with Johnnie and Paddy. Following their deaths, he played less and less. By the time Séamus Ennis visited him to record he no longer even owned a fiddle in playing order. Séamus recalled that on the night he arrived he found Frank very unwilling to play. Finally, after persuading him to record a few tunes Frank had to take the pieces of some dismantled fiddles and build a complete one from them. By the next day Frank was recording. Though the material is of astounding quality and Ennis was openly enthusiastic with the offerings, Frank, pointing to the sorrow of having to play without his brothers finished by saying, "Ní gar ann" - it's no use.

Frank Cassidy was a very shy man and in his latter years remained almost a musical recluse. While he was surrounded by music and musicians on a daily basis through the family's music hall business following the death of his brothers, he rarely ever played. Only when exceptional and kindred spirits were discovered would he invite a playing partnership. Many, like Dr. Malachy McCloskey[1] and James Byrne who heard Frank play masterfully shortly before his death remember that if they wanted to hear him, they would have to be satisfied with sitting in an adjoining room while he, alone and usually in darkness, played.

A single photograph of Frank exists in the Cairdeas na bhFidléirí collection in Glencolmcille which was donated by the O Cuinneagáin family. It was taken in Glencolumcille at a time when broadcastings were being made from the area. Frank appears as a smallish and very distinguished man standing next to John Doherty. In keeping with his very reserved nature, he agreed to allow himself to be photographed providing he did not have to look into the camera. Frank Cassidy died on March 21st, 1961.

The most enthusiastic and loyal supporter of the Cassidy banner was the brothers' cousin, Con Cassidy. Born in Teelin some eighty years ago Con grew up in a house that had a deep and abiding love for music. His parents did not play but both had a great fondness for the music. When Con was a boy he was often sent to the house of his neighbour, Paddy Barron. Paddy was a fiddler who played locally for house dances and would often be out long hours. Con would keep his wife company while Paddy was away playing. Sometimes he would get bored with the adults' chat and sitting next to the fire, he eventually found himself picking up the tongs and poker. He held the tongs like a fiddle and drew the poker across them imitating the playing movements of his cousins and the fiddlers he observed at house dances. Such was the good nature and humour of Con Cassidy that decades later, he would describe to the swelling numbers of admiring young fiddlers that his finest playing was when he was "going at the music hammer and tongs".

Con's father recognised his longing to play and got him a fiddle. He was sent to his cousins to learn and made progress mainly under the guidance of Frank. Eventually he became skilled enough to play for house dances and this marked the start of a long playing career. He could recall at this time there was little communication between the fiddlers of Glencolumcille and Teelin. He and a friend were asked by the local parish priest to play for a dance in Glencolumcille. The two appeared in the hall and went up on stage to play along with a father and son from Meenaneary. The other two began to play and continued starting the sets for the remainder of the night. Con and his partner did not know a single tune and to avoid disgrace had to sit and draw their bows lightly over the strings pretending to play all night long.

This was a minor setback. Con continued to develop in the style of his cousin Frank whose music he held in the highest regard. Con spent some years away in England working as a Geologist's and Drill Engineer's assistant on Construction sites. During these years he did not touch a fiddle though he did keep in contact with the music. Joe Cooley lodged in the same house and Con regularly hosted him for tunes. By the time Séamus Ennis called to Teelin on his collecting visits Con had developed into an accomplished player. Ennis transcribed several of his tunes at this time.

For a number of years he played with a small local band which had a variable line up depending on circumstances and availability of players but it's core was composed of Con and Mickey Gallagher on melodeon. By the Seventies the house dance tradition in Teelin was largely dead and Con's main outlet for playing was in the pubs of Teelin and Carrick. John Doherty was based in Carrick for a number of years and this presented Con with the opportunity of playing with his old acquaintance for an extended period of time. The two developed a striking duet which clearly echoed the powerful recordings of John and Frank Cassidy. Afterwards John moved to Stranorlar and Con played increasingly with James Byrne. At this time the area was becoming the focus of attention of a new generation of Donegal fiddlers and enthusiasts seeking to make acquaintance with the masters of the style so greatly praised by Séamus Ennis and others. In the centre of this searchlight was Con Cassidy.

Con was a gentle man in the old and most noble sense of the word. Those coming to learn from him discovered a man of extraordinarily rare qualities and skills. He was a farmer, a fisherman, a thatcher, a traditional creelmaker, a keen observer of nature and life amongst other things. He had a personal warmth and humour which was entirely magnetic. Con's partnership with James Byrne, Seán Chon Johnnie Byrne, Thomas Cunningham, Dermot McLaughlin and Dermot Byrne became a regular feature of the social life of the area. His tunes were freely passed on through this outlet and he made his repertoire available to all who visited him. It must be said however that his style, which was completely reflective of Frank Cassidy's, remained his own.

Throughout the Eighties Con travelled in wider circles and demands for his playing increased consistently. Despite age and gradually declining health Con's enthusiasm for fiddle playing typically saw him as the last man going to bed at night and first up in the morning at any musical gathering. He regularly ignored the level of attention focused on him as curiosity and modestly described himself as an average Teelin player. This was a harsh self-evaluation and ignored the fact that he was measuring himself against giants. When Con Cassidy died on February 12th, 1994 a large gathering of young players congregated to play for hours with the tremendous zeal that they had found in his music. The huge impact which Con's wit, humour and musical genius had on a new generation of players will be a long time in the measuring.

The rich Teelin fiddle tradition was complemented by a number of other players whose standards and genius in playing would have caused them to be the prime players and pride of any other area. Mick Mc Shane was slightly older than Frank Cassidy. He had learned his fiddle playing from the McConnells during their frequent visits to the area. As such, he was always regarded as being a short bower in contrast to Frank's longer bowing. When Frank was not partnering his brothers at house dances and concerts, Mick was his first choice partner. Francie Dearg O'Byrne often quoted him as being the next best Teelin player to Frank Cassidy. Mick taught Connie Haughey, a contemporary of Con Cassidy who often played with Con in the local band. Though Connie would have been originally influenced by Mick towards a shorter, staccato bow there is some evidence that he later adapted a longer more fluid bowing style from the Cassidy's influence. Connie was usually partnered by Jimmy Lyons for house dances.

Jimmy Lyons was a contemporary of Con Cassidy. He was a tall, thin man and learned his earliest music from the lilting of his father John, who also had acted as a source of tunes for Frank Cassidy. Jimmy was a very enthusiastic fiddler and is remembered as having played at home for hours when bad weather kept him in from fishing. He was regarded by his peers as excelling in highland and hornpipe playing. Séamus Ennis recorded twenty two tracks from him during one of his visits. All of these pieces pay testimony to a man of astounding ability. The playing is classic Teelin style music displaying a great fidelity to the documented music of both Frank and Con Cassidy. It is clear that he adopted the longer bow and rich embellishments that were played by the Cassidys. Jimmy emigrated to England and died there in the Sixties.

Two other players from the area were Francie and Jimmy Kelly who were contemporaries of Mick Mc Shane and likewise learned from the McConnells. Nearby in Carrick the Mac a' Bhairds were also fiddlers. The late Alphonsus and his brother Columba were greatly attracted to both the Dohertys' and the Cassidys' music. Alphonsus was a noted air player following in the line of Frank Cassidy's approach. Columba is now retired from teaching and highly active in fiddle playing. His repertoire appears to be more dance music oriented than that of Alphonsus and he is a good exponent of the highland. He occasionally plays on a tin fiddle which was made by one of the Dohertys. Other fiddlers from the Carrick area include the late Séamus Sweeney, who is still highly regarded by those that remember him in his prime and the late Jimmy McLaughlin. Gerry Breslin, originally from Ardara, is also a noted player and enthusiastic supporter of the music. John Byrne, a Garda serving in Dublin and coming from between Carrick and Kilcar has grown into a talented player often returning to teach at the Francie O'Byrne Memorial Weekend.

THE DEARGS

Two brothers, Mickey Bán and Francie Dearg O'Byrne of Kilcar brought a piping influenced, driving, yet rhythmical staccato style to the virtual borders of perfection. Francie started to learn the fiddle at the age of nine years. His father played the fife and a bit on the melodeon and Francie and Mickey both picked up some tunes from him. House dances were abundant and the two brothers cut their musical eye teeth playing for local dances. With the shortage of space in the houses the boys often played standing up in the corner, regularly supporting each other by standing back to back over the long hours of the dancing. This stance was carried on by them long after the demise of the house dances and untypical of their subsequent younger admirers they continued to play standing.

Francie played at home using his own system of tuning until eventually he was told at school how to figure out the correct tuning[2]. This consisted of imitating the melodic gap between the two notes in the call of the cuckoo over all the strings on the fiddle. Besides his father, he also learned some tunes from his aunt who was a noted lilter. Visitors to their grandfather's house included the pipers Mickey Gallagher, Hugh Doherty and Hiúidaí Gallagher. Two other early and significant influences on both Francie and Mickey were Pat The Nailer Harvey and John Doogan, a blacksmith from Leitir both of whom apparently learned from John Mhosaí. While Pat was a renowned player and had some marvellous airs, it was his bowing ability that amazed the boys. As Francie put it, "he could quiver the bow from stem to stern".

As the boys grew into manhood their fame as players spread throughout the district. They were in demand for playing at house dances seven nights a week. They would regularly take a boat from Kilcar to Teelin to play for a house dance and there they came into contact with the Teelin fiddlers who held an outstanding respect for them. Francie enjoyed a very good relationship with Frank Cassidy whose playing he admired greatly. Frank clearly had a similar respect for Francie as he often invited him to his hall for private sessions and they liberally traded repertoire. They each had the gift of a polite, yet, direct demeanour.

Francie spent a period of time working in Scotland and when time permitted he made as much contact with fiddlers and pipers as he could. Besides the early piping influences he seems to have gathered from visitors to his own and his grandfather's house there may have been some incorporation of the sounds he heard in Scotland into his style. Of the two brothers, there is no doubting that Francie was the superior player. Mickey was quite skilled and well able for dancing but his younger brother formed the backbone of the partnership.

The style of the Deargs is quite unique. The bowing is generally staccato but not as much as in Glencolumcille. The measure of the music is moderate and unhurried with a tremendous concentration placed on enhancing the rhythm by use of intricate pipe influenced double stopping. Possibly the greatest example of this technique in Donegal fiddle playing is to be found in the brothers classic recording of the jig *Rí na bPíobairí* where imaginative double stopped droning seems to carry the tune on to the point of defying the number of bars in the piece. The Deargs thrived on a long bowing double stop to drone portions of a piece. They did this, for example in their reel, *Saitheadh a' Bháid,* where the second finger and the fourth finger are used alternatively to keep the melody playing on the third string while the second string was continuously sounded as a drone. For players raised in the informal system of learning by playing, the technical accomplishments of the Deargs, especially Francie, is astonishing. Complex bowing as well as difficult position playing presented no barriers.

Over the years of playing for dances as well as actively hunting out tunes from a driving love of the music, Francie, in particular, amassed a huge and unique local repertoire. It consisted of some of the richest tunes which Donegal has contributed to the wider fiddle tradition. Prior to my having met Francie I had been led to believe he was a man who would not pass on his tunes. After having had the great pleasure of meeting this distinguished gentleman I am happy to utterly refute such a belief. Francie did record on a number of occasions in the early days of taping devices. As they became more readily available Francie had aged and was well aware of the fact that he was not performing at the dynamic levels he had reached as a young man. As a private man, he was also very shy and nervous around tape recorders. As such, he was loathe to record solely on the basis of performance standards and this was sometime incorrectly interpreted as being protective of his inheritance. On the other hand, those who knew him saw that

Francie was extremely anxious to hand on the tunes which he learned. He did this not by recording them but through a means which was totally in keeping with his own traditional learning background. He simply sat the person looking for the tune down and with extreme patience played the tune repeatedly until he, himself was satisfied the pupil had the tune correctly. This notion of a correctness of a tune was a very strong point with Francie. He was not totally happy with the developments in fiddle playing, particularly with variation and speed, though he could play quite fast himself when the notion was on him. He was meticulous about ensuring the player had the tune as he liked to play it. This method of transferring his tunes was vastly superior to any recording method and any fiddler alive today who learned a tune from Francie Dearg will certainly never forget the experience. Mickey Bán O'Byrne died on December 12th, 1980. His brother greatly missed the presence of such a skilled partner. He continued to play on until his death on June 25th, 1987.

One person who had ample opportunity to learn from Francie Dearg was his son, Pat. His musical, like his facial resemblance to his father is uncanny. Pat certainly absorbed Francie's perfectionist approach to the music and is meticulous about his fiddling. He went through a period where he was more concerned to get Francie to pay and as a result gave less attention to his own activities. Happily, Pat is venturing out more to play and those who have had to depend on tapes for their exposure to the music of the Deargs would do well to listen to Pat. A similar good fortune to learn from a master was afforded to Peter Carr, Francie's grandson. Though only in his late twenties Peter is an accomplished multi-instrumentalist and full time musician. His fiddle playing is of a very high standard and strongly reflects its source. Following the death of his grandfather Peter has come to partner his uncle, Pat, as well as James Byrne at the numerous sessions in Kilcar.

Frank McHugh, a fisherman from Muckros, is another noted player much in the rhythmic and bowing style played by the O'Byrne brothers. Frank was well acquainted with the Deargs and would have become familiar with their repertoire from his long association with house dances. For a player of his ability he is all too rarely heard today and those who have been able to hear him at gatherings in southwest Donegal have been impressed by his ability and fidelity to his local style. The late Barney Doogan of Kilcar is now best remembered through a rare tape of a limited number of recordings he made privately in Kilcar. This playing shows his music to have been fully rooted in the local style. Most of the tunes are either typically associated with the Deargs or alternatively the Dohertys. Peter Cunningham is another player to have enjoyed the great respect of the Deargs. Peter played for house dances with the two brothers and traded repertoire with them. He has also handed on some tunes to Pat Byrne and Peter Carr.

Three players to have sadly passed on very recently without the benefit of having recorded either their music or memories were Bernard Haughey of Dunkineely and James and John McNeilis from Gortaragh, just outside Kilcar. Both of these players were exceptional in their youth. Unfortunately both emigrated and spent the major portion of their lives in England. Had they been able to remain at home they undoubtedly would have flourished as major players. Upon returning their playing activities were very limited. Bernard Haughey was very relaxed and enjoyed playing in the company of Pat Connaghan of Doorin Line.

MUSIC IN THE GLEN

We have already seen one story of the first meeting of John Mhosaí Mc Ginley and Mickey Mór Doherty. A second one is set in Glencolumcille and has the Doherty family entering the glen for the first time. Mickey Mór, who is a young man with some of his sons, stops at a blacksmith's forge in Malinmore which was owned by Pat Boyle. Mickey Mór falls into conversation and discovers that one of the three sons of the blacksmith, the youngest, can play the fiddle. Mickey Mór lends him his fiddle and the young man plays astounding music. He brushes off Mickey Mór's praise saying he cannot play at all but his older brother is the real player in the family. The fiddle is then passed on to him and he is even better. This continues on until all the brothers have played. Mickey Mór is astonished beyond belief. He asks where they learned and they all admit that they are not good players but that their father taught them. The blacksmith plays and he is the best of the lot! Mickey Mór enquires where he got his marvellous music and he replies by saying it was all local music and though he can only half play Mickey Mór should travel to the Mhosaí's forge and listen to John Mhosaí if he wants to hear music. This is done and the famous and astonishing first meeting takes place.

This story is certainly based on real persons; Pat Boyle and his son Con and Jimmy as well as a third. They all had learned to some degree from the Mhosaís. At first glance this story appears to be richly embellished, but, looking at the throng of fiddlers who populated Glencolumcille the tale may be only a slight exaggeration. If the old saying of there being a fiddle in every house in the area was ever true it was true in Glencolumcille. Players were prolific and the quality of their music and depth of repertoire are still legendary by even today's burgeoning standards[3]. They included Seán, Peadar, Séamus and Cassie O Canainn from the Post Office in the village, Matthew Kelly, known as Fear a' Cleaibh, Paddy Gillespie and his son John, John Molloy, who went to live in Glenties, Christie Byrne from Malinbeg, Pádaí na bPingineacha who got his name from charging a penny for playing, as well as Francie Boyle and John McElroy from Malinmore.

In general the style to be found in Glencolumcille differs from that of it's neighbouring area of Carrick and Teelin by being more staccato and attacking style, more in line with that played by the McConnells and the Dohertys. The sole exception to this appears to be Andy McGinley who used a long bow and played something akin to the Cassidys' style. Josie Byrne of Glenmalin, now in his later years, was a noted house dance player. He still prefers to play in the comfort of his own home and as such is rarely publicly heard. He maintains a quiet partnership with James Byrne and many of his tunes, particularly a brilliant piping march, have come back into circulation through James. John Ward was also from Glencolumcille and eventually moved to Ballybofey where he owned the Central Bar. He died a short time ago in Glencolumcille.

Two brothers, Pat (1886 - 1955) and John Leslie were born at Corran, Glencolumcille. The brothers worked as weavers at home and were very active at house dance playing. They were strong, driving fiddlers and some of the most noted players in the glen. They emigrated to Long Island, New York in the late 'Twenties and continued to play there. Pat returned home for one visit, in 1953. The two brothers are still commemorated in the village through a reel which bears their name and popularised by James Byrne.

Mick Carr from Meenaneary who died only a few years ago was another accomplished player whose style was very typical of the area. His repertoire was based on that played for the house dances and continues to be passed on by his son, Micheál, and James Byrne. A cousin of the Mhosaís was Condaí McGinley. He is said to have played with a typical Glencolumcille style. His sons John, Paddy and Con also played in his style. Con is now living in Cheshire, England and is a regular visitor home on occasions such as the Glencolumcille summer school and to Glenties. Con has done a great service to the younger generation of players by opening his repertoire and giving a new lease of life to many of the rare tunes of Glencolumcille. Tony Byrne is another player diagnostic of the area. He has spent most of his adult life teaching in Athy though following retirement he has become a more regular visitor at home. A regular at functions was 'Johnnie the Sergeant' Boyle originally from Kilraine, Glenties who was the local Garda Sergeant for many years. Lastly, a bright emerging fiddler is John Byrne now in his late teens.

THE BEIRNEACHS

From Min na Croise was to come another local dynasty. Peadar hIghne, Padaí Hiuidai Byrne and his relations John and Frank Byrne were exceptional house dance players. Following the decline of the house dance in Glencolumcille the local hall, Halla Mhuire, whose foundation stone was taken from the tumbling walls of the Mhosaí family home, became the centre for social playing. In this venue they continued to thrive. Without doubt the pinnacle of Glencolumcille fiddle playing was reached by John's son, James.

James An Bheirneach Byrne is now in his early forties. He grew up in one of the most musical houses in the glen. He was steeped in fiddle playing and related folklore from his earliest days. His style had little external influences other than the host of fiddlers from his locality. He must have progressed at an astronomic rate as a recording of himself at the age of eighteen along with his father reveals a player of fantastic ability. James' exposure to outside influences remained limited for some time. He became familiar with the Cassidys and other players in Carrick and Teelin. During John Doherty's residence in Carrick he availed of the opportunity to pick up both tunes and technical approaches from him. He continued to play into his early twenties and for a short period gave the music a rest. This may have been a fortuitous strategy because when he returned he was playing with a power that was almost beyond belief. Two important influences on his later development as a fiddler would appear to be the music of Danny Meehan as well as Tommy Peoples for both of whom James has a deep respect. Today, his most constant playing partner is Connie Drost who has developed a strong duet with him based on the music she has learned from James.

James Byrne's mastery of both his instrument and his stylistic idiom are comprehensive. He plays with a short staccato bow, rapid, crisp triplets and employs left hand ornamentation more in the line of ingenious double stopping than the standard rolls which add incredible rhythmic effect to his tunes. His repertoire is highly diagnostic of the area and voluminous.

I have been somewhat critical elsewhere of the generation preceding my own for their general insistence that the zenith of Irish fiddle music was reached with the recordings of Michael Coleman. More recently I have sadly noted in some conversations the point that an analogous situation has arisen with John Doherty in Donegal fiddle playing. Despite being an ardent admirer of John Doherty I am of the opinion that James Byrne has surpassed John's level of playing in that broad style some years ago. I write this not to add up another icon to be frustrated by, but as proof that the music builds on the achievements of the past, moves on and hopefully gets better in the journey. It is not a competition to establish who is best as such a notion totally misses the point. James Byrne is a masterful player. He is humble about his art and has endlessly proven his devotion to the betterment of the music to those who have approached him for guidance in playing. Despite a recent set-back to his playing through an injury to the little finger of his left hand, he has recovered to his full playing potential. While he has already contributed much to the growing attraction to Donegal music as well as the production of a new generation of players, James Byrne will hopefully be inspiring players for decades with his marvellous musical gift and warm personality.

PÁDAÍ BHILLÍ NA RÓPAÍ

Pádaí Bhillí na Rópaí was a native of Kiltyfanad, near the deserted village of Port outside Glencolmcille. His people made rope by boiling the roots of fir trees and then using a traw hook, twisting the loose fibres into rope. They were famous for their skill as the strong sea winds in winter meant that the thatched houses of the area required the best of ropes to withstand the onslaughts. Padaí's name, however, was to be made through fiddle playing. He became one of the foremost players of his time and was in great demand for house dance playing. Though he showed a very deep affection for his native place he spent a short period of time in America where he left a profound impression on Ed Reavey in Philadelphia. Pádaí eventually returned and married Bell Tully. They settled at her family farm in Calhame, outside Dunkineely. The home soon became a popular meeting place for fiddlers. For his wife, this situation, with justification, caused some difficulty and though Pádaí was in demand for playing, coming to an arrangement to get out to play could be difficult. At this time his famous nickname was changed by some of his fellow fiddlers to taunt him. He became locally known as Pádaí Bhell Tully, taking on his wife's maiden name as his new nickname.

Whatever his home arrangements, Pádaí did manage to return and play in his beloved Glencolmcille on occasion. Once he was booked to play at a wedding. He consented and made the long journey back into the glen. Unfortunately he did not return for a few days. In the meantime, the Doherty family was passing through the locality. They knew Pádaí well and were fond of his music. Mickey Mór and sons called to the house looking for tunes and were met at the door by Bell who, in reference to his favourite air and speaking in direct translation from Irish, informed the visitors that he was not within as he was "back in Glen making Blackbirds"!

Pádaí Bhillí na Rópaí who covered the ground from Glencolumcille to Donegal Town and taking in Ardara and Glenties is remembered warmly and with humour by those who were fortunate enough to meet him. He is mostly associated with three tunes today, a highland version of *The Green Groves of Erin* (the original Scots strathspey being *Miss Stewart of Grantully*) which bears his name and is sometimes alternatively called *The Low Highland* as well as the air *An Londubh or The Blackbird* as well as *The Kiltyfanad Reel* made popular by James Byrne. His fiddle, through the efforts of Billy and Marie O'Connor of Donegal Town, eventually passed into the hands of Con Cassidy who proudly did it justice until his recent death.

THE KILLYBEGS AREA

Fiddle playing in the Killybegs and surrounding area was very strong in the past. The McCahills Pat and Willie were very respected players and nephews of Connie Gallagher who taught music locally. As we saw in his association with Danny O'Donnell, Connie was a note player while the McCahills learned their music through the discipline of the house dances. Willie and Pat were some of the most respected players of the area and Pat is best remembered through the reel which bears his name and was popularised by Danny Meehan. They often played for local dances in houses at the Traugh Hall near Fintra where they were partnered by another good fiddler, Connie Moloney, from Fintra Braes.

Con Cunnea from Croagh, an uncle of Dr. McCloskey of Glenties was another important player in this area. His two sons, Gerry, who later became a priest and was active in east Donegal, and Alphie, who became a doctor and practiced in Waterford were also fine fiddle players. A possible relation of theirs from the same area was Davey Cunnea who is remembered by Eddie Keeney of Ardara as having been an excellent player.

As we have seen above, the classical violinist Arthur Darley spent some time as the Church of Ireland organist in Bruckless. While there he associated with the Dohertys and composed the now popular double jig *Bruckless Shore.* Two of his other composition are still played in Donegal.

Today the main players in the town of Killybegs are Paddy Hegarty of Church Road and Paddy McGowan of Donegal Road, Killybegs. Both are quite good players and deserving of much greater attention than they now enjoy. Paddy Hegarty's late brother, Francie, as Dr. McCloskey recalls[4] "was one of the best traditional fiddlers I met and not far behind him was his brother

Paddy". Francie died in May 1942 having sadly reached only 26 years. Peter Cunningham, now in his twenties, is developing into an accomplished fiddler of significant promise.

REFERENCES

1 Dr. Malachy McCloskey. *Reminiscences on Traditional Fiddlers and Traditional Music.* Dearcadh, The Ardara Review. Nollaig, 1992, pp. 102 - 103.

2 Alan Feldman and Eamonn O'Doherty. *The Northern Fiddler.* Blackstaff Press. Belfast. 1979.

3 Caoimhín Mac Aoidh. *An Oidhreacht Cheoil in Iardheisceart Thír Chonaill* (in Oidhreacht Gleann Cholm Cille, Seosamh Watson Eagarthoir). An Clóchomhar Tta. Baile Átha Cliath. 1989.

4 Dr. Malachy McCloskey. Op. Cit.

CHAPTER FOURTEEN

SOUTH DONEGAL

The southern triangle of the county stretching from Mountcharles over to Barnesmore Gap and on to Pettigo then heading south to Bundoran is usually considered the gateway to Donegal. For centuries the plain of Maigh Ena has acted as a transitional zone from the neighbouring areas of north Connacht and Fermanagh. More so than in any other area of the county, diverse stylistic influences have been traded between near neighbours. The contrast between the bouncy, rhythmic fiddle music of north Leitrim and west Fermanagh and the driving music of Donegal is stark, yet where they have blended they have in most cases yielded very pleasant results.

Today when visitors explore this area for fiddlers they are almost always taken by surprise not only by the number of players to be found but also in the quality of the players. This healthy existence of fiddlers has been a long one and the district's contribution towards the development of the music at a national level goes back a long way. In fact the Ballyshannon fiddler William Allingham was to play an important role as correspondent and field collector in collaboration with one of the great names of Irish music of the last century, George Petrie.

WILLIAM ALLINGHAM

Allingham was born in the Mall, Ballyshannon on March 19th, 1824 and within his lifetime gained recognition as a poet of national importance[1]. Although his reputation as such continues to grow even today, few are aware that he was at least a competent fiddler. William Allingham was born into an economically stable family. He received his secondary education in Killeshandra, County

Cavan and at the age of fourteen returned to Ballyshannon to take up employment in the local bank. Shortly afterwards Allingham went to work as a Customs Officer and after a few postings, mostly around the northern half of the country, settled in as Principal Coast Officer in Donegal Town.

As a diarist of some significance he has left us some information about his playing and collecting activities[2]. Whenever the opportunity arose he visited and played music with George Petrie. Allingham was enthusiastic about the cultural revival of the period and made efforts to collect tunes wherever he could, targeting the sad, but nonetheless fertile, grounds of the workhouses. In his diary he informs us that he learned "a large number of tunes from nurses" no doubt employed in the workhouses[3].

An entry dated November 9th, 1847 notes him practising the fiddle. On November 30th, 1847 we find he visited a fiddler by the name of Tom Read in the poorhouse (presumably in Ballyshannon) who played for him *'Ain Kind Dearie'* and *'Paudeen O Rafferty'*. While we learn no more about Read's skill as a player, we get an idea of the psychiatric standards of the day in Allinghams recording how the unfortunate fiddler "kept a piece of iron on his head to do him good"! Again on September 19, 1848 we find him practising from midnight to two in the morning, this time with a fiddler named Hagarty. Confirming the great abundance of players in this area he tells us "fiddlers abounded, pipers (presumably warpipers) were not scarce; the fame of harpers lingered, but I never heard the Irish harp till I went South".

In his book 'The Petrie Collection of the Ancient Music of Ireland' we find George Petrie being "indebted to my accomplished young friend, the poet, William Allingham..."'[4] for supplying the melody, first two verses and the chorus to a local song entitled *It Was an Old Beggarman, Weary and Wet*. In the more comprehensive work 'The Complete Petrie Collection of Ancient Irish Music'[5] which was posthumously edited by Charles Villiers Stanford we find Allingham's contribution of a $^9/_8$ tune entitled *Kitty O Hea*. This tune was used as the melody for one of his rare ballads which he published in broadsheet format, a copy of which survives in the Trinity College Library Broadsheet Collection. This tune can be played as a very nice slip jig.

In this second of Petrie's works, Allingham again is credited with the words and melody of *It Was an Old Beggarman Weary and Wet* as well as the song airs *Van Dieman's Land* and *Mo Chailín Deas Ruaidh.* The latter two were presumably collected locally with the last being written in 6/8 time and temptingly appearing as a jig. This, however, is complicated by the occurrence of an extra bar in the second part.

William Allingham poet, diarist, music collector and fiddler died in Hampstead, England in 1889 and his ashes are kept in Saint Catherine's Church, Ballyshannon, overlooking the town he so fondly praised.

THE EXTENDED MOORE FAMILY

Staying in Ballyshannon, a distinguished father and son partnership gave the town and its rural hinterland access to excellent fiddle playing for the best part of a century and a half. Willie Moore was born in New York City in 1850. When very young his father, a County Roscommon emigrant, died. His mother decided to return to her native townland of Corlea, on the northern shore of Lough Erne between Belleek and Ballyshannon, with Willie and his older brother Eddie. Soon after arriving Willie learned to play the fiddle from Pat McBride who lived in a two storey house in Chapel Street, Ballyshannon. McBride at this time was thought to be in his late fifties or early sixties and was the most highly regarded fiddler for house dances in Ballyshannon. Though he had a small amount of sight he was functionally blind. Whenever his services were demanded he would always be either collected in a pony and cart or alternatively two men would be called upon to walk him to and from the venue.

Another Ballyshannon fiddler of McBride's generation whom Willie often cited as being a very influential player was Eddie Mulhern who lived in the Port. Alec and Mickey McConnell were also known to Willie. He also often spoke of travelling tinsmiths, Tom and Andy McCafferty whose native area he could not recall, but who were popular players and regularly visited Ballyshannon. Of the brothers, Tom was the much more regarded fiddler. Again remembered as adults during the time of Willie's youth were the McCabe brothers, one of whom played fiddle with the other teaching dancing.

Pat McBride's teaching efforts with Willie Moore paid off very well. Willie rapidly took to the fiddle and became known as a player of very high standing in the Ballyshannon and Belleek area. His contemporaries were John Rourke and his uncle, John Slevin. These players regularly came together to provide the music for house and barn dances and regularly played in duet and trio combinations.

Willie eventually inherited his mother's small farm, married and had two sons, Billy and Eddie. Eddie was born in 1902 and showed an early interest in the fiddle. He started to take lessons from Willie at the age of seven and soon was able to play *The Keel Row* for a highland. Eddie's playing grew to gain him a justly deserved reputation as a marvellous fiddler. During his early adult life, Corlea and the rural communities surrounding Ballyshannon and Belleek were active areas where the populations were relatively stable and though centred on small farms, were for the most part holding their own. The communities had built small halls where dances were regularly held and between these, house and barn dances Eddie was in constant demand. In this thriving setting he regularly paired up with his main playing partner, Joe Gavigan, who came from Derry as a youth with his family to live in Corlea.

During the Twenties a branch of Conradh na Gaeilge was formed in Belleek and was very active for three or four years. Meetings were held regularly which attracted people from the town and surrounding areas. At the meetings Irish was taught by a man named O'Grianna from Gweedore and dancing instruction was given by Séamus Mac a' Bháird. The music and dancing proved very popular and it was this element that initially attracted Eddie Moore and Joe Gavigan. After a short period Joe showed a great proficiency in the language, which coupled with his musical abilities, made him a prime target for recruitment as a teacher by Conradh na Gaeilge. Joe showed some interest but his steady job in Belleek Pottery ultimately won out.

Joe Gavigan is remembered as having been a sweet-toned musician whose playing mixed well with Eddie's and who was influenced by the fiddle playing of his uncle, James Gavigan. Unlike many of the Donegal duets of this time Joe and Eddie did not play in octaves. Joe died at about sixty years of age in the Shiel Hospital, Ballyshannon in the early Forties.

Another playing partner for whom Eddie Moore held great respect was his first cousin Harry Carey. Harry was born in Glasgow and came to live in Corlea as a youth with his grandparents and uncles. In this musical family surroundings Harry took to the fiddle with great enthusiasm and quickly became a good player. He accepted a post as an Agricultural Officer in the County House, Lifford at the age of 21 years. While there he became well acquainted with Andy McIntyre, the County Librarian who, as we have seen, was a good fiddler. Harry married a sister of the noted Kilcar fiddler Barney Doogan. They had two daughters Cathleen and Eithne, the latter of whom is herself a well known fiddler and has made great strides in the teaching and development of fiddle playing in Armagh.

Two other playing contemporaries who associated with Eddie Moore were Daniel Kilfeather of Garrison, County Fermanagh who, though best noted as a fiddler, was also an accomplished flute player as well as Johnnie Flynn from the townland of Clyhore, Ballyshannon, who also worked in Belleek Pottery. Johnnie is remembered by Eddie as having been a nice, easy player. As noted above, women fiddlers were almost a curiosity in the past. Mollie McWilliams was an annual visitor to the once famous Harvest Fair of Ballyshannon. Eddie remembers she would play on the street during the fair and always attracted a large crowd. It is not clear where she came from. Other fiddlers familiar to Eddie were the Chisolms from below the 'Breezy Mountain'.

Since the Forties there has been a progressive decline in Eddie Moore's rural community as well as the passing of most of his fiddle partners. The demand for house and hall dances has nearly died out, yet, despite this Eddie has continued to play on. He spent a number of years with Belleek fiddlers Philip Breen, Mick Hernon and Paul Coyle in the Cú Chuluainn Céilí Band. Today hale and hearty in his early nineties Eddie is well looked after by the devoted and attentive staff of the Rock Home in Ballyshannon. He is a mine of information about the fiddle music of the Ballyshannon and Belleek areas since the middle of the last century and with his excellent health he is able to play a brace of reels with the energy of a man a quarter of his age.

JOHN GORDON

As noted in the beginning of this chapter south Donegal is the one area of the county where the cross-fertilisation of styles has been strongest. Also as we have seen, the Belleek fiddler associated with the stone fiddle, Denis McCabe, was a contemporary of the Ballyshannon uilleann piper Patrick Haly and they are known to have been musically associated.

This sharing of local tradition continues quite strongly today. Though proud of his Fermanagh up-bringing, so emphatically has the influence of John Gordon been stamped on the fiddle music of the Ballyshannon area over the past sixty years that to exclude him from any discussion on the fiddling of south Donegal would be laying too much importance on the handful of miles to his birthplace.

John Joe Gordon was born in 1928 at Drumcully, halfway between Belcoo and Garrison, County Fermanagh. He is the grandson of one of four Highland immigrant brothers who came to settle around the south Fermanagh /North Leitrim area. His father, John James, was a noted fiddler as was his mother, Mary McGuire and her brother Francie from Stranagress, Glenfarne, County Leitrim.

John Joe has spent the vast portion of his life in Belleek and has in many senses put that small Fermanagh village on the national music map. Those who have followed his career over the years can remember him as a child prodigy. He started to play when only six years old. His father's fiddle was too big for him to make the stretch so he played it on his knee like a cello. He picked up a number of tunes playing like this and by the age of nine he was able to hold it in the normal position. At this time he entered an open competition for fiddle playing in Enniskillen. Many of the regular dance players of Fermanagh entered as the prize money of fifteen shillings was considerable. By all accounts the only person surprised that day when John captured the title was himself.

At the age of twelve he was brought by his mother to a travelling music and dance teacher Mr O'Donoghue who had a considerable reputation. After hearing John play a couple of tunes he told his mother to bring him home as she would only be wasting her money on sending him to lessons. The teacher admitted that John had already reached a level of playing beyond which he could not take him. O'Donoghue, then having thought a bit made an offer to his mother to hire John to play for his dancing classes. Since those early days John Gordon has been recognised as a fiddler of exceptional talent.

Throughout his formative years it must be said that Seán McGuire made the strongest impact on his playing. This has not, as has been the case with some similarly influenced players, resulted in a style slavishly devoted to the reproduction of the McGuire sound. John has devised a personal style of playing which is marked by staccato, attacking bowing of incredible precision coupled with an astounding sense of melodic variation. In terms of left hand technique his position playing is impeccable and flat keys present no impediment for him. His mastery of the instrument has been so thorough that his playing has left an extensive impact on the musicians of Ballyshannon and Bundoran with whom he regularly plays.

CYRIL CURRAN AND FRANK FANNON

Cyril Curran comes from a very musical family in Ballyshannon. He received some tuition from Mother Dominic at the Convent of Mercy, Ballyshannon. Cyril was one of the most active fiddlers in the town for decades playing with John Gordon, Thomas McGarrigle, Pat Kelly and many others. Before moving to England he also played in the Assaroe Céilidh Band. Cyril commonly partnered John Tierney, from Antrim who had a shoemaker business in Ballyshannon for some years as well as Peter Murphy, from Armagh who played with the Fitzgerald Céilidh Band based in Bundoran. Cyril makes a regular number of trips home each year and renews his old partnerships.

Another Ballyshannon fiddler to have spent years in England is Frank Fannon. He is a highly capable player and now lives in nearby Belleek where he regularly plays at local Cómhaltas sessions and often partners John Gordon.

TERRY McINTYRE

Terry McIntyre, now in his mid-forties, is a native of The Mall, Ballyshannon and one of the areas mainstay fiddlers. Like many of today's musicians in the town he began to learn to play from Mother Dominic at the Convent of Mercy, Ballyshannon with lessons starting about the age of seven years. As he progressed and became more adept in the music he remembers being particularly impressed by John Tierney.

While a student in Dublin he generally found little time to play but towards the completion of his studies there took an increasing interest in fiddling. He began working soon afterwards with Gaeltarra Éireann, initially in the Carrick area where he befriended the boxplayer Mickey Gallagher.

A transfer to Gweedore came in 1973 and this move ideally positioned him for a strong resumption in playing. At this time, Gweedore was a major hotbed of traditional music. He regularly appeared in association with Prionsías and Máiréad Uí Mhaonaigh and was quickly recruited into Ceoltóirí Altan. Terry's playing grew exceptionally in Gaoth Dóbhair and he absorbed much of the repertoire of Prionsías Ó Maonaigh.

In 1980 he returned to Ballyshannon and the demands of establishing his own accountancy practice resulted in less attention to the fiddle. Recent years, however, have seen him returning more to playing and, in particular, partnering John Gordon. His style fits well into the local, bouncy rhythmical pattern. The family-run pub, McIntyre's Saloon Bar, has become a well-known venue for quiet, informal sessions.

THE MEN FROM BUNDORAN

Bundoran, with its seaside walk at Roguey, has been famous as a holiday destination from the earliest developments in organised tourism. Professional fiddlers would often gather in the summer months and play along the cliff route and then later in the evening perform for dances in the town. During the early decades of this century the annual Bundoran Gala Week always included fiddle and dancing competitions. An excerpt from the July 5, 1930 edition of the Donegal Democrat shows that fiddlers were quite willing to travel some distances to the town to compete. The fiddle competition was won that year by P. Mulreaney of Cliffoney, County Sligo and second was J. Harkin of Dromore, County Tyrone.

The greatest contribution to an enviable dynasty of Bundoran fiddle playing began with a fellow countyman of the latter Harkin. Paddy Kelly was born in Fintona, County Tyrone towards the end of the last century and regularly associated with the famous McCanns of nearby Trillick. A masterful player from an early age, he found himself in great demand to play for dances. His fame and reputation spread widely with the result that he found himself being frequently booked to play in Bundoran for the thriving Irish dancing scene there in summer. It was commonplace for him to cycle every weekend during the fine months from Fintona to Bundoran to play for dances. He became a regular feature of the musical scene of the town and over time his playing commitments in the south Donegal area grew to the point where they were lucrative enough for him to establish residence there.

Paddy played in a style which was typical of his locality. It was fast with energetic, staccato bowing. His left hand was technically astute and well capable of position playing. It is interesting to note that these exact same elements characterise the playing of Frank McCann of Trillick who is now in his seventies. Paddy did make some 78 RPM disc recordings which have since been lost. It appears that these were privately produced demo recordings and never commercially released. A single reel to reel tape[6] of his playing made in the early 1950's has recently been re-discovered by his son. It contains four tracks of music formed by three sets of four reels each and another of three hornpipes. The playing is extremely exciting with an abundance of drive and variation. It reveals a fiddler, though at an advanced age, capable of extraordinary and enticing playing.

The repertoire of Paddy's formative years was gleaned from his native south Tyrone. Fortunately this has been very well captured in the manuscripts of Sergeant Bogue, an RIC Officer who was stationed throughout the northern half of the country in the early years of this century. The manuscripts were gathered into a number of bound volumes and these were passed on to local Tyrone players upon Bogue's death. Frank McCann is now in possession of all of these except a single volume containing up to one thousand reels which was passed on to Paddy Kelly. Many of Paddy's tunes can be spotted in it.

The south Tyrone repertoire shows some remarkable differences and similarities with the Donegal repertoire. The very popular Donegal reel, *The Oak Tree* occurs as a close version known as the *Grand Turks March* while the Scots reel *Miss Montgomery,* is very like the version played by John Doherty. Other tunes which exhibit the distinct local Tyrone flavour is an interesting setting of the *Swallow's Tail* (or more correctly titled in Donegal as *The Swallow's Tail Coat* named after the dancing masters' coats) which Paddy called *McKenna's Reel* in reference to its association with a local dancer named McKenna. Two Tyrone reels which Paddy introduced to Donegal are *Hayden's Favourite* and another whose name has been lost and re-christened *The Man From Bundoran* in his honour.

Paddy Kelly continued throughout his life to be a central figure in the musical framework of south Donegal. He formed a marvellous céilídh band which at various times boasted amongst its ranks the famous uilleann piper Felix Doran. Paddy also travelled further afield to most parts of Ireland and Scotland. Following the death of his wife he moved for a short number of years to Perth, Scotland where he continued to play.

By the early 1950's he was still playing with a special vigour. The first All-Ireland Fleadh was organised in 1952. After last minute prompting from friends Paddy decided to travel to it with no other purpose in mind than to play and enjoy music. On the way to Mullingar those in the car managed to coax him into entering the fiddle competition. Paddy wasn't interested but later allowed his name to go forward. He played to his usual high standard and following the adjudication could not be separated from the legendary Sliabh Luachra fiddler Denis Murphy. The two were brought back and both were requested to play an air in order to establish the winner. In the end Paddy Kelly came out on top securing the unique claim to having won the first All-Ireland Fiddle Competition. He continued to play excellent music up until his death in 1959.

The Kelly name lives on in the Donegal tradition however as Paddy's son, Pat, was a worthy pupil of his famous father. Pat was four years of age at the time of the family move from Fintona and bar the short years in Scotland has spent all of his life in Bundoran. He took to the fiddle in his youth and received meticulous instruction from his father. His style is said to be extremely close to Paddy's and comparison with the aforementioned tape-recording of his father confirms this.

Pat's devotion to fiddle playing has been lifelong. Under his er. His reputation both as a solo player as well as in combination with his father spread rapidly. Following years of playing throughout Ireland Pat toured Britain with Seán McGuire. His playing is marked by a great command of the staccato bow with a mastery of variation and position playing. His repertoire is completely typical of that of his father with some influences of the Dohertys. Over the past two decades Pat has cut down on his touring. His playing remains at a high level of excellence and his duet playing with John Gordon which has become more frequent in recent years is very exciting.

THE EXTENDED McGEE FAMILY

The extended McGee family, originally from around Glasgeeragh, Pettigo, produced several fiddlers of note through to the current day. Brothers Pat and John were the primary house dance players in the area. John's sons Hughie, now in his seventies and living in the townland of Cower, and Mick both played. Besides being a much sought-after player, Pat also made fiddles. His daughter, Mary Kate, picked up her fiddle playing from him and eventually married and settled in Ballintra. Her son, Thomas McGarrigle, was in turn taught by her. She was certainly an adept player and teacher as Thomas, now a middle aged man, grew to become a highly accomplished player. His repertoire reflects his mother's store of tunes and his bowing shows some interesting similarities with that of John Doherty. Despite recent problems with his left hand, Thomas has reached an enviable standard of playing. The great demands of his work schedule unfortunately mean that he is all too rarely heard playing.

ANN McGROARY

Ann McGroary from Ballinacarrick Barr, Ballintra is now in her late twenties. She started to play the fiddle around the age of eighteen years finding initial inspiration in the music of Brendan McGlinchey. Though largely self-taught she did receive a great deal of help from the late noted fiddler John Doherty from Clyhore, between Ballyshannon and Belleek, Philip Breen and her uncle, Patrick Travers. Her progress on the fiddle was rapid and she has proven to be a fiddler of considerable commitment. The sustained growth in her playing in recent years has been a delight. Though a performer in high demand for both solo playing as well as in her capacity with the Mountain Road Céilidh Band Ann has made a critical contribution to the playing in the area through her on-going teaching of younger fiddlers.

Another local player is Oliver Thomas who played with the Tirchonnaill Céilidh Band. Significant developing fiddlers in this area include Oisín McCauley, now living in Ballyshannon, who plays with a style distinctly influenced by that of John Doherty, arising from Oisín's up-bringing in Carrick. James McNamee, of Ballintra, has come under the guidance of his near neighbour Thomas McGarrigle while Lorainne O'Brien has emerged as a player of potential under Ann McGroary. Collette McAree from Laghey has been growing steadily as a player and promises to continue to do so in the future.

THE MUSICAL STONE MASONS

Phil McGroarty was born on January 21st, 1897 at Drumkeelan, Mountcharles. This area was the heartland of the then thriving quarrying and flagstone dressing industry. Fiddlers were abundant there and he learned his music at the house dances of his local area. Steeped in the local craft of stone carving he took up employment in Rossnowlagh in 1918, eventually leaving it to work on the construction of the new Basilica at Lough Derg. Towards the end of the 1920s he returned to Rossnowlagh and established a highly successful monumental stone carving business which continues today in the highly skilled hands of his sons. Though having moved away from his home place, he was regularly visited by his old playing partners Charlie McCahill (this name is invariably pronounced on the basis of its older gaelic form to sound like McCaul), Charlie Meehan and Christie Doherty who would cycle the distance for a night's music. Charlie McCahill was one of the most talented of these and died in 1947. These were all well respected fiddlers and most were skilled in stone carving. Phil was a highly regarded fiddler and one of the most important players of his generation in the Ballyshannon area. He appears to have injected a good number of highlands from his home place into the local repertoire. Some tapes were made of Phil's playing but sadly the vast majority of these were burned in a fire. Phil is but sadly the vast majority of these were burned in a fire. Phil is pictured today through an excellent portrait by accomplished Rossnowlagh artist Barry Britton.

Another stone carver was Phil's Drumkeelan neighbour Eddie Monaghan. Eddie was born in the 1890's and spent a period working in America where he was well known in musical circles. He eventually returned home and travelled quite a bit on the strength of his trade, being involved in such large scale projects building the Cathedral in Enniskillen at which time he came to meet and greatly impress John Gordon. Eddie would regularly associate with his old neighbour Phil McGroarty, calling to the house whenever possible. Those who remember Eddie are unified in their praise of his fiddling. Two tunes in which he revelled were *The Sunshine Hornpipe* and *The Copper Plate Reel.*

JOHN JAMES CONNAGHAN

John James Connaghan of The Forge, Doorin Line, Mountcharles was born in 1903. He learned his music at local house dances where he often partnered Charlie McCahill, Charlie Meehan and Christie Doherty, who died tragically in middle age in America. He also was well acquainted with the Doherty brothers, particularly Mickey. John James provided a great service to the archiving of Donegal fiddle music by hosting Mickey Doherty on at least two occasions for a taping session. In the relaxation of a familiar surrounding and in the company of a kindred soul, Mickey produced the best recordings of his music known to exist.

John James' home, referred to as The Forge, was one of the strongest centres for music in the area. Players would travel miles to attend a music night there and in the later years of his life, this venue would attract and eventually impact on such players as Vincent Campbell from Glenties. John James appears to have made a very concerted effort to reach a level of excellence in his playing. The highly respected Sligo flute player, John Egan was stationed in the Mountcharles area for a number of years in connection with the local railway. He came to know the fiddlers of the area very well. At informal gatherings as well as on broadcasts he acknowledged the excellence of the fiddlers of this area and singled out John James for particular praise.

From a series of private recordings now in the possession of his son, Pat, we have a great insight into the marvellous style of John James Connaghan. These show a driving attacking style with a wonderful blend of melodic nuances from the likes of Mickey Doherty's style as well as some of the fiddlers of the southwest. His ornamentation is advanced and freely executed. On occasion he is partnered by Charlie Meehan and Christie Doherty and in these circumstances John James clearly dominates.

To further add to our information about this great player a sheet of paper, now in the possession of his son Pat, made out by John James contains a list of tunes which he played at a local concert. It gives us a good insight into his preferred repertoire. The list, to which I have added some clarifications such as alternative tune titles in parenthesis, reads: *'Repeal of the Union, Mammie's Pet, Tullaghan Lassies, Maids of Mullagh (Maighdean Mhara Mhullaigh Mhór), Paddy's Trip to Liverpool (The Boyne Hunt), Nine Points of Roguery (The Black Fanad Mare), Bean a Tí ar Lar, Mooney's (Paddy Ryan's Dream), Blacksmith's Fancy (reel), Kiltyfanad Reel, the Glen Road to Carrick, (King) George the Fourth (Highland), Ewe with the Crooked Horn (Highland), The Highland Jenny (Highland), The Cock's Tail (a Donegal version of the Dublin Reel), Peter Street (Timour the Tartar), Cuffe Street, Jack Latin (Pinch of Snuff reel), (Bonnie) Bunch of Ferns, Hound and the Hare - Fox Chase, Fanad Lassies, Mol na Tiarna, Boil the (Breakfast) Kettle Early, Stormy Weather, Cat that Kittled in Jamie's Wig (Miss Lyell), Lowlands of Scotland (Jim Kennedy's Favourite), Lough Isle Castle, Bonnie Ann, Roar of Loughros Mór - Atlantic Breakers, Duúamán na Binne Buí, Easter Snow, Pigeon on the Gate, Johnnie's Gone to France (The Sun Behind Glenties), Sailor's Bonnet, the Rising Sun, the Rising Moon, Toss the Feathers, Farewell to Erin, Mourne Mountains, Contradiction Reel, Drowsy Maggie, Heathery Mountains (Braes), Gravel Walks of Grannie reel, Farewell to Erin, Cup of Tay, Miss Patterson's Slippers Reel, The Oak Tree.*

It is almost certain that each tune was not performed as the single pieces listed but rather in sets as they were traditionally played. For example, it may well have been the case that the three highlands listed in sequence *George the Fourth, The Ewe With the Crooked Horn* and *Highland Jenny* were played in that order as a set.

This repertoire is typical of the mainstream fiddle music of John James' locality and the entire list would, even today, find almost total familiarity amongst the fiddlers of the southwest in particular. This set of tunes is also interesting in that it gives some insight into the pieces that John James enjoyed playing publicly as well as giving firm evidence of those who influenced his repertoire. Tunes and their titles which are almost diagnostically associated with Francie Dearg and Mickey Bán O'Byrne in the list include: *Highland Jenny, Jack Latin (The Pinch of Snuff,* though Francie and Mickey exclusively used *Jack Latin* as the title), *Mol na Tiarna, (The Bonnie) Bunch of Ferns* (again a title almost exclusively used by Francie and Mickey) and *Toss the Feathers.*

As for the balance of the list the Dohertys would be more commonly associated with the pieces and their names with two exceptions. The first is *The Blacksmith's Fancy*. This reel was recorded in a powerful duet version by John Doherty and Frank Cassidy for the Irish Folklore Commission. There are also some private solo recordings of John playing the tune and saying that it was from John James he learned it[7]. As John James Connaghan was a renowned blacksmith it would be tempting to conclude on the basis of the title that he either composed or had himself associated with the tune through its title. His son Pat however, who also plays and has a detailed knowledge of his father's repertoire, is certain that John James did not compose it and the title was given to the tune by players older than his father. Thus it seems that although he was the principal source for the tune the connection between the title and John James occupation as a blacksmith is purely coincidental.

The second unusual item in the tune list is the appearance of the title the *'Roar of Loughros Mór - Atlantic Breakers'*. This is a reference to the descriptive hornpipe most commonly known as *Tuam na Farraige*. The name has been translated as The Atlantic Roar or the Atlantic Sounds etc. and is discussed more fully in the chapter dealing with folklore. The appearance of the title the *Roar of Loughros Mór* however suggests that John James may have picked the tune up around the Ardara or Glenties area. As we shall see when dealing with Anthony Helferty, this was the specific name he (Helferty) gave to the tune when passing it onto the fiddlers of that district. This is in contrast to the title *Tuam na Farraige* which is the name characteristically applied in the Teelin–Carrick–Glencolumcille area. Finally two curiosities are to be found in the list, namely, the double appearance of the reel *Farewell to Erin* and the use of alternative titles *Tullaghan Lassies* and *Lough Isle Castle* for the same tune. In the first case, this may reflect two reels with similar titles, namely *Farewell to Ireland* and *Farewell to Erin*. Otherwise, it may be a minor oversight on John James' part in preparing the list, possibly from slight nervousness before the performance. In the second instance, the two tune titles were typically used by the Dohertys' for the same tune.

John James Connaghan's impact on the formulation of traditional fiddle playing in south Donegal has been greatly underestimated for a number of years. His private recordings are now opening the eyes of a new generation of Donegal fiddlers to a player of major accomplishment. John James Connaghan died in 1973. His son Pat is a great enthusiast of fiddling and continues to play as does his two children Neville and Clair.

DANNY MEEHAN

Danny was born just over fifty years ago at Drimalost, Mountcharles. His father, Jimmy (1903 - 1986), played a small bit on the fiddle but was known more for his ten key melodeon playing. Jimmy was keen on the playing of Paddy McDyer and absorbed a good portion of his repertoire. Danny's mother, Nan Sheerin, of Doorin Line also played a bit on the fiddle and was a next door neighbour of John James Connaghan. In fact, Jimmy and Nan first met on one of his visits to John James' house for a musical evening. Danny was always very enthusiastic about music and started to play fiddle with a serious commitment at around thirteen years. While working hard at developing as a player he was always astounded at the musical ability of Michael Coleman and there are some elements of the latter's style in his music. His strongest early influences, however, were his father and the numerous local fiddlers and one of his neighbours in particular, Charlie McCahill.

At the age of fifteen Danny left to work in London and has effectively been away since then. He returned for a period in his mid-twenties and during this time became greatly influenced by the playing of John Doherty. Danny had become a player of exceptional ability at this stage and meeting a player of John's stature provided great excitement and inspiration for him. He absorbed as much of John's repertoire as he could and it appears adjusted his style more towards the Doherty way of playing. By his early manhood Danny had reached a standard of playing which few in Ireland could ever hope to aspire to. His fiddling was wildly passionate. His dance tunes were played fast, attacking and with a spontaneity which defied any form of anticipation. So gifted was he with technical ability that despite what appeared to be a frenetic pace his tunes always rang with an incredible, mastered command.

During the Seventies and into the Eighties Danny was a regular and much sought after visitor at home for fleadhs and family occasions. He had been recruited into the London-based band Le Chéile and introduced a strong Donegal influence into the group's repertoire. Playing with Le Chéile presented him with a few rare opportunities to return to Ireland. London's gain was certainly Donegal's loss and players who revelled in his company such as James Byrne and Tommy Peoples, both of whom have been positively influenced by their association with Danny, regretted not seeing much more of him.

Danny's mature stylistic accent exhibits some of the diagnostics of his native area and the similarity of his playing with someone like John James Connaghan is also clear. His execution of ornamentation in varying a tune has opened up his music, reflecting his abundant enthusiasm for fiddling and his use of an occasional sharpened third finger (say G on the D string or D on the A string) playing shows his links with the players of the southwest. Danny's musical depth is expressed in his ability to understand and show a profound respect for the playing subtleties of many of the older generation of fiddlers with whom he came into contact.

Danny has become a seminal source for other players of his generation as well as the current developing one. The breadth of his repertoire is considerable and his maintenance of older stylistic elements combined with his personal zest have resulted in a player of colossal stature. It would be accurate to say that even despite the prowess of such polished players as John James Connaghan and Paddy McDyer the zenith of fiddling emerging from the fertile area around Mountcharles and Inver was realised in Danny Meehan. He is a highly personable, yet, modest man for someone whose gift is so abundant.

Though Danny has been less inclined to be involved in playing in more recent times his music is one of the most astounding developments in the Donegal tradition. It exhibits a remarkable kinship of spirit with that of Tommy Peoples in terms of its incredible depth, imagination and pure passion. Danny's visits home are all too rare for the many who take delight in the playing of one of the most exciting fiddlers ever in the Irish tradition. Fiddle playing in the Meehan family did not stop with Danny. His brothers Jimmy and Peter and sister Kitty, now living in Newtown Square near Philadelphia also picked up the instrument. His sister Rosabelle, in Donegal Town, is also a tremendous enthusiast of the instrument. With many of Danny's personal traits of modesty and pursuit for the beauty in the music she often underestimates her marvellous local repertoire. Over the past number of years and in Danny's absence her main musical influence has been the sweet playing of Danny O'Donnell for whom she has considerable respect. Rosabelle is also well known for her playing with the Shamrock Céilidh Band in which she is sometimes partnered on fiddle by Joe Freally.

PAT McDYER

Pat McDyer, from Letterbarrow, just outside of Donegal Town, is remembered as being one of the most influential and accomplished fiddlers in this area. He was slightly older than John James Connaghan and was the most sought after performer for house and school dances. So gifted was he that all of the local players strove to pick up his repertoire and technique. This apparently became a problem for Pat and he is reputed as having tried to counter this pressure by becoming slightly protective of his music. This did not thwart the efforts of his admirers however as they would commonly gather outside the windows of the venues in which he would be playing and between the small groups of players they were able to pick up his settings. Two players who greatly admired him and managed to pick up his tunes were Jimmy Meehan and Charlie O'Neill.

CHARLIE AND PAT O'NEILL

Charlie, sometimes known locally as Santa, having been born on Christmas Day is a native of Letterbarrow. He learned his early music amongst the numerous local fiddlers playing at local house dances. He eventually moved to The Moy, County Tyrone a number of years ago. He has kept active in fiddle playing there and has managed through regular visits to maintain contact with his native area. Charlie's repertoire is a rich one for fiddlers with a Donegal interest as it contains many of the old house dance tunes which were specific to his native place. One of his regular playing partners over the past number of years was the late John Loughran from near Pomeroy who died in 1987. Charlie's son, Pat, is a well known fiddler and the two are noted for their intricate duet playing which has appeared on at least one commercially released recording.

Remaining in this area, one of the more eccentric characters is Myles Tinney. Myles based himself in the countryside surrounding Mountcharles. He worked as a migrant farm labourer and is known to have become a competent fiddler. He is largely remembered for his mischievous exploits however. For example, he used to slip into the confessional in the local chapels sometime before the priest would arrive and hear the confessions of many of the local people. Sometimes the evidence gathered would be used for or against the poor penitents depending on Myles' whims. He is best remembered now for his making and playing trapezoidal, or box, fiddles.

Before moving on from Mountcharles, the humorous story of an anonymous fiddler from this area appears in the Irish Folklore Commission's school's folklore collection. It was contributed in May, 1938 by Andrew McGee, then 92 years old of Drumrooske, outside Donegal Town. He tells us[8]:

> A newly established merchant in Mountcharles was visited by a country fiddler who asked him if he stocked everything. The merchant answered 'Oh yes, everything you can name'. 'Well Sir, please give me a yard of buttermilk'. The merchant, not to be outdone, got a bowl of butter and measured a yard across the counter. 'There you are sir'. 'Paper it up if you please'. The merchant turned away in disgust and the fiddler went away laughing'.

PAT HARVEY

Pat Harvey was a native of the Lough Eske area. He was a contemporary of John James Connaghan and certainly played with John while growing up. He was acquainted with John Doherty while his brothers Johnnie and Tom Harvey also appear to have been musical. It seems Pat emigrated to America as a young man and settled in the Philadelphia area. Though he did correspond with John James Connaghan in order to keep in touch with developments at home, very little is remembered about him in south Donegal. During the sixties he did make a tape of his playing especially for John James. This tape includes approximately twenty five sets of tunes which are directly based on the Coleman-Morrison-Killoran repertoire. What stands out on this tape is Pat's incredible mastery of the Sligo style to which he would have been exposed in his adopted city. With a great deal of information on the music scene in America steadily streaming back home from the Thirties onwards it is difficult to understand how a player of what was clearly major talent could have escaped recognition. Pat Harvey may have limited his playing activities to a small social circle but it appears that this was much to the detriment of the larger body of traditional musicians who would have done very well to hear him.

REFERENCES

1. Alan Warner. *William Allingham*. Bucknell University Press - Irish Writer's Series; Associated University Presses, London. 1975.
2. William Allingham. (H. Allingham and D Radford, eds.), *William Allingham - A Diary*. Macmillan, London, 1907.
3. William Allingham. Op Cit.
4. George Petrie. The Petrie *Collection of the Ancient Music of Ireland*
5. George Petrie. *The Complete Petrie Collection of Ancient Irish Music.* (Charles Villiers Stanford ed.) Boosey, London. Parts 1-2 (1902), Part 3 (1905).
6. *Teip Paddy Kelly*. Cárideas na bhFidléirí Collection, An Foras Cultúir Uladh, Gleann Cholm Cille.
7. *Teip John Doherty*. Cairdeas na bhFidléirí Collection, An Foras Cultúir Uladh, Gleann Cholm Cille.
8. *Andrew McGee*. Irish Folklore Commission Schools Collection. An Roinn Béaloideas agus Ceolta Tire, University College Dublin. 1938.

CHAPTER FIFTEEN

THE FUTURE OF THE TRADITION

As we have seen in the early chapters of this work, the Donegal fiddle tradition had remained insular for quite a long time. External influences, compared to other styles, were minimalised by isolation. One of the most striking recent changes in the direction of the Donegal tradition has been the scale of increase in its outward influencing of Irish musicians. In the past fifteen years there has been a sustained growth in the numbers of players influenced by Donegal fiddle music. In some cases these fiddlers have made a national impact.

Dermot McLaughlin, now in his thirties, from Derry started to play at a very early age taking lessons in the town. He became a multi-instrumentalist playing fiddle, uilleann pipes, flute, whistle and melodeon. By his late teens his interests were becoming increasingly focused on the fiddle and pipes with the fiddle eventually winning out. He was strongly attracted to the playing of John Doherty and it is fair to say that John's intricate bowing style has been completely mastered by Dermot. His playing has consistently risen to exciting heights and Dermot now figures as one of the most significant players in Irish music. He is intensely familiar with the tradition and a popular player at any gathering in the county. His musical links have become strongest in the southwest and central portions of Donegal where he has forged strong connections with James Byrne, Vincent Campbell and formed an exciting duet with the late Con Cassidy. Dermot will certainly play a key role in the future development and spread of Donegal fiddling. Joe McLaughlin, a younger brother of Dermot, likewise started out as a multi-instrumentalist. He similarly came down to a choice between fiddle and uilleann pipes but in his case the pipes won pride of place. He still remains, however, an amply gifted fiddler with a strong stylistic likeness to his brother. Though I never had the pleasure of hearing a Doherty brothers duet live, I have heard the next best thing. Listening to Dermot and Joe play two fiddles is to savour exhilarating Donegal music.

A friend of the McLaughlins from boyhood is Peter Tracey. Their link goes deeper than just friendship as Peter likewise has been heavily influenced by the style of John Doherty. His staccato bowing and aggressive drive in playing, again, conjures up the classic hallmarks of John's style. Peter is destined to play an important role for the next generation of Donegal players.

Maurice Bradley of Ballinascreen, County Derry, now in his late twenties, has looked consistently to the Donegal tradition for his influences. He has emerged as a player of tremendous skill and is greatly admired by the older generation of fiddlers from whom he sought to learn. Tom Traynor, from Downpatrick, County Down, is now in his thirties. Married to concertina player Michelle O'Sullivan and living in Kerry, he is admired as a player of great skill and possesses a repertoire which is vast almost beyond belief. Tom was a consistent visitor to southwest Donegal and during his years in England, about a decade ago, he continued to look towards Donegal music for his direction. Again, future players of Donegal fiddle music will find rich rewards in listening to Maurice and Tom. Dublin fiddlers Ronan Galvin, who has family connections in Glencolmcille and Mick Brown have been travelling for some years now to visit and learn from James Byrne. They have captured the style with great maturity and their duets and trios with James have gained great respect amongst the Donegal fiddlers.

As evidenced by these players, Donegal music has clearly been successful in changing from its more inward perspective to an outward looking one and there is every likelihood that like the latter, other players will discover its riches. This change has been a fruitful one, but, there are other changes which its practitioners will have to consider. The history of Donegal fiddle music has taught us anything many things. While it is certainly traditional, in the sense that it has been handed down through oral transmission with all the attendant conservatism of acceptability of sounds and techniques, it is equally sure that some amount of alteration fits into the process.

I would be of the opinion that the rates of change which the music has undergone have been accelerating with time. This is based on some simple observations and assumptions. In the distant past, say between two and three hundred years ago, Donegal fiddlers would have been influenced only by a small range of musical idioms, for example, a minor degree of western classical music. Their influences outside of traditional music would be purely founded on what they heard performed.

This would have remained the case up to the early decades of this century with the bulk of whatever stylistic adjustments and influences on Donegal music arising from within the traditional fiddle influences of Ireland and Scotland. By the 1920s, however, things started to change rapidly. Mass communication, through revolutionary developments in transport, the broadcast and most especially the recording media, meant that Donegal fiddlers had a greater ease of access to music outside their own regional traditions. Conversely, new musical influences such as we noted in chapter two with jazz, could more readily make in-roads into traditional music.

The folk era of the Sixties and Seventies undoubtedly left some impressions on traditional music while rock influences on the music are not unknown. To date some performers have teamed with group line-ups ranging from rock bands to concert orchestras with several outstanding achievements. Other well-respected musicians fully capable of playing within the recognized tradition see themselves as players of broader, yet less well defined idioms, such as New Age Music and Roots Music.

The fact of the matter is that the form of the music and its influences are now changing more rapidly than ever before and this rate of change, or more optimistically, development, will even further increase in the future. The labels on whatever type of music is being played would, to me, appear to be of little importance. What should be the focal point is the quality of the music and the depth of understanding and appreciation of where the music came from. It may be a well-chosen truism to state at this point that it is often impossible to know where you are going if you don't know where you've been.

The future of Donegal fiddle music rests on a small number of factors. These are: the state of the current middle-age group of players, the state of the young players, the natural traditional development processes inherent within the music and finally, the more formal development structures which have been put in place by special interest bodies aiming to further enhance the music.

We have seen that in the past decade, Donegal traditional fiddle playing has emerged from a prolonged period of mis-understanding by the larger body of traditional musicians. It now is widely recognised as an exciting stylistic approach in Irish fiddle playing and the techniques and repertoire are being readily absorbed outside the county and even in the international arena. Unlike the greater portion of Ireland, the majority of middle-aged and younger Donegal players have benefited significantly from their forebears' commitment to pass on the history and folklore related to the body of their music. Donegal fiddle playing can easily be thought of as a fully fleshed out tradition where the wedded traditions of music, history and folklore remain not only intact, but, are being actively reshaped and passed on.

Considering this achievement, as well as noting the standard of excellence of the emerging generation of fiddlers, the short term future of Donegal fiddling looks good. The more challenging longer term outlook hinges, I believe, on one critical point; that of the existence of a sturdy educational structure through which the music can be passed on with all the excitement that is inherent in it. To this aim, the annual Donegal Fiddler's Summer School in Glencolumcille and the annual meeting of Cairdeas na bhFidléirí in Glenties are important achievements. More importantly, however, is the on-going teaching by such persons as Proinsías O Maonaigh, Dinny McLaughlin, Ann McGroary, The Harpers, Geraldine Boyle, Séamus Sweeney, Séamus Gibson, Martin McGinley, Roisín Harrigan, Peter Carr, James Byrne, Paula Doohan and many more. It is this hard and routine work that will in the long run dictate the future of Donegal fiddling. Bodies such as The Arts Council, The Donegal County Arts Committee, Údaras na Gaeltachta, Comhaltas Ceoltóirí Éireann, The Ballyshannon Town Commissioners Arts Programme and Cairdeas na bhFidléirí who by either their provision of or direct support for classes, masterclasses, workshops etc. play a critical role in this future and have much to be proud of in terms of the advancements they already have helped to win.

I have been privledged to meet a generation which produced players such as the Doherty brothers, Hugh Gillespie, Neillidh Boyle, Danny McCarry, the Cassidys, the O'Byrnes (Deargs), John

Gallagher, Proinsías O Maonaigh, Jimmy Hueston, Charlie Patton and Danny O'Donnell. From within a couple of years of my own generation have come Tommy Peoples, Danny Meehan, James Byrne, Vincent Campbell, Frank Kelly, Bríd Harper, Máiréad Ní Mhaonaigh, Cíarán Tourish, Séamus Gibson, Dermot McLaughlin, Paul O'Shaughnessy, the Glackin brothers and Martin McGinley amongst many others. If we get the educational support structures right, I live in unbounded anticipation because the best is yet to come.

APPENDIX

A DISCOGRAPHY
OF DONEGAL FIDDLE MUSIC

I have compiled this discography to include all known commercially released audio and video recordings of Donegal fiddle players. In considering fiddlers for inclusion I have incorporated those players born in the county and who are typically identified with the broad Donegal Style. Furthermore, I have included those players from the county who have concentrated their playing in the styles of other areas of the country. Also included are players who, though not from Donegal itself but by virtue of family connections, natural attraction to the style etc., have greatly rooted their playing in the Donegal style.

Where a player recorded on 78 RPM discs I have listed the tune titles on each side of the disc. The reference numbers and recording labels refer to the original issues. It should be noted, however, that in almost all cases 78 RPM discs were subsequently re-issued on other 78 RPM labels related in some manner to the initial parent recording company. For the sake of brevity, I have not included references to these re-issues. In some cases the 78s have been re-mastered or simply re-issued on modern microgroove 33 & $^{1}/_{3}$ RPM discs. Where this has occurred I have included references to the re-issued recordings.

Lastly, I have included two additional classifications of recordings which have featured Donegal fiddle players and whereby the Donegal influence is clearly evident. The first of these is where the Donegal fiddler appears on a compilation recording. In this case the player performs in a solo (possibly with accompaniment) capacity on a track/s along with other featured artists. In the second case, the fiddler appears with in combination with some group of players of other instruments ranging from duets to full group performance. Those wishing to access a broader discography of traditional music should consult 'A Short Discography of Irish Folk Music' by Nicholas Carolan and published by the Folk Music Society of Ireland in 1987. The following recordings are arranged in the order of title, label and reference number.

SOLO RECORDINGS

John Doherty

Johnnie Doherty, Comhaltas, CL 10; John Doherty, Gael Linn CEF 072/3; *Bundle and Go,*Topic,12TS398; *Pedlar's Pack,* EFDFSS, FSA 60074; *The Star of Donegal,* Folktracks, FSA 60075; *The Fiddler and the Fairy,* Folktracks FSA 60073.

Mickey Doherty
The Gravel Walks, Comhairle Bealoideas Éireann, CBE002;
The Fiddler and the Fairy, Folktracks, FSA 60073.

Tommy Peoples
Tommie Peoples, Comhaltas CL13; *High Part of the Road,* Shannachie 29003; *A Traditional Experience,* Solo, 7012; *The Iron Man,* Shannachie, 79044; *50 Traditional Fiddle Solos,* Walton MNF; *Traditional Music Played on the Fiddle,* Trad (GTD), HC 008.

Danny O'Donnell
78 RPM'S RECORDED IN LONDON IN MAY 1939 FOR REGAL ZONOPHONE:
The Mullingar Races and Drowsey Maggie (reels) IZ1010; *The Tenpenny Bit, Shandon Bells and The Boys of the Town* (jigs) IZ1010; *The Garden of the Daisies, The Blackbird, The Job of Journeywork* (set dances) IZ1024; *The Slievenamon and The Cuckoo* (hornpipes) IZ1024; *The Humours of Bandon and Miss Brown's Fancy* (set dances) IZ1030; *The Rakes of Clonmel* and *Kitty's Fancy* (jigs) IZ1030;

78 RPM'S RECORDED IN DUBLIN IN MAY 1945 FOR REGAL ZONOPHONE:
The Rose in the Heather and *The Bride's Favourite* (jigs) IZ1289; *The Plains of Boyle* and *The Flowers of Spring* (hornpipes) IZ1289; *The Irish Barndance* IZ1290; *The Glendowan, The Copper Plate* and *The Flower of Limerick* (reels) IZ1290; *Colonel Rodney, The Scholar* and *Buckley's Fancy* (reels) IZ1291; *Schottische Medley: Thistle and Shamrock* (highlands) IZ1291; *The Cobbler, Close to the Floor* and *The Rambling Pitchfork* (jigs) IZ1292; *The Barmaid, Charming Katy* and *The Moving Bog* (reels) IZ1292;

The Donegal Fiddler, Philips, 6373030.

James Byrne *The Road to Glenlough,* Claddagh, CC52;

Neillidh Boyle (as Neil O'Boyle)
78 RPM'S RECORDED IN DUBLIN ON MAY 3RD, 1937 FOR REGAL ZONOPHONE:
The Harvest Home (hornpipe) and *The Green Mountain* (reel) IZ721*; *Haste to the Wedding* and *Over the Hills* (jigs) IZ721; *The Blackberry*

Blossom and *The Swallows Tail* (reels); *The Dublin and the Liverpool Hornpipes; The Pidgeon on the Gate* and *Jenny Picking Cockles* (reels)**; *The Connachtman's Rambles* and *Biddy From Sligo* (jigs);

The Moving Clouds - The Enchanted Music of Ireland, Folktracks, FSA 60170.

* Reissued on *From Galway to Dublin,* Rounder Records, 1087.
**Reissued on *The Irish Phonograph,* EMI, GAE 1003.

Hugh Gillespie

78 RPM'S RECORDED IN NEW YORK CITY IN MAY 1937 FOR DECCA:
Master Crowley's Reels 12105; *The Irish Mazurka,* 12105; *The Mullingar Lee* and *The Star of Munster,* 12112*; *Mc Cormick's Hornpipe,* 12112*;

78 RPM'S RECORDED IN NEW YORK CITY IN JUNE 1938 FOR DECCA:
Jenny's Welcome to Charlie (reel), 12164; *Master Crowley's Favourites* (jigs), 12164; *Dowd's Favourite* 12171; *Versavanna* (mazurka), 12171; *Farewell to Leitrim* and *Tom Steele,* 12186; *Mc Kenna's Farewell* (hornpipes), 12186; *Paddy Finley's Fancy* and *Joe O'Connell's Dream,* 12192; *Finea Lassies* and *Gurren's Castle,* 12192;

78 RPM'S RECORDED IN NEW YORK CITY IN JUNE 1939 FOR DECCA:
The Girl That Broke My Heart and *Dick Cosgrave's,* 12213; *Contentment is Wealth* and *Finley's* (jigs), 12213; *The Pidgeon on the Gate* and *The Lady of the House,* 12225*; *The Mountain Stream* and *Parker's Fancy* (hornpipes), 12225; *Dowd's No. 9* and *Jackson's* (reels), 12229; *Jackson's Favourite* and *Kip's* (jigs), 12229; *The Donegal Traveller* and *Miss Montgomery* (reels), 12233; *The Stage* and *The Rights of Man* (hornpipes), 12233.

All the above sides except those marked with an asterisk were reissued on *Hugh Gillespie Topic* 12T364 in 1978.

Bríd Harper

Echoes of Erin, Comhaltas, CL28; Comhaltas on Tour, Comhaltas, CL29; *Come Dance With Me in Ireland,* Comhaltas, CL 31; *Guinness Seisiún,* Comhaltas, CL 35;

Paddy Glackin

Glackin, Gael Linn, CEF 060; *Rabharta Ceoil,* Gael Linn, CEF 153.

Séamus and Kevin Glackin

Na Saighnean, Gael Linn, CEF 140.

Dinny Mc Laughlin
A Rake o' Reels and a Clatter o' Jigs, Robin, ROB/AL/M072.

Francie Dearg and Mickey Bán O'Byrne
Ceol na dTead, Cló Íar Chonnachta, CIC 078

COMPILATION RECORDINGS

Danny Meehan
Paddy in the Smoke, Topic, 12T176 LP.

Paddy Glackin
The Flags of Dublin, Topic, 12TS-383; *An Fhidil II*, Gael Linn, CEF 069.

Séamus Glackin
An Fhidil I, Gael Linn, CEF 068.

Vincent Campbell, James Byrne, Con Cassidy and Francie O'Byrne *The Brass Fiddle*, Claddagh, CC44.

Paul O' Shaughnessy
Slogadh '78, Gael Linn CEF ; *Round the House - Music for the Sets* Volume 1, Na Píobairí Uilleann, NPU 002.

Dermot Mc Laughlin, Liz Doherty, Kevin Glackin, Séamus Glackin, Tommy Peoples, Séamus Gibson, Proinsías O' Maoinaigh and Máiréad Ni Mhaonaigh.

Fiddlesticks, Nimbus, NI5320.

Charlie and Pat O'Neill
Forward and Back with the O'Neills, Blue Stack, Blue Stack 001.

Con Cassidy and James Byrne
O Bhun Sliabh Liag, Forge Brae, FBC 007.

GROUP RECORDINGS

Tommy Peoples
The Bothy Band 1975, Mulligan, LUN002;
Celtic Folkweave, Polydor, 2908013 ; *1691*, Arfolk, SB313;
Molloy - Peoples - Brady, Mulligan, LUN017.
Sounds of Stone/Artists for Mullingar, Burren Action Group, BAGCD 001

Danny Meehan
Le Chéile - Lord Mayo, Inchecronin, INC 7424;
Le Chéile II - Arís, Inchecronin, 7423;

Máiréad Ni Mhaonaigh
Ceol Aduaidh, Gael Linn, CEF 102; *Altan*, Green Linnet, SIF1078;
Horse with a Heart, Green Linnet SIF1095; Albert Fry, Gael Linn, CEFO82 ;

Máiréad Ní Mhaonaigh and Cíarán Tourish
Island Angel, Green Linnet, GL1137;

Máiréad Ni Mhaonaigh, Paul OShaughnessy and Cíarán Tourish Kevin Glackin
Baker's Well, Claddagh, CCF20;
The Red Crow, Green Linnet, SIF1109;

Paddy Glackin
Hidden Ground, Tara,2009; *Doublin'*, Tara, 2007.

Paddy and Séamus Glackin
An Bóthar Cam, Gael Linn, CEF 035.

Martin Mc Ginley
Dervish, Sound Records, SUNC001

Dinny Mc Laughlin
Aileach, EMI, Leaf 7009.

John Gordon
Loughsiders, Top Spin, TSLP 101;
Irish Traditional Music from Belleek, Outlet, SOLP 1042.

P. V. O'Donnell
P.V. has appeared with some groups who have recorded on a little known label based in New York City. It may also be possible that he has recorded solo material for this label.

VIDEO MATERIAL

John Doherty
John Doherty (with Pete Seeger, banjo), Folktracks Recordings, Bristol;
Fiddler on the Road, Ulster Television, Belfast.

Vincent Campbell
Faces of Ulster, Flying Fox Films, Belfast;
Rhythms of the World, Flying Fox Films, Belfast;

Vincent Campbell and Máiréad Ní Mhaonaigh
The Magic Fiddle, Flying Fox Films, Belfast

Paddy Glackin
The Pure Drop, RTÉ, Dublin

Con Cassidy and James Byrne
McGilloway's Way, Ulster Television, Belfast.

Paddy, Séamus and Kevin Glackin and Altan
Bringing it All Back Home, Hummingbird Films, Dublin

GLOSSARY

Allamande – A dance of german origin which spread as far as Donegal where it became completely absorbed into the local dancing tradition with the name being gaelicised in some Irish speaking areas as An tÓllaman.

Convoy – A gathering of friends and neighbours for singing, dancing, playing tunes, story telling, games etc. which took place on the night before a person left the locality to emigrate. This term is used throughout Donegal and in most Ulster counties in place of the more southern term American Wake. Listening to older people it appears that the term may have originated from two possible concepts. Firstly, the night's sport was to lift the sorry spirits of the emigrant and 'convey' the more happily on their journey. Alternatively, many of the party would stay on in the house until the next morning when the journey would begin. They would then walk in convoy some part of the road with the emigrant.

Cotillon – A dance of French origin in 6/8 time which suited traditional Irish dance structures as it appears to have been designed to be performed by four couples as in the typical Irish house dance form. It spread to Donegal and its name was gaelicised in Irish speaking areas as *An Cotilan.*

Fling– This is another term for a highland but is not used by Donegal fiddlers to describe either the dance or tunes. It is occasionally used in the south and west of Ireland where the tunes and dance are much rarer.

German – In my experience, this title is used exclusively in Donegal to describe a Barndance. It is in 4/4 time and played very close to the speed of a hornpipe. A structural characteristic of a German is the occurrence of groups of two or three crotchets to accent the rhythm for the dance which was specifically performed for these tunes.

Highland – A tune in 4/4 time to which a number of dances were performed in Donegal. While they were common in Ulster counties only a few were found in the local repertoires in the remainder of the country. They continue to be most abundant amongst

Donegal fiddlers. Highlands were generated by Donegal fiddlers by adapting strathspeys and where reels were deemed not to standard they were converted to highlands. Highlands are played slightly faster than the Scots play strathspeys but considerably slower than a reel. Extended strings of triplets which occur in parent strathspeys are often simplified but not totally eliminated.

Lancer– A six part set dance which along with the Quadrille were the most popular set dances in Donegal. The set appears to have been introduced via British Army regiments who absorbed the dance from the French who seem to have created and named it after the French Army ' Regiment De Lancier'.

Roll– This constitutes, in the main, fingered forms of ornamentation in Irish music. It is used to grace a crotchet. In the space of the note the player plays five rapid notes which result in a round or rolling sound. The typical note pattern consists of the note to be graced, a note or two above, the graced note, the note immediately below it and finishing on the graced note.

Schottische – A 4/4 dance of German origin which spread as far as Scotland where local composers created Highland Schottisches. By dropping the second word Donegal fiddlers construed them as Highlands. Similarly for barndances Donegal players derived the title Germans from German Schottisches. The word 'Schottishce' is not used by Donegal fiddlers, who talk exclusively about Highlands and Germans. In other Ulster counties fiddlers use '*Schottische*' interchangeably for Highlands, Flings, and Barndances. They pronounce it as *Skot-tish* signifying some perceived connection with a Scottish origin or otherwise as *Set-tessh* possibly indicating some connection with set dances.

Strathspey – A piece of music of Scottish origin which is used for a dance . In 4/4 time, these tunes are characterised by a distinct dotted rhythm and commonly contain successions of triplets. It is played in Scotland at a slightly slower tempo than the Highland is played in Donegal.

Quadrille – A group of five dance patterns performed as a single set by pairs of four men and women with short breaks between each part.